Countering Development

Countering Development

Indigenous Modernity and the

Moral Imagination

•

DAVID D. GOW

Duke University Press • Durham and London 2008

© 2008 Duke University Press
All rights reserved
Printed in the United States of America
on acid-free paper ∞
Designed by Katy Clove
Typeset in Carter & Cone Galliard
by Keystone Typesetting, Inc.
Library of Congress Cataloging-in-
Publication Data appear on the last
printed page of this book.

To the memory of my mother, the incorrigible Betty Gow

Contents

Acknowledgments

Many years ago, I decided to write a book about anthropology and development. I diligently plodded away and sent the first three chapters in draft form to a potential publisher, who responded with the rhetorical putdown, "So what else is new?" Enraged and somewhat insulted, I gave up on the book but revised the chapters, and each one was finally published elsewhere. Although mollified, I still thought I had it in me to write a book, so some fifteen years ago, before I became an academic, I decided to try again. This second attempt was more serious: I spent one year writing, a second year revising, and a third year sending the manuscript to potential publishers. The reviewers for the first publisher did not, in my view, understand what I was trying to do. The second set of reviewers was, in my opinion, too conservative and failed to appreciate the subtleties of my argument. But the third set was devastating and, I had to agree, right on the mark. The principal lesson I drew from this painful experience was that if I wanted to write a credible book about anthropology and development, I had better go and do some serious, long-term research in the field. This book is the result of that realization.

The research was conducted primarily during the summers from 1995 to 2002 in several rural communities in Cauca, Colombia, as well as the city of Popayán, the provincial capital, and included a six-month stint in the field in 2000. In the initial years, the research was supported by grants from the Instituto Colombiano de Antropología e Historia (ICANH) and Colciencias, the Colombian scientific research agency, first for an assessment of the Nasa of Tierradentro displaced and resettled after a devastating earthquake in 1994, and then for a team project on new social movements. For their support and the opportunity to participate, I thank María Victoria Uribe, then director of ICANH; Claudia Steiner, then director of social anthropology at ICANH; and

María Lucía Sotomayor, coordinator of the research team for the latter project. In 1999, together with Myriam Amparo Espinosa, Adonías Perdomo, Susana Piñacué, and Joanne Rappaport, I was awarded an International Collaborative Grant from the Wenner-Gren Foundation for Anthropological Research. Our regular meetings and discussions of each other's work provided a stimulating opportunity for addressing many of the issues discussed here. The grant was renewed in 2001 with the participation of Tulio Rojas Curieux in place of Myriam Amparo Espinosa, who was involved in other projects. In summer 2002 I received a University Facilitating Fund Award from George Washington University, for which I am grateful.

Over the years, many people in Cauca have shared with me their views and perspectives on the processes under way there. They often shared their food with me as well. First and foremost are the members of the communities that form the foundation of this study: in San José and Cxayu'ce, Don Lisando Campo and his family, particularly his son, José Manuel; Don Mario Musse and his family, particularly his daughter and comadre Lucia and his son Rogelio, Omar Pacho, Luis Abelmar Mumucué, and Juan Abel Mumucué; in Tóez Caloto, compadres Felipe Morales and his wife, Mercedes Belalcazar, Don Jorge Inseca, Don Victoriano Cruz, Abelardo Huetia, Severo Atila, and Vicente Pinzón; and in Juan Tama, Don Ángel Yoinó, Don Julio Niquinás, Luz Mery Niquinás, Fernando Huetia, and Celio Vivas. In Juan Tama, Susana Piñacué opened my eyes to the role of indigenous education as a political project.

Equally important have been the members of the Sun and Land Foundation (Fundación Sol y Tierra; FST) established by the Quintines, the demobilized members of the Quintín Lame Armed Movement. I particularly thank Alfonso Peña Chepe, Dumar Ortega, Elber Dagua, Luis Carlos Chala, William "Moncho" Monroy (tragically assassinated in fall 2005), Walter Quiñones, Gerardo Delgado, Clara Ines Erazo, and Albeiro Dagua. The Quintines were the first to take me to Tierradentro and the first to introduce me to the challenges and complexities of development planning at the community level. They were also active in the creation of La María, a place of peace, which opened my eyes to the importance of social mobilization and the need to challenge the state.

I also would like to thank the two reviewers who read the original manuscript. Les Fields's comments, criticisms, and recommendations helped me clarify the argument and reduce the excess verbiage. The librarians of the Bender Library of American University, just a few blocks from my house, were always very helpful and supportive.

There are, however, four individuals I would like to single out without whose friendship and support this study would have been impossible. The first is my wife, Joanne Rappaport, who first introduced me to Cauca, got me involved in doing research there, and encouraged me to write this book. She has been my staunchest supporter and most demanding critic during the whole process. She made this book possible. The second is Henry Caballero, whom I first met while he was still imprisoned. In the various positions he has held over the past decade, as director of FST, as secretary in the provincial government, and most recently as the coordinator of a peace-building program in the region, he has always taken the time to talk with me and share his wide-ranging knowledge and insights about development and politics in Cauca. The third is Lucho Escobar, the first director of FST, and someone who for many years worked closely with the Regional Indigenous Council of Cauca and the indigenous movement in various capacities. A man of independent mind, he has always taken great pleasure, leavened with a healthy dose of humor, in deflating some of my more outrageous ideas and setting me straight regarding the realities of the personalities and organizations that make Popayán what it is. The final person I thank is Vince Peloso, a historian and fellow researcher, whose friendship goes back some thirty years. His support over the years in this endeavor was much appreciated and his tenacity, determination, and persistence in publishing his own work served as a stirring example.

Abbreviations

ACIN	Association of Indigenous Cabildos of Northern Cauca
AICO	Indigenous Authorities of Colombia
AISO	Indigenous Authorities of the Southwest
ASI	Indigenous Social Alliance
CCF	Christian Children's Fund
CECIDIC	Center for Education, Training, and Research for the Integrated Development of Communities
CET	Ethnoeducational Center of Tóez Caloto
CIMA	Committee for the Integration of the Colombian Massif
CNK	Nasa Kiwe Corporation
CRIC	Regional Indigenous Council of Cauca
CRIH	Regional Indigenous Council of Huila
ELN	National Liberation Army
FARC	Revolutionary Armed Forces of Colombia
FST	Sun and Land Foundation
MAQL	Quintín Lame Armed Movement
M-19	April 19th Movement
NGO	nongovernmental organization
NPA	New People's Army
ONIC	National Indigenous Organization of Colombia
PAR	participatory action research
PEB	Bilingual Education Program (part of CRIC)
RLS	Reverse Language Shift

As is well known, Kant posed three questions as being central
to our human condition in general and to the Enlightenment project in particular: what can we *know*, what can we *do* and what
can we *hope for*?–PHILIP QUARLES VAN UFFORD, ANANTA KUMAR GIRI,
AND DAVID MOSSE, "Interventions in Development: Towards a New
Moral Understanding of Our Experiences and an Agenda for the
Future"

This desire for things modern does not, however, necessarily make
them [Third World people] docile, detribalized and depoliticized
consumers of *everything* manufactured in the West. Neither does
this imply the inevitability of processes of cultural homogeniza-
tion driven by Western discourses of development, consumer capitalism and cultural imperialism.–STEVEN ROBINS, "Whose Modernity? Indigenous Modernities and Land Claims after Apartheid"

Introduction:

Beyond the Developmental Gaze

Other Ways of Doing Development

In this book, I refocus the ethnography of development through a
critical assessment of the development practices of local people in Colombia. I examine how three indigenous communities, established after
a devastating earthquake in 1994, wrestled with conflicting visions of development. These communities are located in the southwestern province of Cauca, famous for its history of indigenous mobilization as well
as its resistance to the violence spearheaded by state security forces,
paramilitary organizations, and the guerrilla movement. Relocated from
the more isolated, mountainous part of the province, the communities
were founded in lower lying lands, closer to highways, towns, markets,
and schools. These new communities offered the possibility of research-

ing over time changing indigenous attitudes toward the future and their place in the Colombian nation. What I examine is how development was redefined in indigenous Cauca, moving beyond a myopic obsession with alleviating poverty to promoting a process that would produce culturally different citizens — protagonists in a multicultural nation.

Such a refocusing of development, really a form of counterdevelopment, has involved a redeployment of planning for education and the creation of an arena for thinking through how cultural difference can provide an indispensable hinge for constructing a new indigenous but critical modernity. This means forging a culturally informed *mundus imaginalis moralis* — a moral imaginary — that reinforces and strengthens an indigenous presence in the region but also engages the moral promises of the Enlightenment, complementing the discourse of human rights with that of economic, social, and cultural rights.

Contemporary rural Colombia offers unique possibilities for the study of processes of local development. The previous two decades have witnessed an effervescence of indigenous activism and identity construction, culminating in the 1991 Constitution, in whose writing three indigenous delegates participated. This enabling legislation recognized the multiethnic character of the Colombian nation and codified the administrative forms by which native peoples would henceforth participate in civil society as ethnic citizens. As a result, being indigenous in Colombia has certain distinct benefits, including the right to communal land tenure through the reservation system, self-government through locally elected councils, and official recognition of indigenous languages. The 1991 Constitution granted indigenous people exemption from taxation and military service as well as the possibility of obtaining scholarships for university education. It also granted indigenous authorities control over development and education. Though many of these rights came out of earlier legislation, they were unified in the new constitution. This process has opened new possibilities for indigenous agency in Colombia.

In this project, I study indigenous counterdevelopment by comparing the three communities in terms of their planning discourses and practices. There is no single indigenous approach to development and modernity, not even in the relatively small province of Cauca. How does each community define and employ the concept of culture? How do they engage a concern with culture in the economic and political reconstruction of their communities? To what extent can they refocus the existing development discourses at their disposal, so that they enhance, rather than constrain, their priorities? How can they engage cultural difference without being separatists?

This resistance to the state is not in opposition to it; rather it is the demand to be recognized as indigenous and to be treated as citizens, to become a vital part of the nation. It is more than just a demand for redistribution, for a greater share of the country's resources that are rightfully theirs, as poor, marginalized, disadvantaged citizens — although clearly, as displaced people, they have a right to make such demands. Their quest for justice is a demand that the state be more inclusive, more democratic, encouraging a more active participation of indigenous people as citizens who can transform Colombia, echoing the demands of other marginal sectors (Ramírez 2001a).

The Anthropological Critique of Development

Not for nothing has the academic writing on development, particularly that produced by anthropologists, been called a literature of despondency. The rich get richer, the poor get poorer, and the resulting failures continue to be blamed on the usual culprits: benign neglect on the part of those in power, inappropriate policies and weak institutions, lack of resources, widespread corruption, and growing cynicism and rank opportunism on the part of those supposed to benefit. While the rhetoric of civil society with its mantra of empowerment, participation, and democracy has been presented as a means of providing ordinary citizens the wherewithal to make their voices and opinions heard, the literature of despondency has responded by saying that this is just another way of controlling, of co-opting, of integrating the poor and the marginal into the project of modernity, of mass consumption and market forces (Cooke and Kothari 2001). Only rarely, however, do experts in development listen carefully to what those on the ground actually say about the processes they are experiencing, whether initiated by themselves, external forces, or, more often, some combination of the two. What they do say may confound, confuse, and question the insights of the experts. There has been too little critical attention paid to the nature of development at the grass roots, beyond celebrating its alternative nature.

While anthropological critiques of development, such as those by Arturo Escobar (1995a) and James Ferguson (1994), may argue that development as we currently know it is imposed and does not work, at least for the poor and the marginal, this does not mean that people do not want development. Quite the contrary, as Jonathan Crush (1995) and others have cogently argued, development has lost neither its appeal nor its popularity; development is happening, whether we like it or not. While those who purvey development — be they international institutions, state agencies, or nongovernmental organizations (NGOs) — may be viewed with increasing skepticism and suspicion, there are other ways of "doing development." These "other ways" are what I wish to explore here.

There are several reasons why I think this approach is both important and relevant. First, critiques and discussions of development often leave out or choose to ignore its relationship to modernity and the broader political, social, and cultural context in which development occurs. Modernity is not to be confused with modernization, a rather simplistic, mechanical process of shedding the old and embracing the new, standardized according to terms, conditions, and criteria mandated by those in power. Modernity fosters both convergence and divergence, the intellectual inheritance of Max Weber on the one hand and Baudelaire on the other. From the former comes the belief in societal modernization and from the latter the belief in cultural modernity (Gaonkar 1999). For Weber, the price paid for significant improvements in the material conditions of life must be weighed against the feelings of boredom, despair, and alienation associated with order, rationality, and routine. In contrast, Baudelaire focused on the aestheticization of modern culture and the cultivation and care of the self. For him, "imagination was an ally, and reason was an obstacle" (3). From this perspective, modernity is perhaps best understood as a method of questioning the present. But it can also be viewed as a way of creating the present.

Just as there are various models of development, so are there various models of modernity — in other words, alternative modernities which have increasingly become more indigenized and more critical (Sahlins 1999). By studying these processes and listening carefully to the indigenous voices involved, one can better understand the hopes, fears, and dreams of those affected. "To be modern is to find ourselves in an environment that promises us adventure, power, joy, growth, transforma-

4

tion of ourselves and the world — and, at the same time, that threatens to destroy everything we know, everything we are" (Berman 1983, 15).

My second reason for exploring alternative development strategies is to draw attention to processes under way that may run counter to accepted definitions of development. While they may appear counter-intuitive to conventional thinking, they may signify a radically different way of thinking about development that embodies concepts and practices that reinforce and strengthen our common, shared humanity (Heyman 2003). By countering development and proposing and practicing viable alternatives, a form of critical modernity, these processes may hold out hope for something better for those presently marginalized, ignored, or excluded (Peet with Hartwick 1999).

Third, missing from much of the discussion and critique of development is any acknowledgment of or interest in the ethical or moral dimension of development: What is right and what is wrong? What is good and what is bad? Yet underlying development, or at least the discourses of development, are some implicit assumptions and principles about what constitutes a good society, however we may care to define it. By carefully avoiding such definitional and philosophical challenges, we conveniently legitimize and, to a certain extent, standardize a more technical, more managerial, apolitical approach to development. Nevertheless, the evidence would indicate that the "good society" propounded by the "developers" may differ radically from that desired by those "to be developed," who, if left to their own devices with the opportunity and capability to sift and winnow and carefully select, may propose some form of society in which the moral imagination is accorded its due.

A fourth reason to justify this approach is the opportunity to study development discourse. Until recently, this has entailed close attention to and analysis of the documentation, presentation, and representation of the mainstream international development organizations. But varieties of development discourse are produced by all organizations working in development, be they public or private, multilateral or bilateral, international, national, regional, local, indigenous, or whatever. Hence, it would be more accurate to talk about development discourses (Grillo 1997) and seriously think about "studying down" and analyzing more localized discourses where the potential may be greater for more creative, innovative, and moral approaches to the future. The study of local-level plans, a recent innovation on the development landscape of

Colombia, offers a promising focus of research, since planning is often regarded as the primal act in development—perhaps more important than development itself.

These discourses should be considered within the broader context of contemporary critiques of development itself, specifically the enduring persistence of poverty and the postdevelopmental premise that attaining a middle-class lifestyle for the majority of the world's population may be impossible (Nustad 2001). This premise, of course, assumes that this is what the majority would like, if not for themselves, at least for their children. To deal with these critiques, Nustad cites the critical need to study manifestations of development on the ground in concrete encounters, just as I propose to do here. In a similarly critical, but more creative vein, Arjun Appadurai (1996) has argued that the flow of information generated by globalization has vastly increased people's potential to dream and imagine other worlds and other ways of living. Complementing Nustad, he proposes a serious commitment to the study of globalization from below and a recognition that the word *globalization*, as well as words like *freedom, choice,* and *justice,* are not inevitably the property of those in positions of political and economic power (Appadurai 2000). Both authors, but particularly Appadurai, accept that development can be indigenous in the sense that much of the motivation and creativity may originate locally.

A final reason for studying other ways of doing development is that the researcher cannot ignore (or deny) the political and moral implications of his or her work, a process that should make for a more engaged and provocative anthropology. In Colombia in particular, and, I suspect, in Latin America in general, anthropological researchers, national or international, are regarded with increasing suspicion and distrust. They are viewed by those studied as avaricious extractors of information who will fully exploit what they have gathered for their own benefit, offering little or nothing in return. Some ethnic groups in Colombia, for example, the Guambiano of Cauca, routinely refuse to cooperate with outside researchers, partly because they do not trust them but also because they prefer to do the research on their own. With other groups, such as the Nasa (who are the focus of this study), research requires reciprocity: external researchers are expected and required to contribute through some mutually acceptable form of collaboration. My case was no exception, a situation I describe in some detail in chapter 1.

Such collaboration with the poor, minorities, or the marginalized also has a political dimension that is ambivalent, rather than straightforward, shades of gray rather than black and white. Do we collaborate only with those whom we like, respect, and admire professionally and personally? What about those of whom we strongly disapprove but who may be important and active participants in the processes being studied, such as certain politicians, bureaucrats, businesspeople, soldiers, police officers, guerrillas, paramilitaries, and common criminals? What are the implications of "taking sides," consciously or unconsciously, for the types of research we choose to undertake and the substance of the books and articles we publish? Although there is a certain degree of overlap here between the political and the moral, there is also a personal element. Those of us from the North who choose to study the issues of development in the South are part of the problem. Some will argue that the problems of development, like the poor themselves, will be with us always, and others will argue that the nature and intensity of these problems will only change when we ourselves, individually, collectively, and institutionally, take the initiative to become more accountable and more responsible.

For the past decade I have been listening to what the Nasa have to say about development, about the changes that have occurred in their lives as a result of political violence, government repression, a drug economy, and forced relocation. But the Nasa would be interesting even if all these calamitous events had not befallen them. They are the largest ethnic group in one of the most ethnic provinces of Colombia. Historically famous as warriors, they have more recently been engaged in the struggle for indigenous rights and resistance against the violence of the state and the various armed groups operating in Cauca. Active participants in the indigenous movement, they have spearheaded various initiatives designed to persuade the national government to change its policies and practices towards the poor, the disadvantaged, and the marginalized.

The 1994 earthquake ruined their lands, and communities were resettled on new lands. The lives of the leaders and elders, at least, show few traces of despondency. In one new community, Tóez Caloto, Don Jorge has been responsible for building a Nasa school, where the children, as well as those from neighboring communities, can receive an education. Much respected for his efforts, Don Jorge, an evangelical Protestant, lives in one of the better houses, employs several of his neighbors to work his lands, and sends his daughter to university. Together with some other more entrepreneurial families, he has taken full advantage of the opportunities offered by resettlement. But many families have chosen not to do so. Their communal identity as Nasa is also in flux.

In another new community, Cxayu'ce, three of the elders (the older, more respected members) moved with their people. Don Lisandro, the leader in charge at the time of the relocation and the most political of the three elders, has only one regret about his new life: he can no longer grow opium poppies. Although he used community funds to establish a disastrous bus service, his reputation has not suffered. He has four children, one of whom became a nurse and three of whom are teachers, a pattern that his grandchildren are following. The second, Don Ruben, a farmer well respected for agricultural skills, is married to a school-teacher and has a large family in which the older children, now adult women, while proud of being indigenous, do not identify with an indigenous way of life and have chosen to marry mestizos. The third elder, Don Mario, a small farmer who is also rumored to be a shaman with malevolent powers, has four children, three living in the community; one daughter is a schoolteacher, a second daughter is married to a mestizo and helps him in the fields, and the third, a son, is a small farmer; the fourth, also a son, a teacher in another province, is an aspiring shaman and a strong proponent of indigenous culture. All three families have flourished in economic terms while maintaining a strong indigenous identity.

In the final new community examined, Juan Tama, two of the local leaders who have been very active over the years have few material goods to show for their efforts. For Don Julio, life is a burden that grows no lighter; life before the relocation was better than what he and his family are presently living. While he does not regret the move, he finds life increasingly demanding as he strives to feed his large young family. In contrast, Don Ángel, a well-respected shaman and supporter of indigenous culture, views the present as much better than the past: "Here we are in glory!" For him, the move to Juan Tama has opened up cultural and political opportunities that simply did not exist before in the field of indigenous education and cultural creativity. In material terms, however, he is just as poorly off as Don Julio. Yet both in their own ways have helped establish Juan Tama as the most dynamically Nasa of the three resettled communities. I offer these thumbnail sketches of local leaders and elders to make an important point: while development is happening at the local level, it takes various economic, cultural, and political forms which can only be understood in the broader historical context of what it means to be indigenous in Cauca.

Being Indigenous in Cauca

The province of Cauca is famed for its geographical diversity, ranging from the tropics of the Pacific coast to the temperate climes of the Andes to the lowlands of the Amazon Basin. This diversity has facilitated neither development nor social change. Contemporary intellectuals bemoan Cauca's notoriety as a place of backwardness and poverty, ignored by contemporary discourses of development and controlled by regional elites who, on the whole, are too aristocratic and too feudal to allow the emergence of a dynamic middle class (Barona and Gnecco 2001). Large landowners are faulted for their lack of interest in producing for the market, and likewise the small producers, be they peasant, indigenous, or Afro-Colombian, for their lack of productivity. But this superficial gaze at contemporary Cauca tends to ignore various processes under way, particularly a growing interest and awareness of its cultural richness and diversity, increasing mobilization of large numbers of the population, and growing dissatisfaction with the conventional politics of neoliberalism.

The mainstay of Cauca's economy is agriculture: capital-intensive plantation agriculture and cattle ranching in the warmer, lower-lying north, small-scale coffee and tropical fruit cultivation in the valleys, and labor-intensive cereal and potato cultivation in the higher altitudes. Land tenure and the process of land consolidation have been major problems since colonial times. From 1973 to 1997, the number of farm families with 5 hectares of land or less increased by 82.6 percent, from 84,331 to 154,011, but the amount of land they controlled increased by only 26.5 percent, accounting for only 8.7 percent of total farmlands. Over the same period, the number of families owning more than 100 hectares increased by 27 percent, from 2,110 to 2,678, and the amount of land they controlled grew by 78.5 percent, accounting for 54.2 percent of the total. Within this group, 157 families, less than one hundredth of total farm households, own 36.7 percent of farmlands (Paz 2001, 207–8).

Cauca is famous for its ethnic diversity. It has the largest indigenous population of any province in the country, though precise figures are hard to come by, ranging from a low of 13 percent of its overall population (Paz 2001) to a high of 30 percent (Departamento del Cauca 2001). Indigenous people are organized in *resguardos,* a communal landholding entity that dates from the mid-colonial period and is administered by a *cabildo,* a council elected on an annual basis. These two institutions, the resguardo and the cabildo, together with language — though to a much lesser extent since the majority of the indigenous population in Cauca is monolingual in Spanish — are often regarded as the defining characteristics of indigenous culture and ethnic identity in Colombia (Field 1996). Demographic growth in the resguardos has resulted in increasing pressure on the available resource base, particularly arable land and pasture, and, in some cases, encroachment into the *páramo,* high-altitude humid plains that are usually jealously protected as watersheds.

In addition, Cauca is famous for its political activism. CRIC (Regional Indigenous Council of Cauca), the oldest indigenous rights organization in Colombia, was established in Cauca under the banner of Land, Autonomy, and Culture (Gros 1991). At its founding meeting in Toribío in 1971, the CRIC leadership agreed on a seven-point program that focused on several key themes that have remained constant over the years: the recovery and extension of resguardo lands; the strengthening of the cabildos; the defense of indigenous history, language, and customs; and the training of bilingual indigenous schoolteachers (Espinosa 1998, 116). In the past decade, CRIC has become increasingly involved in human rights, rural development, and the quest for peace and an end to the continuing political violence.

While recovery (*recuperación*) of stolen lands has been an enduring theme, CRIC was also created to defend the lives of indigenous leaders who have been selectively and systematically targeted for assassination over the years by armed groups of the left and right, as well as by the organs of the state, specifically the army and the police. The organization maintains a list of over four hundred members who have been killed over the past thirty years, a reflection of the ongoing state of political violence that prevails in the province, dating from the time of La Violencia in the 1950s and earlier. During La Violencia, an independent republic was established by peasant self-defense units in Riochiqito, one of the more isolated areas of Tierradentro in northeastern Cauca, which, as a member of the Southern Block in 1965, was to participate in the founding meeting of the FARC, the Revolutionary Armed Forces of Colombia (González 1992, 103). This Southern Block is still active on the border between the provinces of Cauca and Huila. The other major active guerrilla group in Colombia, the ELN (National Liberation Army) has long been present in Cauca; one of its major strongholds lies to the west of Popayán, the provincial capital. In the 1980s, the guerrillas made it clear that they would not tolerate alternative voices in the countryside by assassinating indigenous leaders, including shamans, who were regarded as particularly dangerous. In response, the Nasa, the largest indigenous group in the province, established their own guerrilla force, the MAQL, the Quintín Lame Armed Movement, primarily as a self-defense unit. In this, they were assisted by the April 19th Movement (M-19), also very active in Cauca until their demobilization in 1990. In addition, there is a long history of hired killers (*pájaros*) in Cauca, contracted by large landowners and political conservatives to eliminate voices of protest and opposition. Over time, these have become institutionalized as paramilitary units which began appearing in the province around 1990.

Development and Modernity

Development, like modernity, has an ambiguous relationship with culture. Some commentators have argued that capitalism, as the "highest" form of development, can only emerge out of certain cultures, thereby implying that other cultures may actually hinder development (Platteau 1994). As several critics have pointed out, this argument can rapidly degenerate into a racist discourse on the cultural failings of certain peoples (Rapley 2002). When used in the context of development, culture has often been qualified with the adjective *traditional*, a pejorative connotation implying that it is a constraint to change of any sort. More recently the concept has been viewed as more dynamic, flexible, and creative (Rao and Walton 2004). In indigenous Cauca, culture can include fluency in indigenous languages, respect for shamanistic authority, cosmological knowledge, knowledge of the past and present, educational innovation, skills in communication and mobilization, and political representation, to name a few of the more salient characteristics

11

of CRIC leaders (Warren 1998). Incorporation of some or all these elements into the development process not only helps humanize the changes under way but also maintains and strengthens the indigenous political and cultural project.

It is in this sense that *culture* will be used here — as a key element in understanding how people view and critique the world in which they live, as well as how they choose to act in an evolving cultural politics of development. For Escobar (1997), cultural politics is the process whereby social actors, embodying different cultural meanings and practices, come into conflict. In Cauca, this means that different ethnic groups have different ideas about what constitutes development, as do communities within a single ethnic group. In the context of modernity, cultural politics refers not only to attempts to redefine social and political power but also to the more profound process of contesting, negotiating, and formulating the very meaning of modernity itself. In Cauca, the indigenous movement and its supporters argue that if Colombia is to be regarded as a modern nation, then the state must not only embrace difference but also be more inclusive and treat all of its people as citizens with the same rights and responsibilities. Furthermore, it must also live up to the promises and ideals of modernity.

How, then, are we to characterize those who criticize the project of modernity and its most vaunted offshoot, development? The concept of the Other within the project of modernity remains problematic. Anthropology has been charged with the task of defining the relationship between the anthropological Self and the ethnographic Other, but there are various kinds of Others, of which being indigenous is one, Afro-Colombian another, and peasant yet a third (Kearney 1996). Sahlins's proposed indigenization of development, and by association modernity, implies at least some recognition and acceptance of this Other. In his research on the role of agriculture in the making of modern India, Akhil Gupta (1998) defines the condition of the small farmers he studied as "postcolonial," since they demonstrate a distinct lack of fit with the dichotomy of "modern" and "traditional." This is demonstrated by their ability and facility to use and adapt key elements of both, a process of imbrication, of shared knowledges. He borrows the phrase "inappropriate Other" from the filmmaker Trinh T. Minh-ha to refer to them since they straddle both worlds, in a sense belonging to neither yet managing to survive in both (Trinh 1991).[1]

12

The indigenous inappropriate others in Cauca bring more than one perspective to the understanding and resolution of critical social and political issues. CRIC has survived as an institution through its willingness and ability to defy convention and confront the authority of the state directly, but only to a certain point. For example, it was active in establishing armed self-defense units to protect its leaders in the late 1970s and early 1980s. But when these units coalesced in 1984 to form the MAQL, CRIC was obliged to retreat to a more clandestine support role that they were later forced to terminate on account of political pressure from more conservative elements in the indigenous movement. In the 1990s, CRIC mobilized its supporters in Cauca to protest the national government's unwillingness to deliver on its promises, including support for indigenous education. From 1999 to the present, CRIC has regularly appeared on the national stage in support of peace negotiations, an end to political violence by the left and the right, and, most recently, to protest the lack of any public participation in the negotiations over the free trade agreement with the United States. As representatives of the inappropriate other, CRIC has been able to do what other groups cannot or will not do — make their voices heard regionally, nationally, and even internationally.

This tension between the "inside" and the "outside," between the "old" and the "new," between the "proven" and the "unproven" is reflected in the contentious debate over "local knowledge" and its potential "contribution" to development and modernity. Maia Green (2000) suggests that what people "know" generally includes large amounts of so-called Western knowledge, as well as more context-specific local knowledge (see Agrawal 1996). In a similar vein, Anja Nygren (1999) talks about "knowledge encounters" in which the local and the global, the traditional and the modern are intricately intermingled. She also raises the crucial question about the relative importance of these diverse forms of knowledge, whether they can symmetrically coexist or whether alternative knowledges will be inevitably marginalized (282). If arguments in favor of cultural politics and countermodernity are to be taken seriously, then such knowledge encounters in the field of development, as in planning and implementation, offer potentially fruitful areas of investigation.

For some, however, the postcolonial farmers of India and, by implication, other parts of the developing world, should be considered failed subjects of the project of modernity. Their feeling of being "left behind" forms the basis of their mobilization against the dominant vision of national development. Although Gupta (1998, 232) persuasively argues that it would be more productive to think of them "as a disturbing presence that continuously interrupts the redemptive narratives of the West," in the process he downplays the ambiguities suggested by Trinh, particularly the creative and positive potential they offer to the process of countermodernity.

Resistance and the Moral Imagination

For those living at the margin and for those already marginalized, survival often depends on some form of resistance, whether through the carefully calculated practice of the weapons of the weak (Scott 1985) or the more radical and potentially more dangerous avenues of mass mobilization and armed resistance. In widespread areas of rural Colombia, continuing conflict (or at least the perceived threat of it) has become part and parcel of everyday existence, where survival has come to depend on continuing resistance; where local communities have seen no other alternative, violence is selectively used as a form of self-defense. Much of the conflict has its origin in struggles over land, specifically land expropriated from its legal owners, often with the explicit support of the state and its surrogates — the private armies of the powerful — who were the forerunners of today's paramilitary forces.

When communities have organized to legally and peacefully protest the abuses and depredations perpetrated against them, the state has often responded with indifference. The landowners and their hired killers have responded with the assassination of selected local leaders, crimes that often go unpunished. A similar strategy has been followed by the guerrillas. To this day, they continue to assassinate indigenous leaders and occupy indigenous lands. In the period covered by this study, those most affected by this persecution responded by creating their own organization, CRIC, to protect the land, rights, and culture of the indigenous people of Cauca. In turn, this organization and its leaders have been heavily persecuted. On account of their suspected collaboration with the guerrillas for a period in the late 1970s and 1980s, some of the leaders were obliged to go underground, and others were imprisoned. During the 1990s and into the new millennium, the movement has been able to operate more freely and more openly, but always under threat from the armed groups operating in the region.

How do we talk about development in a context of continuing violence, physical and structural, and where the commonly accepted, conventional measures of development — or, better said, lack of development — such as nutritional levels, infant mortality, life expectancy, and rates of schooling, are abysmal?[2] The very fact that people continue to resist demonstrates their refusal to accept the status quo, to fight against their unequal chances, which, real as they may be, are not immutable. Their resistance is more than a protest against injustice, both past and present. It is also a claim for social justice, as well as a demand for recognition, inclusion, and respect. But it is also, as I already argued, a demand for redistribution, for a greater share of the country's resources that are rightfully theirs as poor, marginalized, disadvantaged citizens.

Acknowledgment of this fact can help us understand why the indigenous movement and its supporters continue to struggle, in spite of all the setbacks. In other words, there is a certain moral imagination that guides their actions, a desire and a willingness to care about and empathize with the fate of others, an imagination that not only has some clear ideas about what is right and wrong but also some creative ideas about how these ideals may be realized. In the case of the Zapatistas of Chiapas, Neil Harvey (1998, 35) argues that the creation of new political spaces has been essential in establishing "the right to have rights," to be recognized as a legitimate member of the political community: "It might be argued, therefore, that the struggles of popular movements for dignity, voice, and autonomy are precisely attempts to constitute 'the people' as a political actor; that is, as a people with the right to participate freely in public debate and uphold their right to have rights."

To participate in the larger society, the indigenous people of Cauca have been forced to confront the continuing threat of violence, together with the systematic brutality against their political and intellectual leaders. Their resistance has been forged by violence, but at the same time they have learned to understand (but not accept) that the bloodshed will continue until profound changes occur in the social and political structure of Colombia (which was the long-term objective of many of the guerrilla movements in the country, at least in their earlier years). In no way does this mean that people accept the inevitability of political violence and the possibility of death. Quite the contrary. Many people see it as their responsibility to think beyond violence, to the future of their children, and strive to improve the situation as a form of moral stewardship and responsibility. While the threat and presence of violence are a given, they are not viewed as immutable.

Resistance to violence creates new spaces and new opportunities, in the same way a natural disaster can. The brief biographies of elders sketched earlier capture the ways some families have adapted after being forced to relocate by a devastating earthquake. As a result of the disaster, many other families were forced to leave their communities of origin and move to new lands with state provision of land and housing. In a more general sense, they were offered the opportunity to wipe the slate clean, and start again, to build a new life elsewhere, but one heavily influenced by the past, not just the recent past but also the historical and cultural past. As a type of social laboratory, this process of resettlement offers a unique opportunity to study and understand firsthand the ways in which these new communities deal with the broader range of possibilities that the disaster, somewhat paradoxically, offered them. The communities to be described and analyzed all wished to be relocated closer to urban centers, but not all were, and those that were did not necessarily fully embrace all that development and modernity had to offer. In fact, while there was a certain acceptance of the bricks and mortar aspect of development with its focus on the tangible, be it a feeder road, a health clinic, or a dairy cow, there was an implicit realization and criticism that this was not enough, particularly when considering the future of their children. Though there was an acknowledgment of the obvious importance of some degree of economic and financial security, it did not become an obsession. Equally important (if not more so) was the future of their children and subsequent generations. In their own way, they were confronting a fundamental question that haunts many other similar groups: what is the future for indigenous groups, but particularly their children, in a putative multicultural society such as Colombia in the twenty-first century?

They countered the dominant discourse with one of their own. Like many other displaced, migratory, or diasporic communities in other parts of the world, they opted for education, partly as a means of "entering" and being "accepted" by the larger, dominant society but also as a means of preserving, adapting, and changing their own culture, but on their terms, since they would control the form and substance of the education their children would receive, at least at the primary level. Making this possible called for a combination of political will and cultural pride, both of which had been strengthened by the ongoing political mobilization, the struggle for social justice, and their recognition as indigenous people, legitimate citizens of Colombia. In practice, this form of education is only possible though a kind of local autonomy where the community has considerable control over both the teachers and the curriculum. It also requires a certain degree of courage, as well as the freedom and initiative to be both imaginary and creative, characteristics not usually associated with development, even when broadly defined.

Escobar (1995b) suggests that there are three major discourses for articulating forms of struggle. The first is the democratic imaginary with its focus on economic and social justice, human rights, class, gender, and ethnic equality. Second is the discourse of difference, which emphasizes cultural distinctiveness, alterity, autonomy, and the right of self-determination. Finally, there is the discourse of antidevelopment, which offers the potential for more radical transformations of capitalism and the search for alternative ways of organizing society "of satisfying needs, of healing and living." These discourses are not mutually exclusive, and the indigenous discourses of Cauca in the following chapters embrace elements of all three. The democratic imaginary with its focus on justice, equality, and inclusion occupies a prominent place, and the discourse of difference with its emphasis on culture, human rights, and autonomy is becoming more important. But the discourse of antidevelopment is perhaps misnamed. While the practice of conventional development is questioned and criticized, the proposed alternatives do not call for unrealistic radical transformations. Rather, they offer proposals for countering development, for thinking about it in a different, more human, more constructive, and more sustainable way.

Structure of the Book

The indigenous people of Cauca are well organized and demonstrate a healthy skepticism (if not outright suspicion) of all outside researchers, particularly anthropologists. Therefore, as I argue in chapter 1, collaboration with local people and organizations, whether in the form of sharing knowledge or contributing to ongoing social processes, is imperative. Perhaps more important, however, is the creation of an on-going dialogue about the meaning of these processes with those most actively involved; the people of Cauca were as keen to learn from me as I was to learn from them. Such collaborative analysis shifts the terms of ethnographic fieldwork from an extractive enterprise to a creative one.

In chapter 2, I explain the ethnographic context for my comparative study of the three new communities established after the 1994 earth-quake. During such traumatic events, communities have the oppor-tunity to remake themselves and their culture in innovative ways. But such opportunities may be constrained by those in power, in this case, by both the state and the indigenous movement, with their precon-ceived notions of the place of local indigenous communities in the province and the nation and, correspondingly, the kind of development that is appropriate for them.

Chapter 3 focuses on local planning, comparing the development plans, both process and "text," produced by the three new communities. In its final essence, a plan is produced to convince an audience, some-times internal but more often external, that the community's version of reality and its vision of the future are the correct ones. The plan-ning processes, as well as the contents of the plans, differed significantly from community to community, ranging from passive acceptance of conventional development to active embrace of a more equitable form of change. The differences reflect the communities' changing relation-ships with the indigenous movement and its influence on their evolving concept of culture, a concept rarely treated seriously in development discourse.

Educational planning, in contrast to development planning, draws much of its power and originality from local knowledge. Although this knowledge is dynamic, it can stimulate a critical and more profound understanding of enduring problems and ways to address them. In chapter 4, by comparing the educational plans prepared by two of the new communities, I argue that indigenous education in its conventional form is instrumental in embracing modernity, exploiting the past, and shifting the terms of identity. In its more politicized form, however, indigenous education questions modernity and proposes a more cre-ative alternative that strengthens cultural identity while downplaying the primacy accorded the economic. In the long run, the test will be how well politicized indigenous education prepares the entire community to be active citizens in a multicultural society.

In chapter 5, as a basis for comparison and contrast, I present the experience of Toribío, a predominantly Nasa municipality in northern Cauca, which in 1998 was awarded a national prize for producing the best development plan in Colombia. The people who live there are regarded by their fellow Nasa as being the most radical and best organized group in Cauca. But development planning in Toribío long preceded the 1991 Constitution. In 1980, a local parish priest organized the first development planning workshop in the region. A comparison of the two plans, supplemented by additional information generated at a 1999 seminar on development for young indigenous leaders, shows that the prize-winning plan flattens, homogenizes, and dilutes the everyday world of the Nasa—the price paid for adopting the dominant development discourse. Yet the young leaders continue to raise uncomfortable issues, such as political violence, discrimination against women, and cultivation of illegal crops, which development experts rarely address. Toribío, the successful indigenous vanguard and a model of modernity, has to a certain extent assimilated the dominant development discourse, showing that it is not only at the grass roots but also within the leadership of the movement that counterdevelopment encounters roadblocks.

An ambivalent attitude toward development, an increasing interest in culture, and continuing demands to be taken seriously on the national stage are part of a larger and more ambitious process under way in Cauca, which I discuss in chapter 6. In 1999, the indigenous movement established La María (La María: Territory for Living Together, Dialogue, and Negotiation) as an alternative political space, a subaltern counterpublic sphere where civil society could make its voice heard in the peace process then under way and contribute to decision making about Colombia's future development, specifically the restructuring of the state and necessary social, political, and economic reforms (Fraser 1997). The Sun and Land Foundation (Fundación Sol y Tierra), created by the demobilized members of the MAQL and actively involved in producing development plans with indigenous communities, was instrumental in the creation of La María. Furthermore, it was in La María that Taita Floro Tunubalá, the first indigenous provincial governor to be elected in the history of Colombia, first articulated what was to become the Alternate Plan for Cauca and the surrounding region, the basis for which would be a more just form of development. This was a direct consequence of the 1991 Constitution and the promises it extended.

As I argue in the conclusion, the moral imaginary created by the indigenous movement, when combined with the growing importance attached to the discourse and practice of human rights, offers a different and more fruitful way of thinking about development. From this perspective, development is less integration into the project of modernity and more a creative form of resistance, a form of critical modernity that embraces a radical politics of inclusive citizenship.

This book is about a diaspora of hope, about the possibility of building new lives on the roots and memories of the old, memories that are sometimes pleasant but often are not. It is about the structural factors that constrain people from achieving what Aristotle called "human flourishing," but it is also about human agency, the ways in which people not only resist but also selectively engage with their past and their future as they creatively seek to establish a present that is different and hopefully better. In addition, it is also about the ways people, particularly those living at the historical margins of society, make their voices heard and demand to be recognized and treated with respect and dignity. Above all, it is about questioning modernity, creatively countering development, and working toward viable alternatives to the prevailing assumptions about how life should be lived at the beginning of the twenty-first century.

1

Anthropology as a disciplinary enterprise does not so much harm Indian people (although there are enough individual cases of direct or indirect harm) as conduct studies on issues completely and utterly irrelevant to Indian welfare.—THOMAS BIOLSI AND LARRY J. ZIMMERMAN, introduction to *Indians and Anthropologists: Vine Deloria, Jr., and the Critique of Anthropology*

If anthropologists are not interested in the fate of their subjects, then what use can their knowledge have, either to the community itself or to any genuine "science of man"?—PETER WHITELEY, "The End of Anthropology (at Hopi?)"

More Than an Engaged Fieldnote:

Collaboration, Dialogue, and Difference

Anthropology as a discipline prides itself on "being there," in the sense that the anthropologist goes to the "field" and observes and talks with people. This is anything but simple and straightforward since the anthropologist, whether he or she likes it or not, becomes an active participant in the process he or she is studying. The researcher becomes the major research instrument in the creation and collection of information. If the ethnography produced is to have any acceptance or credibility, it is incumbent upon the researcher to tell the reader how he or she went about collecting the information and also to disclose any personal idiosyncrasies that may have helped or hindered the process.

This first chapter addresses the issue by discussing key elements of my research process in Colombia. The first element is the justification for doing research at all in Colombia, particularly in rural areas, where personal security becomes a major issue. A second and more important element deals with the problems and pitfalls of trying to be a moral and engaged researcher while maintaining a certain objectivity. The third and final element, really an experiment, is an example of how to be actively engaged, moving beyond collaboration in the running of workshops and the production of texts to a more full-blooded but nuanced dialogue about meaning, difference, and responsibilities to those studied.

Who Does Fieldwork in Colombia?

I am periodically asked why I choose to do research in Colombia, the implication being that my choice is somewhat strange, even potentially dangerous. I have no smart, foolproof answer to this question. Nevertheless, it is a question that has concerned me for a decade now, one with which I continue to wrestle. Colombia is a nation at war, particularly in the countryside. This has profound methodological, political, and ethical implications for any serious researcher, but particularly for an anthropologist whose bread-and-butter, if you will, is people. Myriam Jimeno (2001) has argued that the pervasive environment of violence that characterizes contemporary Colombia has produced a climate of personal insecurity and social fragmentation. Daily life becomes less predictable and more circumscribed, thereby underscoring why anthropological fieldwork in inherently dangerous. The researcher may be defined as a spy. People may find it very difficult to understand or appreciate the research topic. Neutrality and objectivity are difficult, if not impossible. The researcher must learn to walk and talk softly, in terms of where to go and what questions to ask, and must continually define and redefine the risks and dangers, not only to himself, but perhaps more important, for those with whom he is working (Sluka 1995).

In the case of Colombia, as elsewhere in Latin America, there is a long, well-documented, and fully justified history of viewing foreign researchers in rural areas with skepticism and suspicion. Why are they there? Who are they working for? What will they do with the information they collect? Given that the U.S. Central Intelligence Agency has a well-established and notorious track record in the region, the assumption is that researchers are working for the "agency," or some similar, potentially threatening entity. Not only are researchers' motives suspect, so are the topics of their research.

In such a politically sensitive situation as that found in Cauca, no "neutrals are allowed."[1] As a result, fieldwork demands a certain degree of engagement on the part of the investigator, whether as scholar, critic, interlocutor, collaborator, advocate, or activist, but such engagement also exacts a price, politically and ethically, because often the anthropologist must choose to take sides, casting his lot with the powerless in their struggles with the powerful, and thus running the risk that the ethnography produced, as part of the public domain, can be used either to benefit or to harm the people described (Greene 1995).

In a review of indigenous rights movements in Africa and Latin America, Dorothy Hodgson characterizes "interlocutors" such as herself: "As scholars who share our ideas and work with indigenous groups in ongoing, constructive, and, perhaps, even occasionally contentious dialogues and debates in an effort to inform and shape their policies and practices, without directly aligning ourselves with one group or faction of the movement" (2002, 1045). She is making an important point here. While quite prepared to share her information, knowledge, and expertise with those she is studying, Hodgson is careful to avoid committing herself to any one particular group. Though this is understandable methodologically, in practical terms it may be impossible, since the willingness to share with indigenous groups is a political statement in and of itself. This is certainly the case in Colombia, and I would question the extent to which one can make these fine distinctions in arenas characterized by long histories of discrimination, oppression, and political violence. Interlocution *and* collaboration may be the sine qua non for undertaking any type of ethnographic research in this context. Such engagement, of course, is two-sided: while it may strengthen the researcher's credibility in the eyes of some, it is guaranteed to make him enemies with others.

Such a decision also requires that the researcher be prepared to take a stand when the occasion demands it. In 2000, I participated in a workshop involving several hundred people to discuss the recently initiated peace process involving the government and the Revolutionary Armed Forces of Colombia (FARC). Also on the agenda was the impending implementation of Plan Colombia, the provision of U.S. military and technical assistance provided to the government for the eradication of coca fields and poppy plots. For the Nasa, many of whom were cultivating these crops, Plan Colombia was seen as being directed primarily at them, the very small producers at the bottom of a long and lucrative production and marketing chain. At the same time, Plan Colombia was viewed in many circles, correctly as it later turned out, as a means for the U.S. government to rationalize a military presence in the country directed at defeating the guerrillas. During the workshop I was interviewed by a major regional TV channel in which I was highly critical of the U.S. government and its potential role in further militarizing the conflict, an act that provided me with face (if not name) recognition in many places. At the request of the indigenous movement, I tried, unsuccessfully, to obtain funds, in both the United States and Europe, to support additional activities in support of peace. Although these efforts did not necessarily create rapport, I am convinced they did help foster some mutual confidence and respect. Even if such efforts did not necessarily open any more doors, minds, or hearts, they did contribute to a higher level of tolerance for my presence at various types of activities.

Both examples clearly demonstrate, however, the ambiguities incurred by the individual researcher who chooses to work in a highly politicized context. By publicly criticizing U.S. foreign policy for Colombia, I was consciously taking a stand against what the United States stood for, while at the same time clearly distancing myself from that policy. By seeking funding to support peace initiatives at the regional level, I was trying to accompany my political stance with something more tangible than mere moral support. In the process, of course, I shed all pretense of neutrality, in the sense that I had chosen to take sides. But had I also jeopardized my objectivity, willingness, and ability to present the facts as I saw them in a reasonably balanced and unbiased manner? Had I perhaps, consciously or otherwise, decided to write about some incidents rather than others to make my argument more convincing? While this is a potential temptation for all researchers, I think it is particularly tempting, if not outright seductive, when studying processes that one sympathizes with if not approves of. Though taking sides may facilitate the research, it also entails certain responsibilities to those one chooses to study and work with. All information is grist for the researcher's mill, but what if some is confidential, controversial, critical, or potentially damaging? The engaged researcher walks an ethical tightrope trying to balance these various concerns to maintain some integrity.

Here I wish to describe and analyze how I went about doing the research on which this book is based, fully aware of the problems involved in foregrounding the author at the expense of the ethnography, while accepting that both are directly and symbiotically related. At the same time, I bear in mind the caveats clearly articulated by Peter Whiteley, addressing similar concerns about his life-long research with the Hopi: "What do reflexive ethnographers *not* tell us about their motivations, feelings, personal histories, fieldwork experiences, inchoate immediate or long-term doubts, and structured positionalities? What do they *not know* about themselves? The apparent ease of introducing the ethnographer as self into the text is, beyond style, more problematic than has been openly imagined" (1998, 18). While the ethnographer may choose to be selective about the subjects of his research, the temptation is to be even more selective about the presentation of self, since he runs the risk of jeopardizing (if not losing) his authority and credibility in the process. Yet this presentation is important because the ethnographer is the major research instrument, responsible for creating and analyzing the information he chooses to present (Ortner 1995). This instrument of the self is, however, also problematic, since it involves not only perceptions but also memories and creativity: "Are memories fieldnotes? I use them that way, even though they aren't the same kind of evidence. It took a while for me to be able to rely on my memory. But I *had* to, since the idea of what I was doing had changed, and I had memories but no notes. I had to say, 'Well, I saw that happen.' I am a fieldnote" (Jackson 1990, 21).

Since this is the case, it is important that the reader have some appreciation and understanding of who precisely the ethnographer is without his necessarily revealing all and producing autobiography rather than ethnography. Of the several points that Whiteley mentions, two are particularly relevant to my own case: motivations and doubts. One can always put up convincing intellectual and political arguments for doing ethnographic research, but there are always other more intangible, less laudable reasons for "going to the field" year after year. There are elements of romanticism, the desire to rub shoulders with people who appear to be doing something socially worthwhile with their lives, a form of vicarious self-righteousness whereby one's personal feelings of guilt are replaced by another's example of virtue. There are also elements of escapism, the desire to be somewhere else where life is simpler because one is less involved and hence has less responsibility, as well as the desire to be someone else. The anthropologist in the field is different from his commonsensical, everyday person at "home." His marginal status provides the opportunity to be more adventurous and shed certain inhibitions. I found these feelings of romanticism and escapism were often accompanied by profound feelings of long-term self-doubt. Given the mixed reception I would often get from people I knew, I used to wonder what went through their heads as they saw me approaching: "I wonder what he wants this time? Does he ever run out of questions? What on earth does he do with all the information he gathers? How can we avoid his questions without being rude, by just ignoring him?" To be totally ignored is perhaps the ultimate insult for an anthropologist in the field.

And this did happen to me, if not on a regular basis at least often enough to make me reluctantly accept that it was not coincidental. I found the research in the communities to be psychologically daunting and physically demanding: daunting because the Nasa are expert at giving outsiders the cold shoulder and demanding because of the discomfort resulting from the diet, the beds, the weather, and the long nights. Though I had survived a similar experience as a doctoral student in the Andes of southern Peru some thirty years earlier, the situation in Colombia was different for two reasons. This was a comparative study which involved four distinct research sites, three new communities as well as one of the communities of origin. As a result, when I was in the field, I was constantly on the move, never staying in any one community for more than a few days at a time. These short-term visits virtually precluded the establishment of the type of long-term friendships that could foster trust, credibility, and reciprocity.

Another factor justifying this approach was the very nature of my research. I was trying to produce an ethnography of development rather than an ethnography of displaced communities. Hence my research concentrated primarily on the process of development, specifically the production of texts, a focus that emerged in the anthropology of development literature of the 1990s (Escobar 1995a; Grillo 1997), as well as in the more applied development anthropology literature (Gardner and Lewis 1996; Nolan 2002).[2] As it turned out, however, my focus on development process turned out to be rather short-sighted, since I could not fully understand it without giving more attention to history and politics, a reality reflected in later chapters.

Writing about oneself, like writing ethnography, can be a creative and selective process that may obfuscate rather than illuminate. It may serve to privilege the author and justify what others could find highly questionable. A case in point is Michael Taussig's (2004) published diary detailing a two-week trip to a small town outside Cali, the capital of the neighboring province, which he has been visiting and studying for thirty years. At the time, the town was occupied by the paramilitaries who, following their chosen vocation, had been killing those local citizens whom they deemed "undesirable," some of whom were known to the author. Taussig justifies the diary's publication by playing on the various meanings of the word *limpieza*, which normally means "cleaning," but has more recently come to mean "cleansing," in the sense of wiping out and killing defenseless people deemed undesirable. But limpieza also has an older meaning, that of healing a person or home, and Taussig examines this double meaning: "Perhaps my diary plays on this ambiguity: that in the process of recoding and detailing this new kind of *limpieza*, the diary might conserve this older sense as well, displacing the malignity of the events it describes. I certainly hope so, and now, looking back . . . believe this to be the reason for having written this diary in the first place" (Taussig 2004, xiii). This is more journalism and autobiography than ethnography, reflecting the author's apparent fascination with violence and his unwillingness to directly confront his own motivation for writing about it. It is difficult to justify writing about the systematic killing of people one has known and liked in the field, without expressing some feelings of guilt, remorse, anger, or regret.

Nevertheless, introducing oneself in the text may help demystify fieldwork and demonstrate just how agonistic a process it can be. How many anthropologists can say that they enjoy fieldwork? Bronislaw Malinowski spoke for many anthropologists in the posthumous publication of his infamous field journal, the frankness of which shocked many of his students and contemporaries at the time, particularly his expression of feelings of self-doubt:

> Went to the village hoping to photograph a few stages of the *bara*. I handed out half-*sticks* of tobacco, then watched a few dances; then took pictures — but results very poor. Not enough light for snapshots; and they would not pose long enough for time exposures. At moments I was furious at them, particularly because after I gave them their portions of tobacco they all went away. On the whole my feelings towards the natives are decidedly tending to *"Exterminate the brutes."* In many instances I have acted unfairly and stupidly. (Malinowski 1989 [1967], 69, cited in Geertz 1988, 74)

The diary, with its author's demonstrated anguish, confusion, elation, and anger, seemed markedly at odds with the stable, comprehensive ethnography of the Trobriand Islanders (Clifford 1988). What the diary underscores is the complexity entailed in Malinowski's total immersion approach to ethnography, over and above the indigenous life being studied: the landscape, the isolation, the local expatriates, the sense of vocation, the vagaries of one's thoughts. It also establishes another precedent, it forefronts introspection: "To be a convincing 'I-witness,' one must, so it seems, first become a convincing 'I'" (Geertz 1988, 79).

The introspection that bedevils fieldwork responds to Whiteley's concern about what anthropologists do not know about themselves or perhaps what they prefer not to know about themselves. In my own case, this meant accepting the fact that for me fieldwork was a form of often persistent and pervasive masochism. I continuously had to remind myself that my research was worthwhile and relevant, but each time I went to the field I never knew what to expect. I would discover that "reality" had changed, and that most people could not care less about my questions and obsessions. Becoming more engaged as a means of assuaging the self-doubt and masochism proved only partially successful, since an anthropologist, by definition, is always an outsider—his strength but also his Achilles heel.

Fieldwork under "Fire"

In the process of conducting doctoral research in Peru mentioned earlier, my family and I were forced to leave the indigenous community that we had been living in because we felt that we were no longer welcome there. People would not speak to us, promised food was not forthcoming, and our belongings were continuously pilfered. This happened six months into the fieldwork, after ample time spent trying to explain, in both Spanish and Quechua, why we were there and what we were trying to study. Some time later, we were invited to live in another community, where we maintained a base for the next two years and continued our research, while at the same time participating in various community activities, accepting certain responsibilities, and, when the situation demanded it, "speaking" on behalf of the community. By so doing, we established an identity for ourselves. We were accepted on personal grounds by building friendships with local people (Bentz

1997). But our "anthropological undertaking" remained unfathomable to the local people.

We ultimately found out why the people in the first community had wanted us to leave. The local teacher, a mestizo, had convinced them that we were there to steal their land. This charge was particularly effective, since the community had only recently regained control over its territory, a consequence of the 1968 land reform law. But it was not just the schoolteacher who was opposed to our presence. A year later, during market day in the local town, I was accosted by the sergeant in charge of the local police force. Armed and drunk, with tunic unbuttoned, he pinned me up against a pickup truck in the main plaza and proceeded to interrogate me about my research. Why had I come there? What was I investigating? Who was paying me? What would I produce? How much money would I make from the book I would most certainly write? Somewhat unnerved, I did my best to defend myself, fully aware that my "scientific" explanation for the importance of studying social change in this isolated corner of Peru rang hollow, more so when I emphasized that I would make no money from the undertaking. That someone would voluntarily choose to live in a mud hut for two years at ten thousand feet above sea level seemed to him an aberration. For the sergeant, as for his fellow mestizo, the schoolteacher, living and working in rural areas was a penance, something that had to be endured. There had to be more to us than met the eye.

In the mid-1990s, when I returned to the Andes, this time in Colombia, I found myself once again subject to the same criticism — not so much from mestizos or whites, but from the indigenous people themselves. On several occasions, I was obliged to defend myself in public, in spite of the fact that I had been officially invited by the organizers to attend the event in question, often a workshop of one form or another. Participants would question my presence, and I would be invited to step up on the stage and explain who I was, what I was doing, who my sponsors were, and what I hoped to "contribute." This form of direct confrontation and interrogation, of being under fire from the people I was trying to study, raised profound questions not only about the nature of my research but also about the expected and acceptable roles of the researcher.

But coming under fire has a more literal connotation in contemporary Cauca. If one chooses to do research in rural areas, sooner or later one will meet representatives of armed groups: the forces of the state, specifically the police and the army; the guerrillas, the FARC or the National Liberation Army (ELN), the paramilitaries; or bands of common criminals.[3] During the period of fieldwork, essentially the summers of 1995 through 2002, with an additional six months in 2000, as a foreign researcher I had most to fear from the last two groups: from the paramilitaries because they were known killers, particularly of those people identified as "sympathizers" of the left, proponents of peace, or upholders of human rights; and from the criminal gangs because they were known to kidnap people and hold them hostage or "sell" them to the highest bidder who would then, in turn, demand a ransom for their safe return. While I had no dealings with either of these latter groups, I had several encounters with the guerrillas, one of which I will describe here, since it illustrates several of the points I wish to make.

I was traveling in a van to Juan Tama, one of the new, resettled communities, with a group of colleagues, all indigenous, when we were stopped just after dawn at a temporary roadblock by two members of the FARC. One of the guerrillas opened the van door and proceeded to ask my fellow passengers who they were and where they were going, and they all identified themselves as members of the Regional Indigenous Council of Cauca (CRIC), working with the organization's bilingual education program. He then turned to me and asked what I was doing there. I responded that I was an anthropologist and that I was collaborating with CRIC. There was a moment of silence before he nodded and waved us on our way. On arrival at our destination shortly afterward, I discovered that my colleagues, for whom roadblocks of this type were not uncommon since the area had been a FARC stronghold for many years, had been much more nervous than I. They had no idea how the guerrillas would respond, and had something unpleasant happened, they would have felt personally responsible. Their fears were not unfounded. The following year the FARC killed a group of young, middle-class trekkers from Bogotá, several of whom were students, in a nearby national park, on the grounds that they thought they were paramilitaries because they were dressed in army fatigues.

Although I had been visiting this area since 1995, this was my first direct encounter with the guerrillas, and while people acknowledged their presence and knew where their camp was, to me they always gave the impression that the guerrillas did not directly interfere with their everyday lives. They claimed that the guerrillas were more interested in outsiders who came to work there and truckers transporting goods, particularly livestock, through the area. While they often referred to the guerrillas as *los muchachos* (the kids), a term of affection and sneaking admiration, this did not capture their ambivalent feelings, since the guerrillas were always a threatening presence. Similar feelings of ambivalence are found in other parts of the world with a long, ongoing history of insurgency. In the southern Philippines, local people expressed similar attitudes about the guerillas. As Jane Margold describes, "References to the revolutionaries were neutral or markedly tolerant: they were spoken of as 'our brothers and sisters in the mountains' or (jokingly, but without sarcasm) as 'the Nice People' (from NPA = Nice People Around). NPA [New People's Army] was also jokingly said to be short for 'No Permanent Address'" (1999, 68).[4]

There were other similar incidents involving friends and colleagues, as well as numerous newspaper reports of guerrilla activities over the years, so it became obvious that the guerrillas were a continuing, pervasive presence, more so in some areas than in others, a powerful, but often circumspect shadow government. Where there was little or no government presence at the level of the municipality, or where the guerrillas had driven the police out, it was usually fair to assume that the guerrillas were in charge, effectively controlling what the local leadership could do. This has been and continues to be a widespread phenomenon in rural Colombia. Of the more than a thousand municipalities in the country, it has been estimated that over the past few years more than four hundred have been obliged to work out a modus operandi with the armed groups, guerrillas or paramilitaries, operating in the area. Although this shadowy presence did not directly affect my fieldwork, indirectly it did since I found it impossible to gauge the level of guerrilla influence in the areas I studied. People claimed it was minimal, rarely volunteered information, and certainly did not encourage me to find out for myself. But I also became aware of the potential danger I posed for my colleagues, as well as for the people who would talk with me.

Given the context of pervasive political violence, I quickly learned to consult friends and colleagues before traveling anywhere, and I usually traveled only when accompanied. As the level and incidence of violence increased, personal security became a major issue, not just for me but, more important, for those same friends and colleagues who would feel morally obliged to do something were anything to happen to me. As a result, I stopped traveling outside Popayán, the provincial capital, after summer 2001. This severely limited the type and variety of information that I could collect. Trying to talk in any depth with a small farmer visiting the city proved to be very frustrating because he was usually there for a specific purpose with little time or inclination to talk freely.

The Moral, Engaged, but Critical Researcher

There has been a reformist tendency present in American anthropology since the early twentieth century.[5] John Bennett (1996), describing the rise of applied anthropology in the United States, suggests that it emerged at the turn of the last century as a form of American egalitarian populism, later updated as a form of New Deal humanitarian liberalism. Yet he is fully aware of the dangers and contradictions of direct anthropological involvement, warning that collaboration with the "subjects" of our research in defense of their rights against encroaching development and globalization is at best an "ambiguous engagement." Such anthropologists were once damned by the academy for participating directly in the processes they are supposed to be studying, and by the morally self-righteous for sitting on the sidelines as passive observers (Bennett 1988).

These different perspectives reached their apotheosis in the Roy D'Andrade–Nancy Scheper-Hughes debate of the mid-1990s. D'Andrade feared that anthropology was being transformed from a discipline based on an *objective* model of the world, which gives information about the object being studied rather than our response to that thing, to one based on a *moral* model of the world whose primary purpose is "to identify what is *good* and what is *bad* and to allocate *reward* and *punishment*" (1995, 399; emphasis original). Among his many criticisms, the major one was intellectual. The objective model provided D'Andrade with a surer understanding of how the world works: "Anthropology can maintain its moral authority only on the basis of empirically demonstrable truths" (408).

For Scheper-Hughes (1995, 416) the issue was more moral than intellectual. "Those of us who make our living observing and recording the misery of the world have a particular obligation to reflect critically on how we choose to represent the human suffering that engages us."

Responding to D'Andrade, Scheper-Hughes agreed that there are two distinctly anthropological ways of engaging with the world: the spectator, neutral and objective, who observes and is above the fray, accountable to "science"; and the witness, active and morally committed, one who takes sides and makes judgments, where the ethical is primary. She writes, "Anthropologists as witnesses are accountable for what they see and what they fail to see, how they act and how they fail to act in critical situations" (419).

If one accepts Scheper-Hughes's argument, how does one put it into practice? One way is through a reappraisal of the potential role of praxis in guiding how anthropologists should conduct themselves. Aristotle used the term to designate the arts and sciences that deal with ethical and political life. In so doing, he carefully distinguished between *theoria* and *praxis*. While the former refers to theories and activities concerned with the production of knowledge for its own sake, the latter refers to theories and activities that create knowledge instrumental in achieving ethical and political ends (Partridge 1987). Theory can only inform practice, and since it is often an exclusive discourse, it is irrelevant for strategic purposes or instrumental action.

Praxis itself, then, is a type of knowledge of the world, partly objective and partly subjective; it consists of negotiation between objective knowledge of the world, operative in a given time and place, and subjective experience of the world found in ongoing human action. From this process emerge implicit patterns that underlie human existence (Baba 1999). But it is also a way of knowing that embodies ethical and political theory and practice as processes of social life. As a result, the practitioner of praxis balances theory with activity, and lives his or her life making ethical and political decisions that matter, a process that calls for continuous adjustment (Partridge 1987). Since praxis is concerned with change, it is oriented more toward the present and prediction of the future, rather than to the interpretation of previous events. It also involves creating the conditions for people to act on their own behalf. Integral to such a theory of practice is an ethics of action, based on commitment to socially responsible work and professional integrity, as well as a willingness to accept a moral responsibility for the consequences of one's actions.

An example of this approach toward "values-oriented action in anthropology" is Sol Tax's Fox Project, inspired by the work of John

Dewey (Baba 1999), which embodied an ethical imperative similar to that of praxis theory. During the period 1948 to 1959, Tax and a group of his graduate students from the University of Chicago undertook to collaborate with the Mesquaki Indians in Iowa in studying issues that mattered to the tribe, the solution of which could improve their lives (Foley 1999). The first phase was characterized by discussions over values, fieldwork, and diagnosis of the major social problems, and the second was more operational and emphasized the need to be collaborative and create activities that the local people valued and managed. These included a media project to change white attitudes about Native Americans, a recreation project with the youth, a cooperative project with the men, and a scholarship program to send students to college. The action anthropologists were to play the role of catalysts and temporary leaders. Tax (1958, 1975) asserted that anthropologists ought to learn and help in equal measure, and that first, the activities undertaken by anthropologists should be "imminently useful" to the people with whom they worked and, second, that the anthropologist should not make decisions on their behalf (Rubinstein 1986). In theory, this means that the anthropologist should provide the group with alternatives from which to choose and allow them the freedom to make their own mistakes. In practice, however, critics have pointedly suggested that this is often nonsense, if not downright irresponsible, and that anthropologists do, in fact, often exert considerable influence (Stull, Schultz, and Cadue 1987). This is so partly because of the power differential, but also because the anthropologist may well have a better understanding of the potential consequences of the proposed alternatives (Kirsch 2002).

For Dewey, all inquiry was communal and should return something of value to the community, something good in a fundamental sense, where the good as defined as "that which enables the actualization of human potential, especially personal growth and development" (Baba 1999, 33). Though some commentators, particularly Bennett (1996, S34–39), strongly question the influence of Dewey, as well as some of the claims made by Tax, others such as Douglas Foley (1999) are more sympathetic, allowing that Tax may well have thought of himself as a philosophical pragmatist. While those most directly involved in the Fox Project claimed that Tax followed a "very democratic, dialogic pragmatist theory of science," Foley, based on interviews and fieldwork some forty years later, states that the action anthropology they practiced was marked by a certain amount of social engineering. The research undertaken was neither very original nor very organized, and there was little symbiosis between theory and practice; project leaders found it very difficult, if not impossible, to be both academic mentors and action anthropologists. Tribal members did acknowledge that the project had helped both the tribe and individual members in various ways, but they also expressed well-founded skepticism about anthropological efforts to "save" or "modernize" indigenous people: "Mesquakis believe that it is their sacred pact with the creator, not the white man's science and religion, that ensures their cultural survival. They chide us to temper such conceits if we are to be good allies" (Foley 1999, 183).

A more relevant and more provocative model is provided by the work of the Colombian anthropologist Guillermo Vasco (2002a), who, among other activities, has worked closely with the Guambiano ethnic group and the indigenous movement in Cauca over the past thirty years. Reviewing the relationship between fieldwork and ethnographic writing, he discusses how Colombian anthropology has addressed these questions (Vasco 2002b). At the end of the 1960s, the group that was to become known as La Rosca, which included Orlando Fals Borda, Victor Daniel Bonilla, Gonzalo Castillo, and Augusto Libreros, was wrestling with how to support the interests of those who had traditionally been anthropology's object of study, specifically indigenous people. The first problem was the nature of the relationship between the anthropologist and those he studies. One approach was to develop and practice more radical variations of action anthropology, such as participatory action research (PAR) and "militant research" (*la investigación militante*). With its emphasis on the generation of popular power, PAR combined techniques of adult education, social science research, and political activism. Methods included collective research, the critical reconstruction of local or regional histories, the restoration and use of popular cultures, and the use of novel means of diffusing knowledge (Escobar 1991; Fals-Borda 1981). Another approach was to privilege practice over theory, abandon the academy, and work directly with the groups under study.

A second problem that La Rosca confronted was how to return the knowledge produced through fieldwork to those who had helped generate it. While the new research methods greatly improved relations between the researchers and their subjects, the results remained in the hands of the investigators, just as they always had. Vasco faults his colleagues for closing their eyes to the political and ideological realities of their work: "These techniques had been developed by social scientists in the service of the enemies of the people in order to reinforce their domination and control over them" (Vasco 2002b, 458).

When Vasco started working with the indigenous movement, one thing that caught his attention was the ways in which meetings of the Guambiano were organized and the importance attached to working in commissions. Although the movement had lifted this term from another context, the way in which they practiced it was radically different. While almost everyone talked and participated in the discussions, they did not prepare explicit conclusions for the final plenary session. Rather, each commission and its members reported on the contents of its discussions, and the plenary session as a whole then took up the discussion. Vasco found this repetition of the discussion perplexing because it proceeded as if there had been no earlier discussion, until it dawned on him that this was how the movement avoided a situation in which the leaders could make all the important decisions, picking and choosing from the conclusions reached by each individual commission. Not only was this more democratic, it also provided an excellent opportunity for doing research: "I understood, then, that the work in groups organized by indigenous people in their meetings were really research meetings, to advance the [state of] knowledge about a problem through discussion, by means of which the knowledge of each member was compared with that of the others in order, finally, to have a global knowledge" (Vasco 2002b, 461).

As a result, each participant in such meetings, which Vasco chose to call research *mingas* (*mingas de investigación*) or knowledge mingas (*mingas de conocimiento*) — minga being the name given to collective work groups in the Andes — became better informed, while at the same time contributing to the transformation of individual knowledge into collective knowledge. This insight was to form the basis of much of the collaborative research that Vasco later undertook with the Guambiano (Hurtado, Aranda, and Vasco 1998). As much of the material presented in later chapters was gathered through observation and participation in workshops of various sorts, Vasco's conclusion is important, since a convincing argument can be made that the proliferation of such workshops has affected the level of knowledge generated as well as the level of participation. To temper the power and authority of the external researcher working with indigenous people, Vasco proposes several key principles which call for a radical change in conventional research methodology (Vasco 2002b, 462).

First, indigenous people are the key intellectual authority. This calls for respecting indigenous thought and explanation, as well as acknowledging its primary role and relevance in indigenous society.[6] In practice, this means above all respecting older people, particularly the shamans, who are usually the bearers of this authority. Second, the opinion of the researcher is only one among many. While this reflects a certain postmodern turn, particularly James Clifford's (1986) call for partial truths, it imposes a certain humility on the researcher, while at the same time arguing for broadmindedness and inclusion. In Clifford's case, however, it is the anthropologist who has the final control over what is produced since he or she ultimately controls what is written. This was not the case for Vasco.

In practice, as I learned, this means that the researcher's opinions, suggestions, or recommendations can be ridiculed or simply ignored. At the same time, however, the researcher must be prepared to argue his case, since otherwise his authority and credibility will begin to erode. Indigenous people may have their own proposals for research, which they may view as more important and more relevant than those of the researcher. In other words, the local people should set the research agenda. While this principle strikes at the heart of academic freedom and the researcher's autonomy in choosing a research topic, it is also the logical conclusion to be derived from a strategy of engagement. The local population, rather than the researcher, decides what the research priorities are. Although the researcher's opinion will be taken into consideration, it is the local population who makes the final decision, and the researcher is expected to comply.

These radical principles strike at the heart of conventional academic research and raise profound and provoking questions about the nature of engagement and collaboration. In contemporary Colombia, a foreign academic or foreign researcher is valued for his knowledge and expertise, which he is expected to share with the local population. This knowledge, in turn, may help identify certain research priorities that are very different from those of the local population, partly because they may never have thought of them, partly because they may not interest them. And who, precisely, is the "local population?" The local shamans, the political leaders, the youth, ex-guerrillas, the wealthy, a local organization, or some combination of these? Just how challenging and problematic this approach can be is demonstrated by my own experience.

In the course of my fieldwork, I participated directly in the preparation of community development plans in two of the new communities, San José and Tóez Caloto, processes described and analyzed in a later chapter. Here I am more concerned with describing and analyzing the complexities, ambiguities, and frustrations of such participation in Tóez Caloto. In 1999, the governor decided it was time that the community made a serious effort to prepare a development plan. Although two earlier efforts had failed (for reasons that remained unclear), he felt the time had come to make a serious, concerted effort involving the whole community. Announcing this at a general assembly of the community, he appealed for widespread support and participation. Tempted by the offer to "make myself useful," I volunteered to help on the spot, based on the assumption that I had something to contribute. I had been studying the planning process in Cauca for the previous three years (Gow 1997, 1998) and had also spent a considerable part of my professional career working as a planner in various development contexts (Gow 1994). Hence, for better or for worse, I felt I had some credibility, some "authority" as a planner. While the governor accepted my offer, all indications were that this would be a community-driven rather than a consultant-driven process, and plans were made to hold a series of workshops over the next few weeks.

I participated in several of these workshops, asking pointed questions, making suggestions, and trying to bring in experiences from similar planning exercises in other parts of the province that I was acquainted with. Nevertheless, I had two particular problems with the process — one more theoretical, the other more methodological — which I raised on several occasions. First, how can one talk about a long-term plan without trying to articulate some coherent vision of the future by answering the following questions: Who are we? Where do we come from? Where are we going? At my suggestion, these general questions were incorporated into the workshop discussions, and the responses varied greatly, from those groups working on education ("our own university") and culture ("our own education that incorporates indigenous culture") who had a clear idea of where they wanted to be, to those concentrating on agriculture and the environment who tended to focus on specifics. In the case of agriculture participants argued for a certain number of livestock, large and small, for each family, and, in the case of the environment, more water and more trees. The community organizer (*promotora*) from the Association of Indigenous Cabildos of Northern Cauca (ACIN), who was facilitating the process, was particularly hard on the latter: "But more trees for what? More training for what? What's behind all these?" From her perspective, these were means rather than ends, and she encouraged the various groups to think more deeply and more creatively about their respective priorities.

My second concern questioned the underlying logic of the model proposed in which the participants, without discussing or analyzing the causal aspects of the present situation, were expected to make a conceptual leap of faith and think about what they would like to do in the future and how they could "measure" what they had done. Many of the participants were confused and unable (or unwilling) to leap. Without this type of discussion and an understanding of why the present situation was the way it was, there was a strong tendency to slide into a cookie-cutter approach to the problem at hand. In the group discussing the economy, for example, one older participant, who complained a great deal about how hard it was for him to make a living, provided a long list of "reasons" for his present situation, ranging from his age, which prevented him from seeking physically exhausting off-farm employment on the local sugar plantations, to his lack of technical knowledge, economic resources, machinery, and equipment! While the reasons for this state of affairs are complex, they are not necessarily resolved by simply "filling in the holes" and providing that which is lacking. Philip Gatter (1993) labels this a reductionist model of economics and agronomy, whereby the "explanation" for a particular problem is independent of any specified social, cultural, or political context. I raised this concern several times, in public and in private, and, while it was duly noted, the planning process continued as programmed. Since the questions I raised and the points I made did not fit neatly into this preconceived framework, my contributions were listened to politely, but largely ignored.

A month into the process, I told the governor that I would be willing to provide some comments on what the community had produced to date, but I received no response. Shortly afterward, during the regular monthly general assembly of the whole community, I attempted to offer some observations and was promptly — and publicly — put in my place by the governor: "People are asking me what you are doing here, always taking notes. Aren't you supposed to be advising us?" I explained that I was only too willing to offer my comments, and let the matter rest. That evening, I learned from a friend, an indigenous schoolteacher in the community, that people had been talking about me behind my back. He wanted to know what the nature of my collaboration was with the community, specifically the *cabildo,* and what sort of arrangement I had made with them. Once I had related to him my version of events, he went on to tell me what he had heard. Someone he knew, an individual "with his own interests" as he put it, had asked him what I was doing there: I had not been invited by the community, and I did not appear to know anything! This latter comment stung, though perhaps I had only myself to blame, since I had consciously chosen not to behave like a typical adviser, by flaunting my "expertise" and telling people what to do.

The following morning I went to say goodbye to the governor in his house, as I was shortly to return to the United States. He was friendly, hopeful that I could help the community find financial support for their projects, and sad to hear that I was leaving. I also gave him some money to defray the costs of the continuing workshops. This was not an easy decision, as I thought it might be viewed as my attempt to "buy my place" and hence legitimate the extraction of information. Before leaving the country, I composed a four-page memo with my comments and recommendations on the planning process, which was delivered to the governor, other community leaders, and the promotora. In the memo, I concentrated on the problems associated with the economy, education, and long-term objectives, suggesting that the community prioritize its problems, concentrate on the most important, identify their causes and consequences, discuss some solutions, and prepare a development strategy. Three years later, in 2002, the final plan had still not appeared.

At the time, I failed to acknowledge that the governor was not operating as an independent agent since he was ultimately accountable to the community, although that did not necessarily constrain him. The production of the plan would provide the community with more legitimacy in its attempts to find financial support for its proposed programs, while the involvement of ACIN would provide more political and institutional legitimacy within the region. Community leaders fully supported the production of the plan, and several were active participants in the workshops. But the support of the "community" was less enthusiastic. There had been earlier efforts that had produced nothing. There was a long-standing suspicion of most forms of external assistance, just as there were certain deep-seated problems which were not really addressed during the planning process, several of which I raised in my memo to the leadership.

Scheper-Hughes and Marietta Baba provide a moral justification for such anthropological engagement, but neither provides much basis for better understanding the social complexities and political realities that such engagement is likely to encounter. In their approach, they assume a level of theoretical, ethical, political, and practical sophistication on the part of the researcher that is rarely encountered. Nor do they provide any guidelines or suggestions as to how the researcher can work toward this. In contrast, Vasco lays out quite clearly what is required. Essentially, he is talking about a radical rethinking, theoretically and methodologically, on the part of both the researcher and the academy, calling for the researcher to relinquish control and for the academy to recognize different ways of doing research. But researchers with doctorates think they know best, and universities are not about to grant equal voice to the undoctored, particularly those from the developing world. Vasco is also calling for the traditional "objects" of research to become much more active participants in the process. While this did partly happen in Tóez Caloto, the questions asked and the information collected were dictated by an outsider. To a certain extent this was inevitable, given that the research was undertaken to satisfy the bureaucratic requirement to produce a development plan. The kind of research advocated by Vasco is only possible in places like Guambía and Juan Tama. Tóez Caloto was used to a more paternalistic approach, consistent with their modernizing discourse.

A Different Type of Engagement

Anthropologists are viewed as a threat — as selfish extractors of knowledge who contribute little or nothing to those who are the objects or subjects of their research. But what if, following the example of Vasco, the research agenda is mutually established and those who are normally studied become researchers in their own right? In the introduction to a history of the Guambiano in which he collaborated, Vasco explains how they formed a history committee in the *resguardo,* taped interviews with the older members of the community, and analyzed their narratives. On the basis of this analysis, they selected key concepts, specific to Guambiano thought, which they proceeded to discuss with a much broader Guambiano audience, including authorities, traditional wise men, adults, leaders, teachers, men, women, and children. The resulting book was written together by the researchers, based on their conversations with many others, and the document speaks with many voices, powerfully, poetically, and prophetically. By recovering their history, they also recover their authority and their autonomy: "That's why we have to recover everything in order to be able to have everything complete. Otherwise, we will never be able to recover our authority and autonomy, but will continue being dependent. We will not be able to walk again the road taken by our forefathers" (Hurtado, Aranda, and Vasco 1998, 269).[7]

But there are also other questions to be addressed about this more collaborative type of research. What sort of relationships evolve among external researchers, national or international, and indigenous researchers? There is the issue of control, referred to earlier, as well as that of epistemology. While I can accept the importance of Mother Earth for the Nasa and respect their views regarding her role in indigenous culture, I wonder what effects such collaboration has on the thoughts and perceptions of those involved. At a minimum, one would look for increasing mutual respect, which could evolve into differing ways of thinking about and understanding reality. This becomes particularly important when dealing with religious and cosmological issues. What sort of dialogue can result from this sort of engagement? To be fruitful, such dialogue needs to move beyond mutual respect to mutual understanding, where there is open acknowledgment of the relevance and validity of various types of knowledge. To what extent can this process alleviate the implicit feelings of guilt experienced by an external researcher? It can help, to the extent that the guilty researcher is willing to relinquish control, listen, and think seriously about how to produce something collaboratively. Finally, who wins and who loses, or is there reciprocity and mutual benefit? The assumption is that such collaboration will not only contribute to the quality and relevance of the research undertaken but that all involved will become better researchers.

From 1999 to 2001, I participated in a collaborative research project with five other investigators, two indigenous, two national, and one international. The two indigenous researchers, both Nasa, were Susana Piñacué, a linguist involved in CRIC's bilingual education program, and Adonías Perdomo, founder of the School of Nasa Thought (an indigenous think tank) and a former member of the cabildo of Pitayó, both of whom were completing a bachelor's degree in ethnoeducation at the University of Cauca. The two nationals were Myriam Amparo Espinosa, an anthropologist at the University of Cauca, who has worked with the indigenous movement, and Tulio Rojas, a linguist at the University of Cauca, who has worked extensively on the study of Nasa Yuwe, the language spoken by the Nasa. The international researcher was Joanne Rappaport, a North American anthropologist who has published widely on the Nasa and who also happens to be my wife.[8]

The objective was to examine the fluid state of ethnic politics in Colombia through an ethnographic approach emphasizing interethnic and international collaboration. While each member had his or her specific research project, the team met on a regular basis to discuss work in progress and comment on the drafts of each other's writings. These team meetings were tape-recorded and transcribed and became part of the research process since they provided insights into how the various team members viewed this collaborative experiment. Although a lot went on during these meetings, I have chosen, for reasons of space and simplicity, to concentrate on those elements that most directly relate to issues of methodology, specifically, the roles of the two indigenous members of the team and my interactions with them.

For Piñacué and Perdomo, there were two major issues with which they wrestled continuously. The first was their relationship to their fellow Nasa, and the second was the ways the results of their research would be used. To a certain extent, both regarded themselves as outsiders, while still remaining insiders — liminal but involved. This was so for several reasons. Both were educated, had spent time outside of their home regions, and, in their different ways, were critical of certain aspects of indigenous society. In her early thirties, Piñacué came from a well-known Nasa family, had studied in Popayán, and had traveled in

Europe. While she identified closely with the indigenous movement, she was highly critical of the politics of the leadership, particularly their lack of recognition of the role of women in the process. She worked intensively and passionately with CRIC's bilingual education program, but she was highly critical of the intellectual elitism she found within the organization. From her perspective, the leadership had become detached from its rural roots and no longer fully understood or cared to understand what she regarded as the harsh realities of everyday indigenous life, tending to romanticize elements of indigenous culture that were, in her opinion, irrelevant.

Her research focus was on Nasa women and their role in the indigenous movement. More specifically, she was deeply concerned about the ways in which women leaders were treated and the double standards that were applied to them, a reflection of the broader male discrimination against women in indigenous society. A leader herself, she sympathized and often identified with all those discriminated against. A natural critic, her feelings about the future of Nasa culture were very mixed, reflecting her betwixt-and-between liminal status. Though passionate about indigenous culture and the importance of studying it, understanding it, and passing it on to future generations, she was fully aware that this was an uphill battle against the forces of modernity, institutionalized in education, music, television and movies, clothes, and development. While indigenous culture was bound to change in the process, she was not convinced that it would necessarily survive in a viable form. A natural skeptic, she tended to question everything.

Perdomo was a natural philosopher. In his late forties, he came from a nonaligned resguardo, one that was not directly affiliated with any regional indigenous organization. Like Piñacué, he had traveled outside the region, to Bogotá and other parts of the country, but he continued to live close to his home community, where he was actively involved in both resguardo and municipal politics. Like Piñacué, he was active in bilingual education and had helped establish such a program in his own community with assistance from CCF (the Christian Children's Fund), a U.S.-based NGO that provides assistance for children. Although an evangelical, he was in no sense a proselytizer and tended to be very critical of organized religion in general. The think tank that he established brought together thoughtful Nasa from various parts of the province to discuss issues of common concern, such as authority, autonomy, and the proper role of the cabildo.

His research focus was on authority and how it was exercised within the communities. Like Piñacué, he was concerned about the future of the Nasa and their culture, though his perspective tended to be more conservative, since he wished to preserve the traditional form rather than accept the inevitability of its change and evolution. His concern was with the loss of culture and the implications for Nasa youth and the future of the Nasa as a group. He once confided to me that he would like to use community funds to send high school students to study at the university in Popayán, where they would stay together in a rented house. They would be guarded by a shaman who would be responsible for protecting them from undue urban influences and ensuring that they did not "lose their culture." While Perdomo also did fieldwork like the rest of us, much of the material for his writing came from careful reflection on his everyday experiences. Although perhaps more "embedded" in Nasa society and culture than Piñacué, who worked and lived in Popayán, Perdomo felt himself to be equally liminal, a reflection of his original mind, his deep concern about the future of the Nasa, his nonaligned status, and his openness and willingness to work with outsiders.

Since they both occupied liminal positions vis-à-vis their fellow Nasa, Piñacué and Perdomo were extremely sensitive to the potential risks they were running by writing about their own ethnic group. This was a recurring theme in many of the team's meetings. What could they say to make people think seriously about their present everyday realities? How much could they say without running the risk of being accused of being traitors to their own ethnic group? How could they reach their respective audiences without appearing too threatening?

To a certain extent, both identified with the person who leaves the community, spends time elsewhere, and then returns to be viewed as a potential troublemaker until proven otherwise. For example, Piñacué implicitly compared her position to that of a returning female migrant, who, it should be noted, is treated very differently from a returning male migrant, implying that women, if not more powerful, are certainly more threatening. "When they [female migrants] return, they become, through experience, a problem. They arrive with other customs that shock the community, so this means that they also become like a threat at the level of the cultural guidelines being generated at the level of community, in the communities 'inside'" (Team meeting in January 2000). The "disorder" has several dimensions, ranging from the more obvious but less threatening, such as changes in dress and diet, to the less obvious but potentially more threatening, such as gender relations, female sexuality, and economic independence. For Piñacué, this "returned migrant" status meant that some viewed her as a threat, while others tried to dismiss her and criticized her for being single and unmarried. But this status also meant that in spite of all her criticisms, she cared passionately about Nasa culture and Nasa society.

For Perdomo, there was an acknowledgment that writing "from the edge" provided the opportunity to open the community's eyes while running the risk of being severely criticized in the process.

> We're simply saying there's a risk. All of us who reach this edge of the boundary come with a series of risks. My idea is that this investigation can serve to awaken our community so that we start to construct some processes, to establish some strategies, to prepare from inside how to relate them to the outside. I would say that what the community has is like a form of envy of the person who goes so far and, when he returns, perhaps they think he is going to change the whole way of being. So the community becomes frightened. On one hand, they are frightened of the people who go very close to the boundary. And, when they return, what proposals do they have? The idea then is to limit this, to control it, so you make a series of criticisms, some of which are pejorative. But "inside" is also like the blood [a question of kinship] . . . "[H]e doesn't know anything about the community," says the community. But also to what extent is it correct when they say to someone that he knows nothing about the community or is it simply a way of controlling, of filtering what he brings? (Team meeting in August 1999)

For him, as with Piñacué, the indigenous researcher is analogous to the returning migrant. On the one hand, the community views him as a potential threat since he may try to change things. Because he is indigenous, his ideas should be taken seriously. On the other hand, however, because the researcher has chosen to situate himself "at the edge," legitimate questions can be raised about how well he understands everyday realities, a criticism that can be used to downplay and denigrate the researcher's findings.

But for both researchers, being at the edge provided them with the necessary physical distance and social space to better understand their own people and to better prepare themselves for addressing contentious, contemporary issues. The research that they undertook, by necessity, had to be both practical and applied: the results not only had to contribute to a better understanding of the issues studied but also had to help generate some practical solutions. To a certain extent, Piñacué and Perdomo were obsessed with this need, responsibility, and obligation to return something to the broader Nasa community, as if this were implicitly demanded from them in return for being "allowed" to do research on their own people. This feeling of obligation distinguished them from many other nonindigenous researchers, but not from other indigenous researchers in the area. The Guambiano working with Vasco, for example, have produced a volume based on their collaborative historical research (Hurtado, Aranda, and Vasco 1998). But whereas the Guambiano research was more concerned with documenting the past, a topic of great interest to many indigenous groups, the research of the two Nasa investigators was primarily concerned with contemporary issues, by definition more provocative, contentious, and critical.

As a result, there was a continuing theme throughout the team meetings: How would the results be disseminated? In practice, the team presented the preliminary results of their research at a special workshop organized at La María and attended by bilingual teachers, university students, CRIC employees, and academics. This was repeated during a special panel organized at the Eleventh Congress of Colombian Anthropology held in Popayán, and the revised papers were accepted for publication in the edited volume, *Returning the Gaze: Collaborative Interethnic Research in Cauca at the Turn of the Millennium* (Rappaport 2005b). For each of these events, the indigenous researchers received "equal time" with the other participants. They were there as fellow researchers. Though it proved to be a grueling experience for both, it helped reinforced their credibility in the eyes of mestizo outsiders and indigenous insiders.

While I shared their concerns regarding the researcher's responsibilities, I did not have to take the same risks that they did nor, try as I did, could I live up to the lofty principles articulated by Vasco. Yet I was still gnawed by a strong feeling of "anthropological guilt," inspired perhaps by the fact that I did not live in Colombia, nor did I have a collaborative relationship with an organization in the same way that Vasco did. What was I contributing to the Nasa communities that I was studying? At this point I decided, perhaps unconsciously, that my two Nasa colleagues would become representatives of the people I was studying. While I could "help" them with their research, they could comment on mine as Nasa, providing a form of reality check, while at the same time learning something about how I viewed the Nasa and in the process hopefully learning something about my perspectives on the Nasa. What I was looking for, perhaps craved, were their opinions and their perceptions. At the beginning of the project I had envisioned our holding long discussions about methodology and epistemology, but these did not occur. Instead, we spent a great deal of time listening to each other explain what we were doing and trying to make sense of what we had found out. As the level of mutual respect and confidence grew, these dialogues gradually evolved into a form of sounding board, where ideas were tested for their logic, coherence, and relevance, and where the objective was not so much to convince as it was to explain.

My own research benefited from their comments in several ways. The relationship was both collegial and cordial, but it was also based on mutual respect, respect for each other's work and autonomy, but also the right to differ. This became clear when discussing each other's written work, in my case the draft of a chapter in our collaborative volume, a revised version of which appears here as chapter 5. In the paper I was attempting to perform a comparative description and analysis of two very different, but very distinct experiences with development in Cauca.

> Well, in this paper I am trying to, I am asking three questions and, as always, they are somewhat large because I am interested in better understanding what the relationship is or what the relationships are between modernity and indigenousness, you can say indigenousness. The second point deals with the role of culture and politics, the role that culture and politics play in this whole process, and third is Susana's favorite question: "What will be the future for indigenous groups, sometimes to a certain extent marginalized?" (Team meeting in January 2000)

I had completed several months of research at the time I made this statement, but I still had problems clearly articulating what I was trying to do, as demonstrated by the vagueness of my first question, trying to relate two already very vague and very contested concepts, "modernity" and "indigeneity." At the time I made this statement, however, I was steadily becoming convinced that the principal question I was interested in answering dealt with the relationship between culture and development. The major problem was that I was unclear about how to realistically research this relationship, given people's propensity to discuss this issue in rather vague and, in my view, unrealistic terms. In some cases, people would provide carefully thought-out answers, but in others they would voice the standard indigenous perspective.

Some of the evidence to bolster my concern came from a workshop for young Nasa leaders in which I had participated the previous year and where I had posed this question directly: What is the relationship between culture and development? I quoted the response of one leader, according to whom culture could always contribute to development as long as the balance with nature was maintained, something which, he argued, indigenous people, on account of their cosmovision, were well placed to do. Piñacué took exception to this generalization on the grounds that people use it more for strategic reasons, that they ignore the cultural diversity that can be found among the various groups of Nasa, and that indigenous leaders were exploiting it for their own reasons.

> I'm a little pessimistic about this type of discourse. . . . These talks are like a utopia in the face of this range of diversity of things they are confronting at the level of all the communities. And, for example, I don't know how they will be carrying out this context in the North [northern Cauca], given that in the North there is also a diversity of cultural dynamics. . . . There are many indigenous communities that have another concept of development and neither is there one, there is not this use of harmony, harmony, we are using it more as a question, more from a more capitalistic scope. (Team meeting in January 2000)

She went on to compare my interest in the Nasa living in northern Cauca, whose experience she did not view as particularly relevant for the Nasa as a group, with the behavior and utterances of some of the Nasa intellectuals associated with CRIC, who, in her opinion, took a totally unrealistic view of what was happening with Nasa Yuwe and its losing battle with Spanish.

A linguist herself by training, very much committed to bilingual education, Piñacué often felt frustrated by the lack of interest on the part of the parents of indigenous schoolchildren, as well as the lack of relevant materials to keep the students' interest in Nasa Yuwe alive over time. While she preferred indigenous music, her students preferred hip-hop and rap. Hence, her feelings about the relevance and sustainability of indigenous education were often ambivalent.

Her view of development was equally critical:

> I don't know how to work this thing and the other is you cannot generalize this discourse of development for all the communities, because for some development is capital, pesos. You have to do projects because you have to sell these projects for so many pesos, because if you don't, then how do we live? But who within the communities are these monies destined for when they arrive and what is the concept of development within the communities, of the women, the shaman, the midwife? One sees a diversity of things here, that I do not understand how to categorize those levels of development dynamics. (Team meeting in January 2000)

She is making several points here. Within Cauca, there are pronounced differences among the various groups of Nasa depending on geography, history, and politics. While the Nasa living in the northern part of the province are often regarded as the most political, they are also viewed as the "least Nasa" in terms of culture because they show low interest in speaking Nasa Yuwe or learning about indigenous cosmovision. Her comments about the Nasa intellectuals within CRIC (of which she, of course, is one) reflect her strong feelings about the unrealities and privileges of an urban indigenous elite telling the rural indigenous masses how they should lead their lives. In her comments she made reference to an earlier meeting in CRIC attended by some of these intellectuals, members of CRIC's bilingual education program, and some rural indigenous teachers. While there was a very interesting discussion about planning and development and what these concepts mean in Nasa Yuwe among the urban intellectuals, the three schoolteachers sat there mute. Nor were they really invited to participate. Her skepticism about development was based on her personal experience of what she had seen happening at the community level: the cult of what was often termed *proyectitis,* the mandate to design projects to get funds, with little clear understanding or transparency about what actually happened to the funds once disbursed. Similar attitudes are found in Nepal, where development is viewed as a provider of employment, rather than a means of improving local well-being (Pigg 1997). In other words, development as practiced in rural Cauca was yet another way for those in power to practice patronage.

For Piñacué, this word *development* was complicated and went against the grain of Nasa thought, as if outsiders were trying to force them to think and to behave in a certain way.

> So, that term [development] appears very complicated to me. That term is like a more schematic vision from outside. It's like we measure precisely the period of the Nasa, what's going to happen in the future, from now until these years the indigenous people will achieve such-and-such, within three, four, or five years. It's like measuring precisely from the outside by means of a schematic question the life project (*proyecto de vida*) of the indigenous people. But from inside, the indigenous people, we would have another way of knowing our future, which is ahead, our future which is behind, and our future which is ahead, it looks a little like the reason for existing on this planet Earth. (Team meeting in March 2000)

For her, the imposition of "development" from outside went very much against the grain of indigenous temporality by mandating a linear approach to change, while at the same time severely restricting ways in which to think about the process. The Nasa have their own way of thinking about the past, the present, the future, and the continuities among all three. Piñacué argued that for them to think about the future in terms of projects lasting three, four, or five years directly contradicted their life project, a way of thinking holistically about their long-term future.

This discussion, and several others that we had, were very much conversations among intellectual equals. The topic in question was one we had all thought seriously about from various perspectives and about which we all had strong opinions. Thinking about the future also raised larger questions about meaning and existence, what she later referred to as *la mirada nasa* (the Nasa gaze) a different way of looking at the world, with different responsibilities to those who came before and those who will come after, writing in the present about the past and the future. She linked this to her own intellectual project.

> I am thinking about who I am going to write for. When you sit down to write you are thinking about that grandfather who left us, about that grand-

mother who left us. We are always yielding to the past, but always thinking about the youth as well, thinking about those two parallels. In that sense it would be like looking a little as if we understand what is planning, development projects, life plan. (Team meeting in January 2000)

Perdomo shared many of Piñacué's opinions regarding development, and elaborated on the idea of a Nasa gaze, pointing out how it had been severely affected by changing political and environmental conditions, as well as by encroaching development organizations:

> That forces us a little to look at how we are going to reorganize that gaze. This is like the crossword puzzle for me, in which perhaps David is [too] entangled to observe. So, what to do? It's true what Susana outlines, that we have a gaze, very special, our own way of measuring time. And our own way of advancing in space. Nevertheless, perhaps in what I wanted to work I have a part, just as those diverse and intercultural relations also allow us to construct authority. (Team meeting in January 2000)

He is acknowledging that the Nasa way of viewing the world has to change in response to various external factors, which in turn have affected the internal workings of Nasa society. He and Piñacué, since neither is overly schematic, can contribute to this process of reorganization and reinterpretation. For him, his contribution lay in better understanding the workings of the cabildos and using this knowledge to strengthen them. But he was also very aware of how easily the state and its surrogates could corrupt the cabildos with offers of easy money, which, reiterating Piñacué's earlier points, were directed at creating jobs for their friends. This had started with the 1994 disaster, when, Perdomo claimed, no less that fifteen hundred NGOs had been formed and had continued thereafter. Though not denying the importance that help from outside could provide, he strongly disagreed with the heavy consumer, materialist approach of most contemporary development.

> Although I always think that the way of measuring development is the other great problem. That we were told that development is to have this chair in this style, these walls in this style, or television sets, or computers, or cars, or all that. So that is another of our errors, the indigenous communities, where we are trying to understand, with a completely false reference, from a view of development as a necessity, as a right, excuse me, as a right but with distinct needs. (Team meeting in January 2000)

Perdomo is criticizing the communities for having so easily bought into the project of modernity with its heavy emphasis on material acquisition, without thinking through the implications of their short-sighted actions. While the communities may have accepted that development is a right, he argues that they have chosen to misinterpret or to misunderstand what this development can entail. He attacks the more obvious elements of modernity, while countering with what he regards as deeper, longer term needs.

These and other comments obliged me to rethink what I meant by development in the context of indigenous Cauca and realize that my approach was too narrow and too conventional. Their approach to social change incorporated other elements, such as health, justice, and education, which they could control to a greater extent. While all three incorporate key aspects of Nasa culture and, hence, Nasa identity, they can also be viewed as part of the project of modernity, as elements of integration, incorporation, and acceptance on terms established by the larger society. But with local control, they can also be used as sites of resistance to dominant discourses and practices.

According to Perdomo, the pursuit of bilingual education offered this potential:

> And now, thanks to Susana, I have become aware of this process of working on [our] own education, above all with CRIC. But it hasn't been done only with CRIC. But also in other places, for example in Tóez [Caloto], they are trying to do the same with the high school. And certainly it's a very different curriculum, but it also has the same type of justification. And this for me has various ramifications . . . [but] the most interesting is the part dealing with education, because perhaps it appears there are possibilities of controlling it to a certain extent. (Team meeting in April 2000)

But this was not education in the conventional sense of preparing students to take their place, to the extent possible, in the larger society. It was a more ambitious, radical project designed to provide students with a better understanding and appreciation of their indigenous roots, while at the same time preparing them to be productive citizens. As a result, the indigenous school, as a locally controlled institution, assumed increasing cultural and political importance within the communities. As both Perdomo and Piñacué were both actively involved in bilingual education, it was perhaps inevitable that I became much more

53

interested in studying education, both the planning and the practice, partly because it appeared to be much more of a grassroots, participatory activity but also because people, specifically parents, felt much more strongly about it than they ever demonstrated about development, conventionally understood.

Our differences, however, were not limited solely to the meaning and practice of development. At the time of our collaboration, and for some considerable time afterward, I was wrestling with the meaning and significance of a new "actor" who had appeared on the regional scene. La María: Territory for Living Together, Dialogue, and Negotiation, was established on the five hundredth anniversary of the Spanish invasion of the Americas. Strategically located on a bluff overlooking the Pan-American Highway, some thirty kilometers north of Popayán, its objective was to create a political space where civil society could make its voice heard in the peace process and the decisions to be taken about Colombia's future development. Since its inception, La María has played host to a series of workshops and meetings: workshops for women and other specific groups; the quadrennial congress of CRIC; meetings of ASI (Indigenous Social Alliance), the political party established by the Quintines, the demobilized members of the MAQL, and CRIC in 1991; and, more recently, as a staging ground for organized, peaceful marches to protest the assassination of indigenous leaders, the pervasive political violence, and the free trade agreement with the United States.

It was to become a major focus of my research and, in various meetings with the team, I tried to argue that La María was a form of moral community that drew its inspiration from the past, recent and more distant, and used this as a basis for both imagining and practicing a different way of thinking about society. My argument was based on close observation of the events organized there as well as the people who chose to participate. The participants were often critical of the government and proposed alternatives to prevailing government policies and practices. They represented a wide cross-section of regional society, including indigenous people, peasants, urban migrants, political activists, social organizers, teachers, high school students, university students, and human rights activists. Women and young people were usually well represented. Pervading the events was a strong element of social solidarity, of people coming together to struggle against injustices of various sorts, while at the same time proposing solutions, some more radical than others.

I proposed to my colleagues that the process under way was also helping strengthen and thicken civil society, a crucial element that has been severely debilitated by Colombia's ongoing armed conflict.

> La María, and what La María has achieved, for me symbolize the best of the indigenous movement, because they worked together, they struggled together, and they carried themselves very well in a relatively anonymous way and they showed the world that when they want to they can do something . . . [In spite of all the setbacks], I am wondering how you can define La María. Is it a place, a territory, a space? But it's much more than that. What is it? (Team meeting in July 2001)

While La María is an alternative political space, it is also part of a larger social movement and appeals to multiple publics, what Nancy Fraser (1997) has called subaltern counterpublics, where subaltern groups invent and circulate counterdiscourses. Such arenas are not enclaves, since they seek to disseminate their discourse to other, broader publics.

My indigenous colleagues took a different perspective which, while not totally debunking my argument, added a much more grounded, more political interpretation. For Piñacué, La María served primarily as a political base and platform for those indigenous leaders, all male, running for political office at provincial and national levels. In practice, this sometimes proved to be the case, but without necessarily invalidating La María's larger role. Although this made her question the leaders' sincerity and commitment to what La María stood for, what particularly irked her was the continuing marginalization of women and their leaders. Workshops there had highlighted the importance of human rights in general and women's rights in particular, but she saw little evidence that women had gained any more political space. The leadership did not encourage the participation of women, particularly if they were strong and assertive, and had, in fact, terminated CRIC's program for women. But Piñacué also blamed the women themselves — and by implication herself — for allowing this to happen. She explained, "Why? Because there is an internal weakness among us as women in the face of that avalanche that we have. So the woman simply exists in that space and our task is to analyze those spaces and how to enter and empower

55

ourselves with those public spaces, while these men present concrete proposals which reflect their interests" (Team meeting in July 2001). For Piñacué, the creation of La María had changed little, except to provide yet another political platform for male leaders, and from which leaders who happened to be women were effectively excluded.

While Perdomo agreed with Piñacué's analysis, he chose to place La María in the broader context of the political and cultural tensions that have historically divided the two major ethnic groups in Cauca, the Nasa and the Guambiano. Chronically short of land and surrounded by the Nasa, the Guambiano have been steadily and legally "colonizing" available adjacent lands. According to Perdomo, the cabildo of Guambía does not allow a Guambiano family to purchase land elsewhere unless there is land available in the new community for at least an additional five Guambiano families, thus ensuring a continuing but growing Guambiano presence. The resguardo of La María is such a creation, which Perdomo viewed as nothing less than an expropriation of lands that traditionally had belonged to the Nasa, but which the Nasa had somehow lost. For him, the key question was: Why was La María established on land provided by a Guambiano resguardo, rather than a Nasa resguardo?

But he was equally concerned about this process of what he regarded as Guambiano expansion in terms of the cultural costs for those involved. From his perspective, this process could only lead to an increasing de-Indianization of the Guambiano. For him, the cultural identity of the Nasa depended in part on their staying and strengthening their home communities. If they chose to leave, this identity would be diluted. The Guambiano of La María, by leaving their home community of Guambía and establishing a new community alongside the Pan-American Highway, had chosen this route.

Perdomo worried about the implications for the Nasa. "One question begets another about La María: Is it a space for diluting the ideological and political content, rather than a space for strengthening it? Because if the Guambiano become peasants, what will happen to us, the Páez [Nasa], when we arrive there and join forces, will we come out stronger or more confused?" (Team meeting in July 2001). From his reading of the situation, Perdomo felt apprehensive about the outcome of continuing collaboration with the Guambiano, fearing that the Nasa could well be the losers. Not only would their cultural identity be threatened, so would their lands. The Guambiano of La María would steadily and inevitably encroach on the lands of the neighboring Nasa. His apprehension, I felt, was an overexaggeration, a reflection of the long-term rivalry that has existed between the two groups, which was particularly urgent for him, as he lives in a resguardo adjacent to Guambía. The appeal of La María to the indigenous movement was its strategic location, and the Guambiano there had willingly offered the land as well as logistical support. While Piñacué remained skeptical, she actively participated in many of the events there. Perdomo, for his part, chose to maintain his distance, at least in the early years.

While I respected my colleagues' opinions, I did not share them, partly because I interpreted the processes under way differently, but also because to accept their argument would have meant rejecting my own, something I was unwilling to do at the time.[9] Their skepticism helped temper my waning romanticism, my quest for the anthropological grail of the "moral community." Moral community there was, but neither as powerful nor as pervasive nor as promising as I had initially wanted to believe. What maintained the mutual engagement was the continuing dialogue, not only about my research and their research but also about other contemporary political events, around which we often had strong and sometimes differing opinions.

For Piñacué and Perdomo, my engagement with them took several forms. First, there was my willingness to read and comment on drafts of their work, comments which they sometimes chose to accept and other times ignored. Second, there was my continuing support for their research to help overcome their initial reservations about the quality and relevance of their work. Third — and this is the least tangible but perhaps most important element — there was the realization and acceptance on their part that not only did I take them and their work seriously, but that I also took their history and their culture equally seriously. And in the process, of course, we became friends.

In this chapter I have provided the methodological context for the ethnography that follows. In so doing, I have demonstrated the problematics of conducting research in a country such as Colombia, which has been experiencing a low-intensity form of civil war for the past three decades. But more important, I have discussed the problematics facing anthropologists who choose to conduct research in politically volatile

57

environments where they are viewed with suspicion, if not outright hostility. Accepting these as a given, as well as the fact that the anthropologist is a free agent who can choose to come and go as he wishes, I propose that one way to reach a modus vivendi is through a form of moral, engaged, but critical research that is both collaborative and productive. The extent to which such an approach may unduly affect the ensuing research and the final analysis will be for the reader to decide.

2

We don't want compassion, nor do we understand charity. We seek
solidarity. We want to share a little tenderness and brotherhood.
—Unidentified victim in the Fundación Sol y Tierra documentary,
Yu 'Up'hku (The Waters Have Given Birth)

Disaster and Diaspora:

Discourses of Development and Opportunity

Various explanations have been offered for the causes of the 1994 earthquake in Cauca. The most relevant have been cultural (that indigenous
society was in a state of crisis) and environmental (that the region of
Tierradentro was ecologically fragile and increasingly incapable of supporting a steadily growing population). Information gathered shortly
after the earthquake indicates that the people living there were vulnerable on several counts, including a limited resource base, low levels of
nutrition, high levels of infant mortality, and low levels of education. To
address the most immediate problems caused by the earthquake, the
national government created a new agency, the Nasa Kiwe Corporation
(CNK). While much criticized by those supposed to benefit from its
formation, CNK did fulfill its mandate and provide unheard-of opportunities to the indigenous communities most affected, primarily in the
provision of land and housing.

The resulting three new Nasa communities are the major focus of this
ethnography. The first, Tóez Caloto, is the most modernized and best
organized of the three, which uses education and selective reinvention
of Nasa culture as the principal means of advancing its agenda. The
second is Juan Tama, named after the most important cultural hero of
the Nasa. Self-conscious, ethnically proud, and socially fragmented,
Juan Tama is the most radical of the three and uses indigenous education
as the basis of what is essentially a cultural and political project. The
third new community is Cxayu'ce, unselfconsciously Nasa, with no par-

ticular ax to grind, except to make the most of the opportunities offered. They have achieved this quietly and unobtrusively.

Discourses of Displacement and Development

Anthropology has staked out a specific niche in the field of human displacement in particular, and refugee studies in general, and this interest stems from several factors peculiar to anthropology and its engagement with development. There is the historical factor, the traditional humanistic concern of the discipline and its identification with the underdog, ranging from the conventional brokering role to that of actively campaigning on behalf of the human rights of ethnic minorities (MacClancy 2002). While historically resettlement has often been viewed as a logistical and engineering problem, it is now increasingly perceived as involving social, cultural, and economic issues (Horowitz et al. 1993). In the early twenty-first century, where there is an increasing prevalence of war, violence, and mass displacement there are also anthropologists, eager to study but also to help (Malkki 1995). Then there is the research factor: the possibility of studying rapid and often traumatic change at close hand, an opportunity that occurs rarely in the more sedate world of academic investigation (Oliver-Smith 1996). Finally, there is the developmental factor: the possibility to exert direct control over the process of change, a type of "anthropological laboratory" (Cernea 1993).

In discussing the ways in which anthropology can more effectively influence change, Michael Cernea (1991) distinguishes between the enlightenment model, in which knowledge is disseminated through education, and the social engineering model, which is much more purposive and directed.[1] He criticizes the enlightenment model for being "a tortuous, uncertain, and slow way to return the benefit of social knowledge to society and influence its progress" (29). In contrast, he praises the social engineering model for its ability to transform this knowledge into "new knowhow and change tools" to be put to practical use for the benefit of society. Social engineering, as a contemporary variation on Auguste Comte's belief that there are natural laws that social science can "discover" and "understand," provides both a rationale and a justification for a conventional, conservative, top-down approach to development and social change, particularly in emergency situations (Cowen and Shenton 1995). But this discourse of displacement is also a discourse on governmentality, the belief in the central, determining role of the national government in solving a country's development problems through mechanisms of control and domination (Foucault 1991). The careful analysis of this discourse can provide a basis for understanding and analyzing the mechanisms through which authorities seek to administer the lives of individuals and collectivities, such as resettled people, and ways in which they respond.

This discourse accepts the process of displacement as a given, whether instigated by human actors or the natural elements, while at the same time proposing a solution based on a "risk and reconstruction" model of the society and culture affected (Cernea 1997). Although calling for "social justice and planning with an equity compass," the model itself is largely inductive, based on accumulated empirical evidence from various parts of the world. It is also mechanistic: if there is a lack of A, then the way to resolve the problem is to provide more of A — enough, at least, to replace what is lacking. In short, the system is not the problem for Cernea.

But what if the landlessness and the presumed poverty accompanying it have more deep-seated structural causes than those highlighted by a disaster? What if there are important, perhaps insurmountable political and social constraints affecting why people's livelihoods were and continue to be so vulnerable? What if those displaced are victims of structural violence that "manifests itself in a deep and widening inequality of life chances; corruption, arbitrariness, and impunity; the permanence of social and economic exclusion; lack of access to information, education, health, and minimal basic needs; and an authoritarian and condescending state and aid system" (Uvin 1998, 107)? Replacing what was lost may be a more complex and more politically challenging task than Cernea and his model are prepared to admit, particularly if those to be most directly affected are regarded as already "disposable" on behalf of the "greater good." An internal World Bank report on forced resettlement makes precisely this point.

> All governments care for the poor, but the question in the end is, where will the tradeoff be, who will get the priority? This varies from government to government. In India, there is tremendous concern for the poor — there is a democratic environment and the poor have a vote. But if there is a tradeoff

between resettlement of two million people and a dam, and the government does not have the resources, what do you do? . . . In the end the government for the benefit of *all* will perhaps vote for the dam and make the two million people worse off. (Billson 1993, 29, cited in Fox 1998, 323)

The social engineering model is most problematic in the ways the social and cultural components of displacement are categorized, analyzed, and diagnosed. These components are identified as a cluster of inter-related losses, a direct consequence of the process of displacement. The first is marginalization, when families experience a process of downward social and economic mobility. The second is the loss of access to common property, when the poor, particularly the landless and the assetless, experience a deterioration in their income and livelihood. The final component is social disarticulation, which "tears apart the existing social fabric . . . [and] generate[s] a typical state of anomie, crisis-laden insecurity, and loss of sense of cultural identity" (Cernea 1997, 1575). Cernea admits that these three components and ways in which to address them are often ignored or overlooked by planners (1581–82).

One explanation for this myopia can be found in the development discourse of planners and developers, with its self-serving rationalizations for external intervention, which tends to simplify culture, depicting it as something fixed and static that is waiting to be acted on by development (Pigg 1997), and using it to reinforce and naturalize socially produced conditions of difference, based on class, ethnicity, or geography, to name only the most common (Gupta and Ferguson 1997). But this discourse may also choose to totally ignore culture, on the grounds that treating it seriously, positively, and perhaps constructively may raise profound questions about the need or justification for "development" in the first place (Crush 1995). In mainstream development discourse, culture has usually been prefixed with the adjective *traditional,* itself a pejorative term, and often "blamed," to a lesser or greater extent, for the continuing problems of "underdevelopment." Viewed from this perspective, culture then becomes just another element of the developmental mix that can be acted on and manipulated by external forces (Harrison and Huntington 2000).

Yet as several authors have pointed out, it is precisely during traumatic events of displacement, moments of total crisis, when "all hell breaks loose" (Warner 1947), that anthropology can move from being the study of "the ordinary, the everyday, the routine" (Malkki 1995) to the study of the extraordinary, when people have the opportunity to remake themselves and their culture (Oliver-Smith 1996). Theodore Downing, concerned about the lack in Cernea's model of any theoretical explanation of how and why social disarticulation occurs, suggests that culture provides the answers to what he calls "primary questions," such as "Who are we? Where are we? Why do people live and die? What are our responsibilities to others and ourselves?" (1996, 36). In the process of displacement and resettlement, refugees are forced to reexamine these primary cultural and philosophical questions, while drawing on their culture to help them adapt to changing conditions.

This framework provides a context for beginning to understand how the state, in this case the national government, responded to the 1994 disaster, but it does not explain the different discourses offered by the state and other involved agencies and how these changed over time. Nor does it explain the different ways in which the three resettled communities chose to respond to the opportunities offered or the differing discourses they articulated to justify their priorities. These discourses of development can only be understood and explained within the broader political, social, and cultural context within which the disaster occurred.

Disaster as an Act of God, Nature, or Man?

On June 4, 1994, the region of Tierradentro, located in the northeastern part of the province of Cauca, was partially destroyed by an earthquake measuring 6.3 on the Richter scale. The earthquake was followed by a series of avalanches and numerous landslides, which flattened houses, buried livestock, blocked roads and trails, killed more than a thousand people, displaced 20 percent of the population, and ruined some forty thousand hectares of land. The municipalities affected were inhabited predominantly by the Nasa, the largest indigenous group in the province. The earthquake struck at four in the afternoon on a national holiday. Already geographically isolated, access by road was almost impossible, and the organizations that wished to help had to rely initially on helicopters to rescue people from the devastated communities. The rescued were housed in temporary camps, prior to their resettlement on new lands, often located at some distance from Tierradentro. As a result of the disaster, the Nasa, whose identity as a community has always been closely interwoven with their links to territory, were forced to deal with several interrelated issues simultaneously: the search for new lands; the development of new community structures and institutions; linkages with their communities of origin; and their visions of the future, of development and modernity. In short, they were obliged to redefine what it is to be Nasa, to be indigenous, in contemporary Colombia, but with the concrete possibility of being able to act on their resulting redefinitions (Rappaport and Gow 1997). Paradoxically, the tragedy offered them the opportunity to break with the past and start fresh.

In more general terms, displacement is usually caused by natural disaster, political strife, government intervention, or government neglect, operating individually or in combination. Government neglect may also be one of the major factors responsible for natural disasters, as in the case of Tierradentro. Groups that are economically and politically marginalized are more likely to have to live in areas that are more vulnerable to catastrophic events (Lubkemann 2002). This was not always the case. Historically, floods, earthquakes, and tornadoes were viewed as signs of God's displeasure, a natural evil resulting from a moral evil (Neiman 2002). An examination of the sermons written after the New England earthquakes of 1727 and 1755, the latter felt over some three hundred thousand square miles, found that the ministers blamed a "moral imbalance in human behavior" for their occurrence, and the author concludes that "earthquakes, especially tragic ones, were not merely luckless occasions for the chance sufferer; they were deeply meaningful punishments and conspicuous warnings" (Van de Wetering 1982, 422, 436; in Steinberg 2000, xxi).

The Lisbon earthquake of 1775 was said to shock Western civilization more than any event since the fall of Rome (Neiman 2002, 240–50).[2] It was one of the world's wealthier cities, strategically located on the edge of Europe, a natural point of departure for exploration and colonization. The wealth lost was vast, including gold and silver, works of art, and thousands of books and manuscripts. More than fifteen thousand people died. Theologians at the time regarded this particular earthquake as a double gift from heaven: on the one hand, a punishment for particular transgressions, and on the other, a manifestation of God's continuing role in the world. But if earthquakes were regarded as paradigms of natural evil, what kind of moral evil had Lisbon committed to produce this one? Traditional sins like ordinary greed and licentiousness provided sufficient explanation, and survivors were given the opportunity to repent before the general apocalypse visited everyone. But this interpretation did not go unchallenged. When the unhappy king of Portugal asked his controversial prime minister what should be done after the earthquake, he is said to have replied, "Bury the dead and feed the living" (Neiman 2002, 248). This pragmatic thinking has also prevailed in the United States. By the end of the twentieth century, only religious fundamentalists continued to draw moral lessons from such disasters, and the trend toward secularization has been strengthened by the state's increasing role in rationalizing disaster.

If this is the case, then why bother to distinguish between natural disasters and man-made ones? Ted Steinberg (2000, 184) argues that this is a way for the state to subsidize pro-development interests and uphold the prevailing economic order. Thus the federal government can rationalize its assistance to the victims of hurricanes, earthquakes, floods, and tornadoes, "events beyond human control — unpredictable and unforeseen acts of nature or God," while conveniently ignoring the social, political, human, and cultural factors underlying such calamities, as happened in Tierradentro. Nevertheless, there is a growing movement to deemphasize the importance of the "natural" in the study of disasters, and a growing emphasis on understanding the historical and sociopolitical context in which such disasters occur (Hewitt 1983). In the case of Tierradentro, some have argued that until twenty-five years ago there was a balance between population and available resources. Over the ensuing years, however, a growing population exerted increasing pressure on an already fragile environment, resulting in increasing degradation and decreasing productivity. But Tierradentro was and still is to a certain extent a region of refuge. Isolated, inhospitable, and difficult to access, it has been a place where indigenous people could feel relatively safe from the economic and social discrimination exercised against them elsewhere by mestizo society.

While there are often major differences in the reasons that people become displaced, there are significant similarities in the immediate effects of their displacement. They lose their households and their productive assets; their domestic economies are disrupted, if not destroyed, together with their social networks and sense of community; they are forced to move to other areas where they may not be welcome; they are often severely traumatized by the experience of becoming a refugee; and, in the case of ethnic minorities, their identity may be threatened.

In recent years, those displaced within their own country, internally displaced people, have increasingly become a "problem for development" because the agencies involved in ameliorating their situation, rather than just providing immediate emergency relief, are also increasingly expected to provide long-term development assistance. Consequently, there is a risk that the discourses of development, as perpetrated by development institutions, may colonize the discourse(s) of displacement, as practiced by relief agencies, and downplay (if not outright ignore) the role of politics and history. In this way, the process that gave rise to the displacement in the first place is never acknowledged and never addressed, and the situation never really improves (Malkki 1995). In the case presented here, the majority of relief and development efforts were directed at the new communities elsewhere, and few activities were focused on Tierradentro itself. Those displaced from their communities of origin were given priority because their needs were greatest. Also, at that time in Cauca's history, camps of displaced people were a political embarrassment. Those who remained in Tierradentro suffered the same fate as they did before the disaster. From the perspective of both provincial and national governments, they were effectively out of sight and out of mind.

Gustavo Wilches, the person initially in charge of resettlement activities, a native of Popayán and a widely respected authority on disaster relief, regarded the Nasa as being in a state of crisis at the time of the disaster, but so did Chucho Piñacué, president of the Regional Indigenous Council of Cauca (CRIC), and himself a Nasa from Tierradentro. But this crisis — if indeed it was a crisis — must be viewed in the broader context, particularly economic and cultural, in which the tragedy occurred. A CRIC documentary produced shortly after the disaster argued that the cultivation of illegal crops, such as coca, marijuana, and opium poppies, had been brought on by the widespread impoverishment experienced by indigenous people — in other words by their vulnerability (CRIC 1994). Using the Guambiano, another local indigenous group, as an example, the documentary shows that in a community where arable land is scarce and productivity low, illegal crops can complement the existing household economy, providing cash for the purchase of family necessities, including the costs involved in sending children to school. While such crops can be grown in all sorts of soil, the high-altitude *páramo,* with its very sensitive ecosystem, is favored because of its isolation and abundant water. People are well aware that activities of this sort have potentially dire environmental consequences, but they continue to exploit these fragile resources.

Although the occurrence of earthquakes may demonstrate punishment for human errors, they may also symbolize hope for the future. The earthquake of 1994 was not the first of its kind. There had been earthquakes at regular thirty-year intervals throughout the twentieth century, in 1907, 1937, and 1968 (Gómez and Ruíz 1997, 109). Earthquakes have also played an important role in the cultural history of the Nasa. All of Tierradentro's culture heroes were born in highland streams, the progeny of the stars. Juan Tama, for example, was born in Vitoncó in the Stream of the Morning Star. Rescued by the shamans, he was entrusted to virgin nursemaids, whom he killed by sucking their blood. Among other achievements, he laid down a set of laws for the Nasa to follow, laws they still quote today. At the end of his life he disappeared into Juan Tama Lake, the most sacred Nasa site and one which continues to figure in the most important contemporary rituals. According to contemporary Nasa, he still lives there, waiting to be called on should the need arise. Most recently he returned to aid his people after the La Violencia (Rappaport 1998 [1990], 154–55).

Earthquakes, then, are associated with the possible birth of a new *cacique* or leader (Gómez and Ruíz 1997, 156). Such was also the hope in 1994, except for the fact that the shamans gave no warning of this possibility. While the shamans were roundly criticized for this failure on their part, specifically for providing no warning of the impending disaster, Piñacué, in his dual role as a Nasa and president of CRIC, announced that "the avalanche did not bring with it the birth of a cacique but the announcement and warning that the Páez [i.e., Nasa] should prepare themselves for his coming, that's the reason why they have to support the shamans and be very unified to assume the reconstruction autonomously" (Gómez and Ruíz 1997, 157).

But the shamans themselves were aware of their failings. Don Ángel María Yoinó, a well-respected shaman from Juan Tama introduced briefly in the introduction, dreamed about the earthquake a year before it happened. The falling rocks and words of the ancestors convinced him that he was going to die. Filled with a great sadness, he was unable to understand what was happening.

> The problem was that I couldn't understand what the rocks meant. The dream did mean something bad, because then I realized that the signs [*señas,* literally bodily vibrations] indicated that I would just die. Then I asked myself what these signs were, but there was no one to discuss it with, because nobody at the time believed in such things."[3]

But Don Ángel was not the only one to experience visions of foreboding. Herinaldy Gómez and Carlos Ariel Ruíz (1997, chap. 5) collected a series of stories and dreams associated with the disaster, but with rather more ambiguous implications. In "The Cross and the Serpent," a story recorded in Vitoncó, the narrator sees a Christian cross, the symbol of domination, and a serpent, a symbol of the Nasa, being swept down the River Páez. But the cross passes on the right-hand side of the river, an ominous sign, whereas the serpent passes on the left-hand side, a favorable sign. A year after the tragedy, after a ritual of purification (*refresca-miento*) in the neighboring community of Wila, also hard hit by the earthquake, the officiating shaman was asked what this story meant and what its implications were for the future of the Nasa. He responded with a guarded optimism, reflecting the historical and cultural roots of the Nasa and their capacity to take the long-term view (Gómez and Ruíz 1997, 200).

The attitudes of those displaced toward their communities of origin in Tierradentro have varied considerably. In a documentary made by FST just after the tragedy, in which various Nasa leaders (specifically cultural activists and shamans) express their opinions about what happened, the narrator states that the ultimate aim of Nasa culture, its ideal, is to achieve a state of harmony, a balanced relationship among people and their environment, Mother Earth (FST 1994). The concept of *pta'nz,* that which works against this state of harmony, is key to understanding Nasa culture and the role of the shaman, since he is the only person with the necessary power and knowledge to recognize its presence and deal with it through the observance of certain well-established rituals.[4] This state of discord has its roots in human failings. Pta'nz "is then everything that generates disharmony or disequilibrium as a result of the actions or behavior of the individual or the ethnic collectivity or the actions undertaken within the territory by non-indigenous people who live there or by strangers passing through" (Gómez 2001, 342). What is being emphasized here is the importance of balance and harmony, not just between people and their natural environment but also among the indigenous people themselves, as well as between them and nonindigenous people. Hence, such potentially disrupting activities as the cultivation of illegal crops, such as coca and opium, or the creation of armed self-defense units are all viewed with suspicion until such time as the shaman, the recognized mediator, resolves the potential discord. For this reason among others, shamans have often been the targets of those who would do harm to the communities.

Those interviewed during the documentary, all Nasa, agree that something had gone very wrong. The most eloquent, Manuel Sisco, an intellectual with close links to shamans, concludes that the Earth no longer regards the Nasa as her children, because they have chosen to disregard her advice and go their own way. He tells the story of a shaman who fell asleep after the earthquake and was visited by Mother Earth in the form of a very old grandmother. She tells him that she is very upset and tired out by the transgressions of her children who no longer love each other or respect either her or the natural environment. In fact, they are no longer Nasa. She concludes by issuing an ultimatum: "I'm tired of you. I am going to turn the other way. I'm going to turn my back on you now so that you'll realize what it's like to live without a mother."

The Ethnographic Context

Formerly called the Páez, the Nasa live in the northern and eastern regions of Cauca and the western part of the neighboring province of Huila, but they have also migrated as colonists to western Cauca and the provinces of Caquetá and Putumayo. Traditionally, anthropologists have described the Nasa as a community of indigenous cultivators who live in dispersed settlements across the hillsides of the Cordillera Central and cultivate coffee, sugarcane, corn, and beans or potatoes and other Andean tubers, depending on the altitude (Rappaport 1998).[5] The center of Nasa country is Tierradentro, an isolated and mountainous zone on the eastern slopes of the Cordillera Central. Since the time of the Spanish invasion in 1536, the Nasa have been stereotyped as warriors who fiercely resisted the Europeans and who, when defeated on the field of battle, continued to fight those in power in the courts.

In the twentieth century, the struggle for land was led by Manuel Quintín Lame, a Nasa sharecropper. From 1910 onward, there were increasing confrontations between the elites of Cauca and the growing landless indigenous population, fighting to maintain or reestablish the *resguardos* (Rappaport 1998, 113). It was not only the loss of land and the increasing impoverishment of the people that motivated Quintín Lame. He was also incensed by the conditions of semi-slavery in which they were forced to live and work, and the loss of human dignity that this entailed. Lame's demands covered five points, which reverberated throughout the indigenous movement for the rest of the century: when CRIC was established in 1971, its proposed program covered essentially the same points (Castillo 1971, xviii): While primarily nonviolent, the contemporary struggle first emphasized grassroots organization and, under CRIC, the occupation and recovery of stolen lands and the implementation of development projects. The Nasa have been and continue to be respected for both their persistence and their resistance (Findji and Bonilla 1995).

In spite of existing ethnographic stereotypes, there is great diversity among the Nasa. Significant numbers of people have been living on the western slopes of the Cordillera Central since colonial times, an area characterized by sugar plantations, cattle ranching, agroindustry, land disputes, wage labor, and a long history of political violence. Here, the struggle for land has been much more intense than in Tierradentro, involving not just the Nasa but also other groups, such as Afro-Colombian and mestizo peasants (Espinosa 1996). Because history and politics and the experience of modernity have been so different there, chapter 5 presents some comparative material from the Nasa municipality of Toribío. There is also a considerable degree of difference and diversity within Tierradentro itself. In the communities lying in the Moras Basin, one of the major watersheds in Tierradentro, the levels of Nasa monolingualism or Nasa-Spanish bilingualism are higher than those found in the Páez Basin, the other major watershed, where the levels of formal education are higher (Rojas 1994).

Furthermore, the levels of historical awareness, closely linked to participation in the indigenous movement, also vary between the two watersheds. While some communities deploy their knowledge of the past within the framework of the ethnic movement, others have, until recently, refused to have anything to do with the politics of the regional indigenous organizations. The Nasa displaced by the most recent earthquake come from both regions of Tierradentro. Diversity between Tierradentro and the other Nasa zones, as well as among the communities within Tierradentro itself, has played an important role in determining how the Nasa have responded to the disaster and the solutions they have proposed. The resettled communities, which are the focus of this study, come from both regions of Tierradentro, and their continuing differences stem partly from their divergent histories.

What the stereotypes omit is any reference to the vulnerability of the Nasa. Vulnerability can be defined in general terms as a group's level of preparedness, resilience, and health for dealing with a disaster (Cannon 1994). People who are vulnerable are more exposed to risks, shocks, and stresses, and hence are less capable of coping with sudden changes (Chambers 1997). Those most affected by the disaster in 1994 were highly vulnerable in material terms, as are many of those who continue to live in Tierradentro. While the level of preparedness in Tierradentro at the time of the disaster was nonexistent, the levels of resilience, as indicated by livelihood security and health, were and continue to be extremely low. Underlying theories of vulnerability is the concept of powerlessness, that people at risk, with few rights and little protection, often lacking in adaptive capacities, are found to be politically vulnerable: "Vulnerability due to powerlessness arises from the social order" (Hewitt 1997, 153). If this is the case, then vulnerability may have its roots in social, economic, institutional, and cultural variables (Maskrey 1994, 47).

Shortly after the 1994 disaster, a survey was conducted of the affected communities in Páez and Inzá, the two major municipalities in Tierradentro, collecting information on the environment, production systems, housing, and health (Wilches Chaux 1995b). The results indicated that the population was suffering from extreme poverty, a situation that made them very vulnerable when dealing with a disaster as serious and widespread as the one that had just occurred. The basis of their domestic economy is the *minifundio,* small-plot agriculture, averaging from 1.7 to 1.9 hectares per family, on land characterized by steep slopes and heavy erosion (Carvajal 1995, 32). In Páez, 95 percent of the soils are poor and unsuitable for agriculture, and the situation is assumed to be similar in Inzá. Soils such as these are more suitable for forestry than agriculture (López Garcés 1995, 30–32). As a result, agricultural yields are low, and

CAUCA MAP

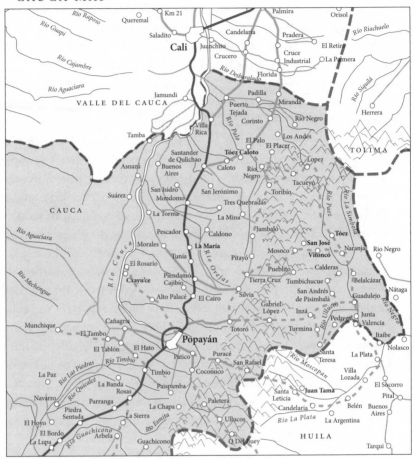

Map 1. Map of Cauca

Legend:

— Pan-American Highway

— Paved Roads

- - - - Unpaved Roads

— Other Roads

- - - Department Boundaries

▱ Department Capital

○ Other Cities

▨ Department of Cauca

people have increasingly turned to the cultivation of opium poppies on a small scale to survive (Gómez and Ruíz 1997). Another study conducted at the same time concluded that only 13.7 percent of the area affected, some 172,000 hectares, is safe for permanent human settlement (Ingeominas 1995, 2).

The quality of life is also low, as measured by standard indicators such as mortality and education. Life expectancy in Tierradentro is fifty-three years, whereas for the country as whole it is sixty-seven years. Mortality rates are also significantly higher for infants and children: in Páez, the mortality rate for children under age five is three times higher than for Cauca as a whole. Data on nutrition are equally alarming: the number of children less than one year old who are underweight is double the national average (Puerto Chávez 1995, 40–43). The situation looks even bleaker when education is taken into consideration, since there is little opportunity for schooling beyond the first years of primary education, though this has improved somewhat (FST 1995b, 9). With perhaps this sole exception, there is little evidence that these basic indicators have changed for the better in the intervening years.[6]

There are some twenty new settlements, both large and small, of displaced Nasa who have been relocated on new lands purchased by the national government in Cauca and the adjacent province of Huila, in addition to settlements of displaced members of other ethnic groups.[7] In some communities, such as Tóez, the epicenter of the earthquake, the houses and surrounding lands were almost totally destroyed by the disaster, forcing the people to relocate with little hope of being able to return and live in Tierradentro, although they still dream of one day being able to at least work their lands. Nevertheless, the people chose to call their new settlement Tóez Caloto to demonstrate their continuity with the past.

Other resguardos, such as San José and Vitoncó, were partially destroyed; some of the population continued living in the community of origin, while the remainder now lives in settlements far from Tierradentro, in Cxayu'ce and Juan Tama, respectively (see map 1). These settlements were not established as new entities, independent of their communities of origin, but rather as extensions of existing resguardos (CNK 1995, 7). Although all three of the new settlements viewed the disaster as an opportunity to improve their situation, the ways they have chosen to do so and the discourses they have employed have varied considerably.

CNK: The Institution of Resettlement

CNK was created by the Colombian government to assist with the rehabilitation of the region and to supervise the relocation of the people. A parastatal, it was created immediately after the disaster in 1994 as the state agency responsible for resettling the people who could not return to their communities, normalizing the situation of those who were able to remain in the zone, providing assistance to other affected zones in the form of land purchase, provision of housing and basic services, the opening of roads, the promotion of productive projects, and environmental rehabilitation (CNK 1995, 10–12). Its name, Nasa Kiwe, reflects its preoccupation with the Nasa and identification with their needs and priorities: "Nasa Kiwe" means "Nasa territory" (Wilches Chaux 1998, 89).

CNK policy toward the indigenous communities revolved around several related objectives (CNK 1995, 5–10; Wilches Chaux 1995a, 1995b). From the very beginning, the agency tried to establish the settlements in areas that were ecologically complementary to the communities of origin in Tierradentro, acknowledging that while the settlements could not replace the original lands, they could serve as extensions (*ampliaciones*). While acknowledging that conflict over land was endemic in Cauca, the agency wished to avoid exacerbating a tense situation by establishing the new settlements in areas where there was little conflict, although in practice this was not always possible.

> In the selection and purchase of lands for the permanent resettlement of the displaced communities, we shall take into account the absence of natural risks (landslide, avalanche), environmental risks (deterioration of critical ecosystems as a result of the settlement of new communities) and social risk. To the extent possible we shall avoid relocating the communities in zones where previous conflicts over land tenure continue and we shall give priority to the voluntary and agreed-upon negotiation of the properties based on administrative expropriation. (CNK 1995, 8)

In addition, CNK believed that Nasa culture was in a state of crisis and specifically, that the loss of traditional values and the decreasing authority of the *cabildos* and shamans brought on by the economic boom in Tierradentro in the late 1980s and early 1990s was a direct consequence of poppy cultivation (Wilches Chaux 1995b, 130). In a 1996 interview, Jesús Enrique Piñacué, the Nasa president of CRIC at the time of the disaster and later a senator in Bogotá, indicated that an important section of CRIC's leadership had reached the same conclusion. An ethnography of the Nasa published about this time provides one of the first detailed anthropological accounts of the advantages and disadvantages of poppy cultivation and discusses the disruptive social effects in some detail: increasing levels of violence, consumption of alcohol, and criminal acts, accompanied by decreasing participation in communal work and reduced cultivation of food crops (Gómez and Ruíz 1997). On a more positive note, however, poppy cultivation has provided employment opportunities for young men who would otherwise have been obliged to migrate or throw in their lot with one of the various armed groups. The authors argue that the area hardest hit by the disaster, which included Tóez, was the most "modernized" and the most susceptible to cultivating poppies, given its strategic location on the highway and the lack of any strong dissenting voices in the form of the cabildo, the shamans, or CRIC.

CNK's objective was the defense and preservation of a culture under threat: Nasa culture was to be maintained by encouraging the participation of the shamans, community authorities, and indigenous organizations. By creating the new settlements in far-flung isolated areas, the agency could ensure the continuation of "traditional culture," uncontaminated by the pervasive influence of urban centers. In this way, the government could demonstrate a serious commitment to improving the situation for indigenous people. But to do so, they needed to work with people who were rural and indigenous, rather than urban and increasingly "de-Indianized," since the latter were no longer regarded as being authentically indigenous. All this was to be achieved though a deliberate effort on the part of the agency to encourage the active participation of those most affected, by having indigenous members on the CNK board, offering employment to the Nasa, and paying close attention to the opinions and demands of the indigenous communal authorities, who, at least in theory, would have the final say in the major decisions to be taken.

To better understand CNK's influence, it is more productive to think

75

of the agency as an organizational hybrid. A parastatal organization created by the state, CNK was free of many of the limitations under which public sector institutions usually function, such as an excessive bureaucracy and continuing budgetary shortfalls. Furthermore, it combined a variety of functions rarely found within a single organization — a type of regional authority responsible for indigenous development, specifically the purchase of productive land and the provision of adequate housing, as well as support for primary education and basic health care. In fact, Gustavo Wilches Chaux, the first director from 1994 to 1996, suggests that CNK combined some of the responsibilities of two then-active national organizations, the Colombian Land Reform Institute and the Division of Indigenous Affairs (Wilches Chaux 1998).

In contrast to these institutions, CNK had more financial and political power. Its financial power was demonstrated by its ready access to funds and its consequent ability to pay a large percentage of the purchase price of expropriated lands in cash, rather than in the bonds traditionally favored by the government which steadily decreased in value over time. Its political power was reflected in its mandate to unilaterally expropriate lands should conditions demand it, as well as its ability to do away with much of the bureaucratic red tape that normally hinders land transfers. However, CNK rarely had to expropriate land, since landowners, particularly those with poor or unproductive lands for which there was little demand, were only too willing to sell.

By necessity, CNK depended for its survival on political support from a variety of sources, including the national government, the provincial government, CRIC, and the indigenous communities themselves. Yet in the final essence, CNK was responsible to the national government, specifically the Ministry of the Interior, which created it. Initially it was believed that CNK could complete its mission within a year, but increasing budgetary constraints severely limited the agency's activities, and it managed to survive from one presidency to the next. In his campaign speeches in 1998, President Andrés Pastrana indicated that if elected, he would in all probability terminate CNK once its five-year mandate expired. But this never happened, and at the next presidential elections in 2002, CNK survived, but barely. While it still survived in 2005, it was a shadow of its previous self.[8]

The literature on resettlement recommends working with existing organizations to the extent possible (Wilches Chaux 1995b). At the time of the disaster, one such possibility was CRIC, which, since its founding in 1971, had become an important actor on the regional, national, and international stages. From the moment disaster struck, CRIC, together with other regional entities, played an instrumental role in creating the basic infrastructure required to satisfy the needs of the refugees, a role that diminished after the creation of CNK. Nevertheless, CRIC did control certain of the basic services provided for the displaced, including the coordination of the health program in some settlements (working with local shamans and medical doctors) and provision of teachers to some bilingual schools. It channeled funds from international organizations, providing loans to the refugees for the purchase of livestock, vehicles, and other necessities. CRIC also played a political role in CNK through its participation on the board of governors where the indigenous members continuously struggled with CNK staff in defense of their constituents.

CRIC's relationships with the resettled communities have been ambiguous, a consequence of both political and historical factors, as well as the fact that CRIC initially supported the resettlement policies promoted by CNK. At the time of the disaster, CRIC was in a state of limbo, weathering a crisis of institutional identity and survival, which entailed less support for its constituents. This was partly a response to the organization's political role. On the one hand, many of its leaders had been either imprisoned or assassinated in the 1980s, and on the other, there was a perception on the part of some that CRIC was too closely identified with the guerrilla movement, particularly the Quintín Lame Armed Movement, as well as with the Communist Party of Colombia (Cardona 1995). Though the constitutional reforms of the early 1990s provided some political space and legitimacy for the indigenous movement, they also provided the opportunity to become more involved in local development with the discourse of decentralization, local planning, and the provision of resources directly to the resguardos (Gow 1997). This tended to blunt the political agenda of CRIC and encourage the policy of *proyectitis,* always thinking, even obsessing, about projects. Subregional associations of cabildos have appeared, entities which have engaged in development planning and the creation of new political linkages at the local level, sometimes supporting CRIC but at other times questioning its authority. To a certain extent, the survival of the organization in the mid-1990s was due to the resources received from CNK, as well as the pressure from the new cabildo associations to change its well-worn discourse of ethnic and class oppression and replace it with a new discourse of sovereignty or peoplehood.

Given the ambivalent perceptions of CRIC, the national government's response to the disaster was to create a new institution. In the days immediately following the earthquake, the government responded in a state of confusion and gave the strong impression that it lacked the relevant information and did not know what it was doing. It was unclear what was happening, who was in charge, and how the government proposed to proceed. This reflected badly on Colombia's international image, as well as on the domestic political situation. President César Gaviria had only two months of his term to serve, his popularity remained high, the second round of the presidential elections was to take place shortly, and he had just been elected secretary general of the Organization of American States, a distinct honor for Colombia. Hence, the decision was taken to nip the mounting criticism in the bud. Three days after the disaster, the government announced the creation of CNK, thereby demonstrating to the public, both national and international, that the president and his ministers were actively involved and taking the situation seriously (Cardona 1995).

While CNK was always controversial, particularly in its earlier years when there were so many demands made on it, most critics would agree that it did help improve the situation. In 1997, three schoolteachers from Mosoco, a resguardo close to San José at the western entry point to Tierradentro, sent a letter to CNK, listing what they regarded as the positive contributions made by the agency (Guegia Hurtado, Caicedo de Cachimba, and Dorado Zúñiga 1997). In addition to the more obvious, such as the purchase of land and the provision of infrastructure, they mention more intangible aspects, such as strengthening community organization, revalidating indigenous cultural values, and increasing the capacity of indigenous groups to negotiate directly with the state. In other words, CNK had made a major contribution toward establishing the new communities, strengthening their values and capabilities, and providing them with the wherewithal to survive on their own. These are large claims that the available evidence does not necessarily substantiate. What is clear, however, is that CNK did provide the basis for the new settlements to exercise their own agency regarding how they and their children would choose to live their lives.

Dreams of Development and Modernity

With varying degrees of success, the three new settlements to be discussed, Tóez Caloto, Cxayu'ce, and Juan Tama, rejected the CNK policy of trying to preserve Nasa culture through a process of isolation and purchase of lands similar to those in Tierradentro. In contrast, these communities opted for greater social, economic, and political integration into the larger regional society in the years immediately following the disaster. After centuries of isolation and extreme poverty, they wanted to be able to take advantage of the window of opportunity offered by the disaster and CNK to improve their lives. Their objectives all centered around land in one form or another. They wanted land that was productive, with ready access to markets. They wanted to establish the new settlements in areas which were ecologically complementary with the lands in their communities of origin, so they could both exchange and market products with the people who remained in Tierradentro. Finally, they wanted to relocate their families near larger urban centers, which offered more educational opportunities and the knowledge necessary to take full advantage of their new lands, as well as the proximity to markets. This initial focus on land had several dimensions. As the communities argued, it would provide the basis for a new home and a continuation of indigenous culture and identity. Its productive potential would provide a more diverse and secure economic base. Finally, the strategic location of the land would provide access to improved information and infrastructure, which in turn could offer increased economic and educational opportunities.

The most dramatic example of this process has been Tóez Caloto, whose members decided to relocate the whole community to the north of Cauca, an area with which several community leaders, including the then-governor, were already acquainted. The new settlement received assistance from ACIN (Association of Indigenous Cabildos of Northern Cauca), a subregional grouping and member of CRIC. ACIN did not support CNK's resettlement policy, preferring to push for an increase in the number of Nasa in the zone of Caloto, an area of conflict with large landowners and a growing problem of land purchases by drug lords associated with the then-powerful Cali cartel. In fact, representatives from the north sought out the displaced families of Tóez and offered them the temporary use of land in Huellas, a resguardo close to the town of Caloto, until they could secure new lands of their own in the vicinity.

For the displaced, the move offered the opportunity to escape from the isolation they felt in Tierradentro. According to Don Jorge Inseca, one of the local leaders mentioned in the introduction,

> Means of transportation — don't even think about it. We did not have means of communication. Let's say we are in a half-developed indigenous zone. It needs a lot to become developed, but you get things by struggling. The future here, even for the indigenous people of Tóez, the indigenous Páez, they say here that yes, we want to study: the universities are closer, there are more alternatives for studying, you can study at night, you can make a career. In any case, they are key points for the future, aren't they? Business is easier: not only does what you plant stay here, but you also you remove it for sale. So all that is looking toward the future and that we have in concrete in the community.[9]

Both CNK and CRIC opposed the relocation of Tóez to Caloto for a variety of reasons: the land, located in an area of large cattle ranches and sugar plantations, was too expensive; the people lacked the necessary technical expertise to work the land efficiently; there was already a high incidence of violence, which the presence of additional Nasa would only exacerbate; and by living on the outskirts of a city, little more than an hour by road from the industrial center of Cali, with a population of over two million, the Nasa would run the risk of "losing their culture." Instead, CNK advised the community to move to Santa Leticia, where there was land similar to that in Tierradentro and where they could live surrounded by other Nasa.[10]

Nevertheless, in spite of the opposition of CNK and CRIC, the cabildo of Tóez Caloto refused to accept the corporation's plans, arguing strongly that the asking prices for the haciendas for sale in the immediate vicinity could be negotiated down to a level more acceptable to CNK, in line with the prices the agency was willing to pay for land elsewhere.[11] By negotiating directly with the owners of the farms they wished CNK to purchase for them, the cabildo showed that it was possible to lower the prices. Over the next few years, the corporation purchased a total of four haciendas for the displaced families, while the cabildo succeeded in attracting funding from a variety of sources for several types of productive activities, such as raising livestock, fish farming, and corn cultivation. Though not directly addressing the criticism concerning their lack of technical expertise, this success did indicate a certain degree of institutional confidence in the new community's potential. Also, the leaders indicated their interest in being able to produce a variety of crops in an environmentally sustainable way. According to Jorge Inseca:

> It's lazy [not to work the land], I said, because here you can produce everything: corn, beans, papaya, grapes, everything you can produce here. So the key is to work, that's what I look for with the idea of giving the [same] motivation to the community and looking at what the alternatives are for the rest of the lands. . . . We want to buy the lands that are [available] so that they remain in reserve because nowadays people are working a lot with ecology, [and] we can't go and seize that hill and make the hoe fly, causing the earth to crumble and making for more erosion. So, I was looking at the level land for agriculture, the productive aspect, the productive aspect.[12]

Regarding the incidence of violence in northern Cauca, the leaders responded that it was no worse than in other areas proposed for resettlement. They cited the examples of Rio Negro in Huila, at that time famous for its large extensions of coca, and Santa Leticia, on the borders of Cauca and Huila, a Revolutionary Armed Forces of Colombia (FARC) stronghold for many years.

But their response to CNK's final objection that Tóez Caloto might "lose" its culture was more radical, more visionary, and as it turned out, more opportunistic. They promised to build their own school, grade school through high school; they proposed to establish an indigenous university; and they would have their children learn Nasa Yuwe. The fact that they would be surrounded by fellow Nasa would safeguard them against "cultural loss," although their new neighbors, who had been living there since colonial times, regarded themselves as "de-Indianized" and "less indigenous," less Nasa. As a result, the northern resguardos welcomed Tóez Caloto into their fold with the hope that the inclusion of this new community would stimulate their own cultural project, given that they perceived its origins in Tierradentro as projecting a more "traditional" aura, in contrast to their own monolingual Spanish-speaking communities, which were highly integrated into the regional market economy.

This stereotyping of Tóez Caloto, however, was not without its iro-   81 nies. At the time of the disaster, Tóez was viewed as one of the more "modernizing" resguardos in Tierradentro. This was so for several reasons: (1) its proximity to the only highway linking the northern and southern parts of Tierradentro, making travel and transportation relatively easy; (2) the high incidence of monolingual Spanish speakers, indicating a lack of interest in Nasa culture; (3) an important minority of evangelical Protestants within the community who eschewed Nasa traditional medicine and, by association, shamanic knowledge in general; (4) its nonparticipation in CRIC and its general lack of interest in indigenous politics, but not local politics. At the time of the disaster, the elected mayor of the municipality of Páez was a Nasa from Tóez. Finally, and somewhat paradoxically, Tóez was the site of a well-respected vocational high school. Established after La Violencia, this high school attracted indigenous students from Tierradentro and other parts of the province. Prior to the disaster, however, the indigenous families of Tóez had shown little interest in the high school or in sending their children there to study. The school, like most of the other buildings in the community, was totally destroyed by the earthquake. But the teachers survived, and the majority of them accompanied the displaced families to their new settlement in Caloto.

Tóez Caloto has been characterized by strong leadership, particularly in the earlier years, political astuteness, and a strong feeling of communal solidarity (reinforced by the fact that most people lost everything in the disaster), but what has distinguished it from the other two settlements is its strong vision of the future, one which would uncritically embrace modernization. While they were still living in the refugee camp in 1995, leaders were already talking of building their own school, in spite of the fact that schooling was readily available in the nearby town of Caloto, four kilometers away (Asociación de Damnificados del Resguardo Indígena de Tóez [ADRIT] 1995; Centro Etnoeducativo Tóez 1997; Mulcué and Yasnó n.d.). By 2002, the school, three imposing red brick structures and still under construction, dominated the landscape. Classes were available through eleventh grade, and the first class was due to graduate at the end of the year. Of the 240 students enrolled, approximately a third came from neighboring communities. Plans for the future envisaged the construction of dormitories, the enrollment of boarders from more distant Nasa communities, and the creation of a learning center that could form the foundation for an indigenous university.

Nevertheless, Tóez Caloto's relations with its community of origin have not been harmonious, partly a result of disagreements over the distribution of *transferencias,* cash transfers from the national government. The new community has felt that it rarely received its due from the home community, which had the final word over their allocation. But more important was the attitude of Tóez Caloto toward those families who chose to return to Tierradentro. In 1997, a dozen families, constituting 10 percent of the overall population, chose to leave the community and return to Tóez. People offered various reasons for their departure. Some of the families cited personal reasons, and others said they were unable to adapt to the different climatic conditions, particularly the heat encountered in the new, lower altitude environment. Some community members accused them of being lazy, unwilling to take advantage of the opportunities offered, while others accused them of wanting to return and dedicate themselves to the cultivation of opium poppies. This matter was discussed during a general assembly involving the whole community in Tóez Caloto, including members of some of the families who proposed to leave. Responses from the community ranged widely, including outright choleric condemnation, particularly from one of the older leaders, Don Victoriano, who was governor at the time of the disaster and had led his people to Caloto. For him, such an activity was a betrayal of Nasa culture, and he started his diatribe by establishing his credentials: "I am Nasa thought" (*Yo soy el pensamiento nasa*). Another leader, Don Jorge, suggested a more moderate line, reminding his audience that he had been governor in the early 1990s when people had started to seriously cultivate poppies. At that time, he had warned them of the impending danger if they continued this practice, and eventually his prediction had come true in the form of the avalanche following the earthquake.

Although these leaders' concept of Nasa culture is colored to a certain extent by the fact that they are evangelical Christians, both strongly believe in the importance of hard work. In Nasa culture, this is regarded as an end in itself, proof that people are reliable and industrious, and not as a means to material success. In contrast, for the evangelicals, who include several of the local leaders, hard work is a means to an end, as a way to achieve material success in the secular world. So when Don Victoriano accused those who wanted to return as being traitors to their culture, he was attacking them on two fronts simultaneously, first for choosing the "easy life" associated with poppy cultivation, and second for rejecting an emerging, constructed Nasa culture adapted to local circumstances.

The community as a whole was very upset at the departure of these families. They were viewed as breaking faith, as fracturing the communal solidarity that Tóez Caloto had established over the preceding three years, in marked contrast to the factionalism that had prevailed prior to the disaster. Those who left were also regarded as fools, not only for choosing to turn their backs on all the resources (particularly land and houses) and services (particularly health and education) that had been provided free but also for turning their backs on the community's vision of indigenous modernity. This striving for modernity through modernization is what distinguishes Tóez Caloto from the other new communities — a conscious effort to simultaneously distance themselves from their past while at the same time adapting and reconstructing certain elements of their culture to make themselves more appealing to a broader public, both indigenous and nonindigenous. More recently, given Tóez Caloto's lack of interest in maintaining legal ties with their original community and a distant municipality in which they no longer reside, the new community has actively pursued the possibility of being declared a new resguardo, thereby legalizing the relationship with their new municipality of residence, a strategy that could provide both economic and political advantages. The official recognition as a new resguardo was finally achieved in 2004. The cultural cost, if any, that such a severing could entail has yet to be determined.

A convincing argument can be made that for the people of Tóez Caloto, their vision of the future focuses much more on the education of their children and preparing them for dealing with the twenty-first century, than on their own, more immediately pressing economic problems (Gow 1997). In spite of the fact that they received productive lands — much more so, say, than the lands received by Juan Tama in Santa Leticia — the lands have not yet proven to be as productive as originally thought. To get the most from the land requires irrigation, machinery, and technical knowledge, and only a few of the families, particularly those of the better-off leaders, have been able and willing to take advantage of the opportunities offered. But the community itself has not been prepared to make the necessary investments, either in technical expertise or in machinery, preferring to purchase a truck rather than a tractor. There are several local mestizo middlemen with the necessary technical expertise about suitable crops, their technical requirements, and their marketing possibilities, but such expertise must be paid for. The production of sugarcane on communal lands, for example, did not prove to be profitable due to a combination of intense competition, relative inexperience, and lack of rainfall. Their herd of communal livestock, purchased with a grant and managed by the community, has been more successful, partly because families already had experience with this activity. As a result, people must look for wage employment outside the community, as laborers on the neighboring sugar and livestock haciendas, or as unskilled workers in the urban centers of Santander and Cali. While the building and staffing of their own school helped establish their indigenous credentials, their economic aspirations have proved to be more conventional.

In contrast, their political agenda has tended to follow the more radical demands of ACIN and the north in general, whose discourse is based more on social and economic justice than on cultural rights and ethnicity. Though the people of Tóez Caloto are self-consciously Nasa, the reconstruction of their indigenous identity has been a means by which they have been able to secure favored treatment in their quest to modernize and to embrace modernity.

The experience of Juan Tama, the resettled people of Vitoncó, has been very different, starting with the initial quest for new lands. In its earlier years, CNK's objectives in certain ways reflected the traditional stereotypes applied to the Nasa, specifically their reputed aggression and traditionalism, referred to earlier. Implicit in the agency's desire to avoid establishing settlements in areas of conflict, a virtual impossibility in the violence-ridden provinces of Cauca and Huila, was the acceptance of the "conflictive" label attached to the Nasa. This stereotypical image was still widespread, as the displaced families from Vitoncó discovered to their cost when they unsuccessfully attempted to negotiate the purchase of land close to Popayán. The impending settlement of 250 Nasa families in the same location was viewed as threatening. By the same token, the proposal to relocate these families in distant areas, such as Santa Leticia, demonstrated the extent to which the agency accepted the

stereotype of the Nasa as "traditional," as people who had to be "protected" from the dangers of the broader society, rather than as historical actors who have always engaged in regional processes (Rappaport 1998). El Cabuyo, one of the sections of Vitoncó, had been a
center of CRIC's organizational activities in Tierradentro since the late
1970s. Earlier, a member of El Cabuyo had been personal secretary to
Quintín Lame, the famous indigenous leader in the first half of the
twentieth century.

Ironically, perhaps, the municipality of Santa Leticia has been and
continues to be a traditional FARC stronghold. With little government
presence in the area, the guerrillas have effectively controlled what happens there, from "taxing" trucks transporting livestock to "approving"
all forms of external assistance, including that offered by CNK and CCF
(the Christian Children's Fund), an NGO that operated there for several
years. Located on the border between the provinces of Cauca and Huila,
far from urban centers, Juan Tama is the site of an earlier colonization
effort by mestizo colonists. The eroded and deforested hillsides are
suitable for small-scale livestock production, but with limited potential
for agriculture. Although it sits beside the main highway linking Popayán with La Plata, the respective provincial capitals, it is isolated. A
frontier area, people are also concerned about the presence of *delin-
cuentes* and the widespread incidence of theft, robbery, and banditry. It
is also a dismal and inhospitable area. During the rainy season, the paths
and trails within the settlement are transformed into a sea of mud, and
the low-lying clouds and mist contribute to a general air of desolation.

The people of Vitoncó only reluctantly agreed to settle there, finally
succumbing to prolonged pressure from CNK and CRIC. This was a
long, drawn-out, and painful process, in which the displaced families
were shunted from one place to another, partly because they were such a
large group. According to one participant:

> Three days after the tragedy they evacuated us to the resguardo of Mosoco
> where we were not well received because they thought that we were going to
> stay there; after three days' stay, they moved us to the section of Escalereta
> where we stayed for 20 days. . . .
>
> In this place beside the páramo of Moras, covered by its thick clouds and
> freezing breezes, approximately 600 of us arrived from the resguardo of
> Vitoncó and after having passed some time, many returned to the zone of the

disaster, their motives and reasons were many, but it was obvious that nothing was clear. (Comunidad de Juan Tama 2002, 8–9)

After a month spent there, they were moved again, this time across the páramo to Silvia, where a regular camp had been established. By the time they arrived, their numbers had dropped to 480. After five months in the camp, they finally obtained land in Santa Leticia.

From the start, there were major differences among the various sections of Vitoncó resettled there. Each one had its own particular ideology and religion, and each enjoyed relationships with distinct movements and institutions, factors that severely affected their long-term commitment to resettlement and the building of a new community. The sections of La Troja and Vitoncó, for example, were allied with the traditional Catholic Church of Tierradentro, which until recently had maintained a stranglehold on education and the cabildos in Tierradentro, downplaying (if not denigrating) the role of indigenous culture in everyday life in the process. This constituency clashed continually with El Cabuyo, a section that has enjoyed a long-standing association with CRIC, having established an experimental bilingual school there some ten years before the disaster, which was later reconstructed in the new settlement; the fact that the original CRIC school was secular, staffed by Nasa, and promoted indigenous culture earned its proponents the label of communist. In the reconstructed school in Juan Tama, the curriculum was designed and taught by local Nasa, based on Nasa culture and history, with assistance from CRIC's bilingual education program. While there were other issues to be addressed in the new settlement, such as what crops could be grown, how they could pressure CNK to provide more productive land, and how to attract additional resources, it was initially the school that proved to be a major bone of contention. Its Nasa-centered curriculum posed a threat for the Catholic religious instruction championed by some families (El Cabuyo/CRIC 1996; Camayo and Niquinás 1997). Also crucial was the fact that teachers from the church-sponsored schools of Tierradentro could not and would not work with CRIC teachers, since they were forbidden to do so by their religious superiors.[13]

The struggle over community education was compounded by a fight over transferencias that unfolded between the home community and the new settlement, given that the majority of the resguardo remained in

Tierradentro and thus had the necessary clout to deny what Juan Tama regarded as its fair share of funds. In 1997, differences unresolved, more than a hundred families allied with the Catholic Church finally moved to another settlement in Itaibe, within the boundaries of Tierradentro.[14] Those who opted to leave were from precisely those sections of Vitoncó allied with the Catholic Church, thus projecting the ideological struggle taking place in Juan Tama over a vaster terrain.[15]

During the years since it was established, the leadership in Juan Tama has devoted much of its time and effort to fighting CNK, Vitoncó, and one another. There has been little leadership within the community and little effort to articulate some vision of what the future might look like. It is a place where people have complained a great deal about the government, CNK, the lack of economic opportunities, and the poor quality of the land. Over the years, however, the land has become a little more productive and a little easier to work, with the help of intensive organic fertilization and extensive plowing by tractor. As a result, families now plant a wider variety of crops and fruit trees in their individual plots and house gardens, although their main interest continues to be livestock. But men and women still have to leave in considerable numbers to find work elsewhere, usually on a seasonal basis. Given their ongoing differences with their home community, and their overall feelings of frustration and partial abandonment, the people of Juan Tama, like their counterparts in Tóez Caloto, have opted for secession, seeking government approval to declare themselves a new resguardo and join up with CRIH (Regional Indigenous Council of Huila), a newly created organization in the neighboring province, founded, ironically, by disaffected ex-members of Juan Tama.

Nevertheless, in spite of their periodic unhappiness and continuing isolation, the people of Juan Tama are proud of being Nasa and of being indigenous. Coming as they do from Vitoncó, the Nasa heartland, gives them both authority and credibility which, although they wear them lightly, they are not afraid to flaunt should the need or the occasion arise. Although the creation and establishment of their own school has proved to be contentious, bilingual education is a reality there, and the school actively promotes and disseminates a Nasa spirituality (*cosmovisión*) as a vehicle for viewing the world which effectively links the past and the present as a way of dealing with the future (Camayo and Niquinás 1997). In a sense, the school holds the community together, since it embodies many aspects and components important to Nasa culture. One way in which this is achieved is through the cultivation of the *tul,* the school garden, a replication of the individual family tul, which is viewed as an integral model of the cosmos. A recent history of CRIC's bilingual education program warns the reader that a family without a tul is experiencing a cultural crisis. "It has lost the mechanisms of cultural resistance because its cosmogonic symbols can no longer be seen" (Bolaños et al. 2004, 115). By the same token, this cosmovision can serve as a foundation for the survival and adaptability of the community.

The importance of self-conscious Nasa culture in Juan Tama as an integral part of everyday life takes many forms. For example, the shamans have been actively involved in various activities. They were consulted about the site of the new settlement before the final decision was taken to move there. In consultation with the school teachers, they created a nursery for medicinal plants. Most spectacularly, they supervised the collective painting of a series of vivid murals depicting the life of Juan Tama on the outside walls of the Council House (Casa del Cabildo), where the previous landowner used to live. This building, visible from the road, dominates the settlement.

The third new settlement, Cxayu'ce, was established in the municipality of Cajibío, an area populated by small-scale mestizo farmers, approximately an hour's drive west of Popayán. The displaced families came from the resguardo of San José in Tierradentro, a place of infamy, since this was the second time in less than fifty years that the community had been forced to flee. The Communist Party's peasant leagues had been active in Tierradentro in the 1940s and, during La Violencia in the early 1950s, government troops, with the active support of the Catholic Church, slaughtered local indigenous leaders, accusing them of being communists and supporting the guerrillas, an event that eye-witnesses can still recall today.

> One day around six in the morning the village appeared to be surrounded. A commission entered to get the people out. They wanted to vacate the houses in order to burn them. Those who didn't manage to get out were burned inside the houses. The army assembled the people in the village. Two managed to escape: Sebastián Tumbo and Pío Tumbo. At midday they took the people towards Mosoco. When they reached the bridge, they separated the men and women. First they made the men pass, they were calling them one

by one and killing them with bullets and knives. Others, they cut off their testicles. About 11 men died, but they let the women live. Another called Rubén escaped from them at the bridge, pretending to be dead and falling in the river but he escaped from them by swimming underwater. (Resguardo de San José 1999, 6)[16]

Decades later, witnesses can still vividly recount what they had seen and the fearful impact the massacre exerted on them. While these two disasters did not necessarily make the community fatalistic, they certainly made the members more cautious and more realistic. While they were quite prepared to take full advantage of the opportunities offered by the disaster — specifically the possibility of obtaining more productive land in the warmer lowlands — they viewed this as a continuation, hopefully an improvement, on their everyday lives in Tierradentro. They did not view it as a radical break with their roots, nor as an opportunity to develop a distinctive agenda or discourse of their own. There was neither the need nor the desire to stick their necks out and prove anything to anyone. They were who they were and would continue to be so.

At the time of the disaster in 1994, San José consisted of some one hundred families living in two sections, Botatierra, predominantly evangelical, and San José, predominantly Catholic. All of those who chose to move came from the latter, because it was more seriously damaged and people lost their sources of water. Like their counterparts in Tóez Caloto, the displaced families refused to accept the conditions laid down by CNK, and the leaders were adamant that they wanted their new lands to be lower lying, warmer, more productive, and nearer Popayán. The leadership is also said to have done its best to fully exploit the opportunities offered by CNK — new lands and new houses for all those who chose to move.[17] But the families in Botatierra, whose houses and lands were also damaged less extensively in the disaster, decided to stay, in spite of the fact that CNK made them the same offer. During a planning workshop held in Botatierra in 2000, the people indicated that their arable land was so poor and so limited in extent that their only means of survival was to obtain additional land in the warmer lowlands. When asked why they had decided to stay in 1994, they confessed they had miscalculated: they had assumed that as their neighbors in San José moved out, they could move in and take over their land. This had not happened because the displaced families in Cxayu'ce had not given up these lands. They would return on a seasonal basis to work them, often planting opium poppies. The people of Botatierra regretted their short-sightedness and lack of initiative. For them, the resettled families in Cxayu'ce had become a model of how to extend one's territory and gain access to and control of warmer, more productive lands. Another small section in San José, consisting of a dozen families with lands up in the páramo, has followed the example of Cxayu'ce and used their share of the annual transferencias to start purchasing land in the lowlands.

In 1995, a year after the disaster, the displaced families in Cxayu'ce were still living in tents in extremely unpleasant and unhealthy conditions, just like their displaced counterparts in Juan Tama.[18] They were well aware of the challenges that lay ahead in having to adapt to a radically different physical environment — learning to cultivate tropical crops such as coffee, plantains, and sugarcane — and also to a radically different political environment, surrounded on all sides by small-scale mestizo farmers, in an area that is one of the traditional strongholds of the National Liberation Army and, more recently, the paramilitaries and the FARC. When asked how they would learn to cultivate these new crops, they responded that they would learn by working with their mestizo neighbors. Over the years, they collaborated with their neighbors and learned through practical experience how to do tropical agriculture and how to deal with tropical pests, specifically the voracious red ants endemic to the area. Compared to the families in the other two resettlements, they have taken full advantage of their available resource base.

Cxayu'ce has received assistance from various sources. A herd of livestock was provided by CRIC on credit and managed on a communal basis, with most of the new community participating. Funds for the new school were provided by a European donor who visited Colombia shortly after the disaster. Cxayu'ce was selected because one of the leaders happened to be in the CRIC office when the donor representative was visiting. CRIC provides the teachers. The Missionary Sisters of Mother Laura, a religious order very active in education, helped find support for an embryonic women's bakery. And CNK, in addition to purchasing land and providing building materials for houses, building a health post and providing health promoters — something which it did for *all* the new settlements — also provided financing for the installation of a *panelera* or *ramada,* a small mechanized complex for crushing sugarcane and producing *panela,* bricks of unrefined sugar. When boiled with water, this produces *agua de panela,* a drink much beloved by the Nasa and most other Colombians.

While Tóez Caloto and Juan Tama wished to sever legal ties with their communities of origin early on and establish themselves as new, independent resguardos, Cxayu'ce, in contrast, maintained close ties with San José, its community of origin, and there were few disagreements over the distribution of transferencias. The older people of Cxayu'ce still regard San José as their cultural home and, when they return from a visit there, comment on how much they enjoy the beauty, peace, and quiet, as well as the cooler climate and tastier diet. Their return visits also have an economic rationale: they have to tend their opium poppies, which are ideally suited to conditions there. But those who chose to stay in San José view Cxayu'ce as a model of how life should be lived in the future. Hence, the new community has both territorial and economic potential that draws its cultural inspiration from San José. Nevertheless, Cxayu'ce became a new resguardo in 2004.

The following was written by fourth-grade students in Botatierra in 2000 for their school newspaper, stuck on the outside wall of the school in the plaza, no doubt with some assistance from their teacher, under the heading "The Indigenous Person and Nature":

> The land is our mother and mother of us. That's why the mountains, the rivers, the plants, [and] the animals are our brothers. We do not try to destroy them but have them serve us rationally according to their laws. Nevertheless, many of us have been penetrated by "white" thinking about profit and exploitation and changed our relationship, destroying the natural resources. Why do they think that man is made to "dominate and exploit nature"? For indigenous cultures domination of nature is not important because we consider ourselves part of it and as such, [part of] our own life.

The students are presenting a somewhat romantic and idealized version of people's relationship to the environment in Tierradentro. While this type of balanced relationship may well have existed in the not-so-distant past, it has changed significantly in the past fifty years, thanks partly to external influences but also due to local, individual initiatives, which have served them well in their new environment. The displaced families, in spite of being surrounded by communities of peasant farmers, have been accepted, not only as hard-working, successful fellow farmers but also as providers of primary education to local children. While Cxayu'ce has its own school, education there is not the obsession it is in the other two communities. The teachers are both Nasa and mestizo, and the school accepts all local children who wish to study there. When they graduate, Nasa children who want to continue their studies do so at the local high school in the nearby town of El Rosario.

But the indications are that this harmonious relationship between the new community and the old will not hold across generations. In spite of the poppy bonanza, young people in San José see little future for themselves there, and their counterparts in Cxayu'ce, although they may like to visit San José, have no desire to live there on a permanent basis. Yet in the decade following the disaster, it is the people of Cxayu'ce who have taken full advantage of the opportunities offered by displacement and successfully adapted to the local environment. They have achieved this from an unselfconscious Nasa perspective, without apparently having to dilute, reinvent, or tout their indigeneity. Admired by their relatives and fellow Nasa in Tierradentro, they have been peacefully accepted by their neighbors in Cxayu'ce. They were small farmers in Tierradentro, and they are still small farmers in Cxayu'ce, albeit more economically successful. In contrast to the other two communities, the families have achieved this in a quiet and unobtrusive manner.

Discourses of Opportunity

Although the indigenous leadership may have regarded the disaster as some form of punishment for the individual or collective failings of the Nasa, those most directly affected, the displaced families, do not. While they clearly remember the trauma and shock of the event itself and the initial chaos and confusion, they tend to focus on the events that followed: the temporary camps, the search for available lands, the buildings of houses, and the creation of new communities. In this long process, which started in 1994 and still continues, CNK has been a key player — buying land; providing materials for the construction of houses; building schools, health centers, and roads; paying teachers, health workers, and agronomists; and financing productive activities (CNK 1995, 2005).

CNK was expected to do a little of everything, but in the final essence its primary responsibilities were the provision of land and housing. And for this it was roundly criticized from the very beginning. There was never enough land, and the materials to finish off the houses properly were never provided. For the displaced Nasa, land was important not only for economic reasons but also for cultural reasons, since their identity as Nasa was intimately related to communal ownership of land and harmonious relationships with their environment. Early in the life of CNK, the director made a statement that was to haunt the agency for years to come. He promised that CNK would try to provide each displaced family with up to eight hectares of land, and this became the lightning rod against which all of CNK's subsequent activities were measured (Wilches 1995b). Because the document in question never clearly specified the type of land, irrigated or rain-fed, flat or hilly, arable or pasture, woods or forest, there was ample room for negotiation. While the three new settlements continued to demand their eight hectares per family as a right, the agency exercised considerable skill in negotiating the number down to an acceptable compromise. In the case of the houses, CNK provided the construction materials and the families the labor. There were complaints about the design of the houses and the long wait involved until all the materials arrived. But both land and houses were provided for free.

Initially, the discourse articulated by CNK emphasized the preservation and maintenance of existing institutions and existing standards of living within a context defined as "indigenous" and nonthreatening. Nevertheless, in spite of the rhetoric about participation and letting the people "speak," this discourse essentially forced the Nasa into nominal acquiescence by imposing its own form of reality, albeit with very different implications for the three communities. Since CNK controlled the resources, they also controlled the discourse, but one that each community chose to interpret in its own manner. Tóez Caloto chose to elaborate a self-conscious modernizing discourse, Juan Tama a self-conscious culturalist discourse, and Cxayu'ce an implied and unselfconscious Nasa discourse that combined culture and agriculture.

But the discourse of CNK was never monolithic. From the very beginning, it articulated and practiced key elements of "alternative development": small-scale solutions, awareness of environmental issues, popular participation, and a central focus on the community, a discourse more frequently associated with the NGO community (Cowen and Shenton 1995; Nederveen Pieterse 1998).[19] This was due partly to the active involvement of sympathizers with the indigenous movement, often with a background in anthropology, NGOs, and community development. But it was also due to the active involvement over the years of members of some of Popayán's social and political elites, with their own ethic of public service, and their own ideas about development and modernity.[20] In addition, though less directly, the resettled communities were affected by the discourses of the indigenous movement, specifically those of CRIC and FST.

In this chapter I have argued for viewing the 1994 earthquake as an opportunity for constructive change for those most affected. I have presented several of the key actors. CNK was an important player from the very beginning and enjoyed political support and received adequate funding, at least in its initial years. As the major institution working with the displaced, it was never monolithic in its approach, in part due to its hybrid, parastatal nature as well as its staff of well-qualified local professionals, many of whom supported the indigenous movement.

The other important actors are the three resettled Nasa communities: Tóez Caloto, Juan Tama, and Cxayu'ce. Each has taken advantage of the opportunities offered in different ways, partly a reflection of historical factors but also a consequence of location, where they managed to obtain new lands. Tóez Caloto is less than an hour's drive by road from Cali, Colombia's third largest city, and Cxayu'ce is less than an hour from Popayán, the provincial capital. Juan Tama is located in a no-man's-land on the borders between Cauca and Huila.

3

Before the Constitutional Assembly in 1991, we were ignorant, we knew nothing about planning, and we knew nothing about projects.—LEADER FROM SAN JOSÉ, 2000 interview

Development Planning:

Slaves of Modernity or Agents of Change?

A comparison of the development plans, both process and "text," produced by the communities of Cxayu'ce (and its community of origin in San José), Tóez Caloto, and Juan Tama will demonstrate that it is possible to talk about processes of indigenous planning. These processes can be distinguished from other planning processes by certain defining characteristics — specifically the underlying tensions and contradictions that stem from being indigenous, a topic that will be explored here in some detail. Nevertheless, in spite of these commonalities, the three plans *do* differ in various ways, a consequence of both historical and cultural factors, which partially explain their differing attitudes toward development and modernity. While participants view the plans with a certain degree of skepticism, whether as a necessary evil or as a means of self-expression, local community leaders regard them as a way of legitimating their relationship with the state and other institutions. A plan is an indication of a community's "high seriousness," proof of a certain level of organizational capacity. As a form of discourse, a development plan offers some insight into how a community sees itself and its place in the larger society. More important, however, is how it wishes to represent itself.

The Gospel of Planning and Participation

The study of development can take many forms, although the focus is usually on results and the causal factors involved, as determined by outsiders. But given the complexity of development and the lack of historical information, causality is often difficult to demonstrate. Furthermore, development is viewed as something that "happens" to people, rather than a process that people themselves can make happen. Thinking of development in this depersonalized way means that the opinions and perceptions of those most directly affected, though often solicited, are rarely taken seriously. When they are, it is often only the voices of the powerful that are attended to. While planning for development, in contrast to actually "doing" development, can suffer from the same drawbacks, it does offer the opportunity to better understand local perceptions through study of the process followed and the documentation produced.

As the intended results of development have proven increasingly problematic and elusive, planning itself has come under fire, based as it is on the assumption that there is some direct causal relationship between a plan and its implementation (Friedmann 1987). Planning has been criticized for being too complex, detailed, and rigid (Rondinelli 1993). It has been analyzed as a system of knowledge that seeks to impose its own version of reality on those to be "developed" (Ferguson 1994), by choosing to highlight certain elements while ignoring others, often at the expense of local history and culture (Crush 1995). For some, planning produces texts that are fictional, authorless, and open to (mis)reading (Roe 1994). Ultimately, planning is seen as linked to fundamental processes of domination and social control (Escobar 1992). Contrasting approaches to planning have been proposed, emphasizing participation, local knowledge, and empowerment, replacing more top-down, authoritarian, and technocratic methods. In their more extreme form, these approaches have been called "alternative development." They incorporate ideas of community, local control, and ecological concerns (Cowen and Shenton 1996), forming part of what could be called "the indigenization of development," which calls for the intellectual emancipation from Western development paradigms and the generation of new forms of development based on the knowledge and needs of local people (Brohman 1996; Conroy et al. 1996; Sahlins 1999).

The 1991 Constitution granted indigenous people rights they were previously denied, the most important of which were local control over development, health, and education, as well as the right to exercise customary law (Rappaport 1996). Control over development was in-

stitutionalized through the provision of *transferencias,* direct cash transfers from the central government, which could only be obtained after
the preparation and presentation by the *cabildos* of detailed plans. As a
result, the 1990s witnessed an efflorescence of indigenous planning and
a plethora of documentation, usually produced through a process of
consultation and participation involving outside consultants, "experts"
responsible for providing the community with the finished product
(Espinosa and Escobar 2000). This is the first time that development
funds have gone directly to the *resguardos,* to be controlled by the cabildos. While these transferencias are the major source of government
financing, they are not the only one, since they serve as a means of
leveraging funds from other public and private sector sources.

The major piece of legislation, Ley Orgánica del Plan de Desarrollo
(Law 152, Article 32), clearly states that the cabildos are free to choose
their own development priorities. They are also free to choose the ways
in which they wish to do this planning "in agreement with their uses
and customs" (*de acuerdo con sus usos y costumbres*), while conforming to
the general principles mentioned above (Article 31). This stipulation
contradicts the requirements listed in Ley 60 de 1993 (Law 60, Article
24), which mandates how the transferencias are to be distributed: education (30 percent), health (25 percent), and drinking water and sanitation (20 percent), with some flexibility in how the remaining 25 percent
is allocated. In fact, indigenous leaders quote this phrase, "in agreement
with their uses and customs," as a justification for *not* following those
stipulations. Indeed, the concept of "uses and customs" is sacrosanct,
an integral component of the discourse of national indigenous leaders,
and it appears in most of the significant indigenous legislation (Dover
and Rappaport 1996). Law 152 mandates that both municipalities and
resguardos must prepare such plans before any funds are disbursed.

Indigenous leaders in Cauca, in contrast to the state, distinguish between a "life plan" (*plan de vida*) and a "development plan" (*plan de
desarrollo*). Though these terms are often used interchangeably, there
are important differences between them. A life plan offers a long-term
strategy for the integral development of the resguardo, dealing with all
aspects of indigenous society and culture and laying out a vision for the
future by implicitly answering three questions: Who are we? Where do
we come from? Where are we going? In a movement documentary on
development planning, indigenous leaders also suggest that a life plan

should include information regarding people's views about progress and ways to live and organize (FST 1998). In contrast, a development plan is viewed as externally imposed and deals primarily with the short-term needs of the resguardo in predetermined domains. The regional Indigenous Council of Cauca (CRIC)'s Tenth Congress elaborated on this distinction proposing that the resguardos focus on life plans rather than development plans: "We recommend that you talk about Life Plans and not Development Plans *so that we can talk about our destiny from the perspective of our own logic*" (CRIC 1997, 51; emphasis added). The Congress emphasized that life plans use indigenous epistemology for understanding and explaining the resguardos and their problems, thereby producing a much more nuanced but complicated type of document, for use internally rather than externally. Nevertheless, resguardos are expected to produce plans before receiving transferencias, and the type of plan that most produce is a development plan, rather than a life plan, although there are exceptions.

As the incidence of participatory planning has become more prevalent and more widespread, so have the criticisms. The more widespread such planning becomes, the greater the potential for dilution and cooption, whereby the process may help consolidate power rather than to question its basic ground rules (Woost 1997). The concept of indigeneity itself has been subjected to increasing critical scrutiny. Akhil Gupta (1998) pinpoints one of the more glaring internal contradictions: if indigenous or local knowledge is shown to have adapted, borrowed, and changed over time, what does this imply for the "essential core of authenticity" that will identify this knowledge as "indigenous"? The logical implication of this argument, then, is that culture is *always* hybrid (Herzfeld 1999), and that epistemologically it makes little sense to distinguish between various types of knowledge. Nevertheless, it does make political sense from a minority perspective: "More usual and more interesting is the interplay, even mutual constitution, of different forms of knowledge generated and practiced in different sites" (Peters 2000, 4).

Indigenous groups in the Americas have become increasingly sophisticated in the ways they can creatively manipulate this interplay. Writing about Native American groups in the United States, Les Field (1999) describes how they have learned to represent themselves in ways that are understandable and acceptable to outsiders and to their own constituencies, both indigenous and nonindigenous. Such representations may involve the judicious but flexible combination of essentialist approaches, which focus on those aspects of culture that demonstrate difference with the dominant culture, with constructivist approaches and their emphasis on cultural reconstruction and the struggle for recognition as independent political actors.

San José and Cxayu'ce: A Plan in Hand

In spring 1999, the resguardo of San José in Tierradentro, together with its new settlement of Cxayu'ce, contracted with a firm of consultants in Popayán to help them prepare their life plan, which in fact turned out to be their development plan, for the period 2000 to 2005.[1] The consulting team was already working in the region on the preparation of development plans for other resguardos; two of the members had broad experience working on various aspects of rural development in Cauca, while the third brought community development experience from elsewhere in Colombia. All three were mestizos who closely identified with the indigenous movement and tried to practice many of the tenets of alternative development, with its emphasis on participation, local knowledge, and empowerment.

The information to be included in the plan was to be gathered through a series of three workshops in the community, led by the consultants with the collaboration of a local teacher, attended by all inhabitants, and conducted in Nasa Yuwe (which none of the consultants spoke) and Spanish. Each workshop would start with a general discussion and agreement about the topics to be discussed, and the assembled participants, usually a reasonable cross-section of the community in terms of age and gender, would divide up into working groups to discuss the topics in more depth. While the topics were selected on the basis of discussions between the consultants and the community, they invariably followed the guidelines and priorities laid down in the legislation. Each group would select a coordinator to lead the discussion and a secretary to record what was said and what was agreed on. Sometimes the consultants coordinated the discussions, other times they sat quietly listening. Two of them were excellent listeners, knowing when to keep quiet and when to intervene, but the third, perhaps the most militant of the three, found it difficult, if not impossible, to sit peacefully and let the dialogue and discussion evolve. At times he became so frustrated at the slow pace of the discussion that he would harangue the participants who, to shut him up, would respond with resounding negatives to most of the questions he raised. When he walked away in frustration, participants would then proceed to talk, rectifying the curt responses they had earlier offered. At the end of the day there would be a final plenary session, when each of the working groups would report back, presenting in summary form what had been discussed and agreed on. While there was usually little or no discussion during these final sessions, there were sometimes interesting and spirited public discussions within the working groups, just as there were in more informal behind-the-scenes contexts, such as around the fireplace in the kitchen in the evening.

Because these workshops were community-wide events, a considerable amount of planning and logistics was involved in setting them up, since participants from several sections were involved, three in San José itself (La Palma, Botatierra, and San José), and the fourth from the new settlement of Cxayu'ce. In addition to providing accommodation for the latter, all participants had to be fed at midday, as well as being offered snacks in the morning and the afternoon. Time and weather were also important factors to be considered. Weather permitting, the workshops were held outside, often in bright sunlight, with participants sitting on small, wooden chairs borrowed from the school, which were not designed with adults in mind (see figure 1). After a while, they became extremely uncomfortable, providing an effective brake on endless discussions. When it rained, as it sometimes did, people would scurry with their chairs inside the nearest available building, usually the school, and continue the discussion until the shower had passed. As a result of these factors, the number of participants, as well as their level of participation, would vary during the day as well as from day to day. But since this was a community event, the levels of interest and participation were high.

The plan was based on the information gathered during these sessions, as well as additional information provided by the cabildo, and a series of ongoing discussions with the more interested members who provided contextual details as well as differing perspectives on the community's future and its relationship to modernity. The issues discussed include access to more land in lower lying, warmer areas, a road to Botatierra, and the installation of electricity and a telephone system. What is important to note is that all these processes, with the exception

Figure 1. Community planning in San José

of the installation of a telephone system, were already under way to a lesser or greater extent, a result of earlier initiatives undertaken by the community. The lower lying lands were purchased with transferencias, the electricity was to be provided by a Pilton Wheel (provided by a sympathetic priest) that community members had carried on their shoulders over the mountains, and the road was being bulldozed by the Nasa Kiwe Corporation (CNK), a result of continuous petitioning by the community.

The final document, written primarily by the consultants but also including written inputs from the community, appeared at the end of the year (Resguardo de San José 1999). The first section, some forty pages long, provides the basic background information. An introductory chapter dealing with the history and general characteristics of the resguardo is followed by three chapters on the two sectors of health, education, organization, and culture on the one hand, and land, economy, and the environment on the other. The second section, much slimmer at just six pages, lays out the policies, objectives, and strategies for each of these sectors in summary form that provides no details. The final page details how the transferencias will be divided up among the four sections of the resguardo in the following year — three in San José and the fourth in Cxayu'ce.

Three points are worth considering here. First, when attempting to describe and analyze the plan as a text, there appears to be no readily apparent logical relationship among the three sections. Each stands alone with little or no reference to the other two. As a result, the document is disjointed and hard to read. This would indicate a manifestation of a blueprint, a standardized approach to planning or the meeting of a bureaucratic requirement, rather than a serious effort at a more contextualized understanding. If this is the case, then questions need to be raised regarding which parts of the plan should be taken seriously, which ones articulate the interests of the participants rather than those of the consultants. Second, there is little record within the plan of the discussions (both public and private) that its production generated, nor of the differing views presented. Though this is to be expected, the fact that there is no mention whatsoever of the substance of these discussions paints a picture of flat consensus that papers over productive and stimulating alternatives. Third, while the plan proposed certain activities in 2000, those actually implemented bore little relationship to the ones planned. In other words, planning on paper and planning in practice diverged considerably.

The first and longest section of the plan, a form of "thick description," contains a large amount of information, collected and condensed to fit into several preconceived categories that are general enough to include a broad array of topics. The health sector, for example, touches on nutrition, housing, sanitation, potable water, drainage, and the aqueduct. The education sector deals primarily with the internal organization of the resguardo; the actual and potential tensions among teachers, cabildo, and parents; and classroom space and furnishings, but only in passing with the curriculum and what actually happens in the classroom. Long on description and short on analysis, this sector identifies few problems, much less the reasons for them.

The discussion of the economy is more explicit and highlights the deteriorating economic situation, together with the worsening environmental conditions, as factors that have been responsible for the increasing cultivation of opium poppies.

> The inhabitants of the community identified the low income of the families as one of the principal problems. This is one of the reasons why some farmers have chosen to grow opium poppies on a small scale. Among the other problems identified were the shortage of lands suitable for agriculture, on

account of either the growing incidence of small farms or the very steep topography. (Resguardo de San José 1999, 37)

The situation is exacerbated by the slash-and-burn system of agriculture, which, in this type of environment, contributes to soil erosion. Together with shortened fallow periods, this helps lower production and productivity. This is one of the very few references the document makes to poppy cultivation, a characteristic it shares with many other development plans. It is important to note how delicately the problem is handled, giving the impression that farmers have been "forced" to cultivate it out of economic necessity, and then only, as the people themselves would claim, to "complement" ongoing, regular agricultural activities. In fact, over the years, the amount of land cultivated in poppies has steadily increased, often replacing rather than complementing existing crops. As a result, many of the young men no longer have to migrate seasonally in search of off-farm employment. For obvious reasons, this is not discussed in the plan. Instead, an ambitious if somewhat unrealistic list of solutions is proposed, based more on concepts of alternative development than on hard-nosed economic realities, which the plan clearly articulates.

> The poor quality of the soil, the steep topography which does not favor well-weeded crops, the difficulty with ways of communication, the shortage of technical assistance and the absence of economically viable alternatives, have "pushed" the producer to cultivate small areas of opium poppies, motivated by a growing and unsatisfied demand, "good" prices, ease of transportation, favorable climate, and, in some cases, credit. (32)

The first solution proposed is the production of indigenous crops, mainly tubers, to achieve food security. Potato cultivation, the staple of the indigenous economy, has decreased over the years, thanks to population pressure and soil erosion, resulting in lowered productivity. Production can only be maintained through the use of increasingly expensive inputs, such as fertilizer and pesticides. The second solution, complementary to the first, calls for the introduction of organic farming, agroforestry, and agropastoral systems of production. In theory, this approach could address the problems of economic survival in an ecologically fragile environment. However, it would require considerable investments of time, money, and technical expertise. The third solution proposes taking advantage of the ready availability of fresh running water for the establishment of fish farming. Though this activity could be environmentally benign, it also requires time, money, and technical expertise. Furthermore, it calls for marketing expertise in a context where an increasing number of indigenous communities, strategically located closer to urban centers, are already producing fresh fish for the market. In a more realistic vein, the plan also recommends the purchase of additional lands elsewhere, a strategy already being pursued by certain families who have used their share of the transferencias to make down payments on lands north of Popayán.

In this first section, which deals with several topics including organization and culture, there are several voices speaking — those of the authors, the three consultants with their specific areas of expertise, as well as those of local community members. For example, there is straightforward reporting of what they heard during the workshops, in this case the discussion dealing with internal organization and authority.

> They also discussed the forms of sanction and the problem of authority in general. Some were thinking about re-instituting the *cepo* [stocks introduced by the Spaniards] but others are opposed and think they should leave it for Tierradentro [i.e., send people there to be punished]. Others think you can re-establish it but only as a symbol of authority. (24)

> In agreement with the conclusions that came out of the workshops, we see that the internal relations among sections [of the resguardo] and among their own institutions such as parents, teachers, and the cabildo are not the best. (21)

There is also written and oral information provided by participants, as well as notes taken during the workshops and observations made based on more spontaneous, informal conversations.

The chapter dealing with education starts with the history of the establishment of one of the schools in the small section of La Palma in 1993, based on a written document prepared by community members.

> In the year 1993, the idea of the importance of education came from Señor Leonardo Pacho, a well-respected leader, and that's why they found the teacher Floresmiro Yandi, a person from the same resguardo, who was also preoccupied with advancing the [accreditation] of the school and encouraging education in this sector. (21)

The following two paragraphs talk about what happened in the succeeding years, as well as after the disaster in 1994. Then the text jumps to the history of another section of the resguardo, Botatierra, and the arrival of two U.S. missionaries from the Christian Alliance Association who came to establish a school and convert people to evangelical Protestantism. The first chapter of the plan, dealing with history in general, also talks about how this particular school was founded, although the details differ. In sum, the first section is repetitive, reflecting different voices and little editing.

The second section, only six pages long, is very different — a document written for the bureaucracy, either the municipality that has to approve it, or the development agencies, public and private, that could potentially provide financial support to implement it. The first three pages are in the form of a preamble spelling out the legal context for the plan, quoting at some length from the relevant legislation. The substance of the plan, however, is contained in the last three pages. Under Organization, the objective is to undertake activities that will strengthen the community, according to the principles of "autonomy, identity, community participation, respect, and consensus in decision-making" (47). This discourse combines concepts from the indigenous movement, such as autonomy, identity, and respect, with concepts taken from theories of alternative development, such as community, participation, and decision making. While the two sets of concepts are not necessarily antithetical and can be viewed as complementary, they remain conceptually and practically distinct. Those from the indigenous movement are long-term goals, whereas those from alternative development are process, ways in which to achieve these goals.

The plan provides few practical details about how this will be done, preferring instead to offer rather vague prescriptions. According to the plan, the major way the community will be strengthened is through institutional networking, by strengthening ties, and presenting project proposals, the nature of which is not specified, to existing regional, national, and international organizations. By proposing to strengthen institutional ties, the plan calls for a radical change in the organizational life of San José, a resguardo that historically has chosen not to actively participate in the various institutional options available, whether at the municipal level or at the provincial level with CRIC. A good argument can be made that San José's strength and survival over the years have depended to a certain extent on its self-conscious, deliberate autonomy, a low-profile means of survival. At the same time, the plan calls for the study of the changing role of the cabildo over the years, as well as the continuing study of customary law and its relationship to local auton-omy and the Colombian legal system, both important issues for the indigenous movement. As a result of the changes introduced by the new constitution, the responsibilities of the cabildo, particularly the gover-nor, have increased exponentially. Since the cabildo was never a very viable institution in the first place, these additional responsibilities have tended to exacerbate the situation. In the case of customary law, ca-bildos are often unsure about how to proceed because there is continu-ing uncertainty about how extensive their mandate is.

The page dealing with education focuses on policy and objectives that emphasize autonomous educational programs which support commu-nity tradition and culture, while at the same time strengthening political identity and cultural diversity (48). Once again, this discourse reflects the influence of the indigenous movement, but ignores the educational realities on the ground in the various sectors, where competing educa-tional philosophies prevail. Since this diversity is not even mentioned, the educational proposal is bland and generic, calling for the design of a program that respects educational autonomy, where the community controls the appointment of teachers. The plan says little about the substance of this education, nor how educational autonomy will be achieved.

The third section, dealing with health, housing, and public services (48), reads more like a broad statement of the desirable, rather than a plan detailing the possible. It lays out a combination of political, cultural, and practical policies. These range from the achievement of equity, and the recovery of local foods and indigenous medicine, to the provision of adequate housing, drinking water, and basic sanitation. Here, there is a combination of three discourses, the indigenous (equity), the alterna-tive (local knowledge), and the developmental (infrastructure).

The final section, on production and the environment, is the longest and the most detailed. Its major objective is to "strengthen the house-hold's agricultural production, emphasizing the food security of the population of the resguardo through the utilization of low-cost organic systems, searching for a better way to exploit their own resources" (49). This is to be achieved through a combination of fish farming, livestock raising, and the organic production of indigenous crops. Though there is no history of fish farming in the immediate area, there are fish farms, individual and communal, in neighboring areas, about which families have direct knowledge and experience. While fish farming can make significant contributions to improving the local diet, fish farmers face substantial problems in the field of marketing, partly because it is a perishable commodity and partly because of strong competition from other small-scale producers. Livestock production is widespread throughout the area and one of the principal factors contributing to the increasing incidence of environmental degradation, a factor discussed during the planning workshops. Likewise, farmers have no qualms about using modern technical inputs, such as fertilizer and insecticide for their corn and potatoes, nor about using their most productive land for growing opium poppies.

Though there were various expressions of regret about the state of the environment voiced during the workshops, there was no indication that producers intended to change their habits then or in the immediate future. Organic farming and the recovery of local crops, particularly various tubers whose production has significantly declined, did not arouse much interest. These reflect a form of Andean nostalgia, felt more by the consultants than by the participants, a combination once again of the discourses of CRIC and alternative development.

The final section of the plan, one page long, details how the transferencias were to be distributed in 2000. Almost 50 percent was allocated to the resguardo as a whole for general administrative costs, the balance distributed proportionally among the sections, according to population. In the case of Botatierra, the largest section, more than half its budget was allocated to education, for the construction of classrooms and a sports field, as well as the purchase of equipment; the balance was earmarked for sewage, electrification, and livestock. For the other three sections, the focus was on agricultural production and the purchase of livestock, as well as electricity in San José and paying off the debt for the lands purchased by residents of La Palma. Some of these activities were mentioned in the plan, others not at all. When the resguardo did distribute the transferencias, this list was a reasonable indicator of what the respective sections tried to implement with the money received.

During the workshops there were some very interesting and provocative discussions, the details of which do not appear in the plan. One such discussion revolved around why the families in Botatierra at the time of the disaster refused to take advantage of CNK's offer to provide them with new land. By reluctantly admitting that the resettled families in Cxayu'ce were a model of how to extend one's access to more productive lands, they were also implicitly embracing another vision of the future. Growing poppies was viewed as no more than a "bonanza," a short-term palliative, a windfall that would contribute nothing to their longer term survival, unless the proceeds were invested productively, an unlikely occurrence, given the limited local opportunities.

During the planning process, a second vision of the future was expressed by the governor, a poppy grower who came originally from La Palma, the section that had bought new land near Piendamó, north of Popayán. After one of the workshops, over supper beside the kitchen fire, he brought up some priorities that had not yet been mentioned, to wit, roads and bridges, electrification, and a telephone system. Since the national government wanted to preserve much of their páramo land as a natural reserve, he argued that the least the government could do would be to provide electricity so that the people "could do things in the evening." By the same token, he was also implying that improved infrastructure would make life in the resguardo a lot more tolerable. The following day, the consultant leading the workshop brought these topics up, and participants became extremely vocal; the intensity of their discussion in favor of this new infrastructure, particularly roads and bridges, completely overshadowed the previous day's discussions about their interest in purchasing additional arable lands. At that time, there was no road to the resguardo, and residents had to make an hour-long trek along bridle paths from Mosoco, where the closest road and telephone lie. CNK had been working on a road of sorts for the past several years which would eventually link Botatierra with the highway south of Mosoco. Several bridges had been destroyed by the 1994 disaster; the most important, on the road to the municipal capital of Belalcázar, had still to be replaced. This meant a long detour by foot, where previously people could travel by truck. In the long run, San José decided against a road, although Botatierra has one.

Neither of these visions of the future appear anywhere in the plan. Their nonappearance became even more paradoxical the following year, when the new governor, a teacher in the community, and his cabildo proceeded to implement the plan. While agreeing with most of the 109 priorities established, they nevertheless pronounced that *their* vision was to develop an indigenous curriculum for the local school, something they had been working toward for several years. While this had been mentioned briefly in the plan, there had been little discussion or debate about it during the workshops. In the course of six months, then, the community had either discussed or presented three distinct visions of the future, one that emphasized land, a second infrastructure, and a third education. They were by no means mutually exclusive, but none figured prominently in the development plan.

There are several possible explanations for these contradictions. The political process within the resguardos, whereby the governor and the cabildo are elected on an annual basis, works very much against any long-term planning. The community leadership changes every year, and while education had not been a priority for the previous officeholders, it was for the current cabildo. But the leadership had not changed that radically; those being groomed the previous year, such as the lieutenant governor, now held a more important position of responsibility, providing him with the possibility of implementing *his* vision, one hopefully built on some sort of communal consensus. Another explanation for these contradictions is the possible perception that in their eyes "development" involves "planning from without," mandated by the government, a process which produces documents that are often interchangeable, blueprints that highlight similar problems and offer identical solutions. If that is the case, then only the last section, itemizing how the transferencias are to be allocated, is to be taken seriously, and the team of consultants who wrote the plan can be seen as interlocutors who know and understand what the state will accept. While there were local expectations regarding the responsibilities of government for the provision of infrastructure and additional land, their solution lies beyond the capacity of the resguardo. Hence they are not included in the plan, which focuses on local problems with local solutions.

Tóez Caloto: Participatory Planning, But No Plan

In 1999, the governor of Tóez Caloto announced at a general community assembly that it was time they made a serious effort to prepare a development plan and appealed for widespread support and participation. All indications were that this would be a community-driven, rather than a consultant-driven process, and plans were made to hold a series of workshops over the next few weeks. At the first planning workshop held shortly afterward, the community was introduced to a *promotora* from the Association of Indigenous Cabildos of Northern Cauca (ACIN), one of the more radical, subregional cabildo federations in Cauca. Indigenous herself, although she did not speak Nasa Yuwe, the promotora was pursuing a bachelor's degree in anthropology through a distance learning program. Though she had been invited to "facilitate" the process, it became quickly evident that ACIN was in charge and that the community would be expected to follow the ACIN model of development planning, already successfully implemented in neighboring communities (Municipio de Toribío 1998). They would have to follow ACIN guidelines, generate information requested by the promotora, and hand over all data collected. ACIN would be responsible for producing the final document. This was not the understanding at the beginning of the process, however. When the governor introduced the promotora, he stressed that it would be the community who would collect the information, analyze it, and produce the final plan. Over the next few weeks, however, the promotora admitted that ACIN had been trying to gain a foothold in the community for some time, and that it had always been their intention to publish the plan.

The model proposed followed a standardized format of sectors to be analyzed: education, health, sport (which also included culture); the family, land use, and economy and the environment; and institutional development. Certain key factors, such as growing political violence by guerrillas and paramilitaries, as well as the increasing cultivation of illegal crops locally and in Tóez, were completely omitted. As in San José, discussion of such activities in official development plans was studiously avoided; first, out of fear of reprisal, and second, out of respect for those community members actively involved. Both activities are, quite literally, life-and-death matters. Each sector was to be analyzed, in turn, in an identical fashion according to: (1) the present situation; (2) the well-known trilogy of achievements, weaknesses, and strengths; and (3) a final section dealing with expected results and ways in which to measure them. Over the next several weeks, the community organized a series of workshops in which a broad cross-section of people participated, including residents of all ages, men and women, teachers and health workers, as well as several respected community leaders.

At the first two-day workshop, which was conducted entirely in Spanish, seven working groups focusing on particular planning sectors were formed, each of which selected a coordinator responsible for facilitating the discussion and a secretary who was to keep notes and summarize the key points of the discussion, to be presented at the end of the day when each group "reported back" to the whole workshop (see figure 2). Those chosen to be coordinators, both men and women, were usually in their twenties, with a proven record of public service and some knowledge, understanding, and commitment to the topic under discussion. For example, of the two young men chosen to coordinate the group dealing with the economy and the environment, one was an ex-governor studying economics at the University of Cauca, and the other was the secretary of the cabildo, who had just completed a course of study in organic agriculture. Attendance at the workshops was high, and the participation of women, as both coordinators and discussants, was impressive.

The working groups met in and around the health center, which, with both a hall and several adjacent rooms, provided shade from the broiling sun. The groups of ten to fifteen people formed a circle, and the coordinators made a conscious effort to involve all the participants, sometimes by going around the circle person by person, other times by asking specific individuals for their opinions. At midday, lunch was provided by the cabildo, and participants lined up with plates in hand to be served large helpings of food that they quickly consumed. Others took the food home with them to share with family members, returning early in the afternoon to continue the discussions.

To provide a context for the proposed plan, on the first day each of the groups was asked to think about the following questions. From the perspective of each sector, how were things before the disaster? Where did they want the community to go in the next twenty years, that is, what did they want for their children? As is generally the case with such activities, the discussions within the groups were always interesting and sometimes heated, while their presentations to the workshop varied greatly in terms of both style and substance. Some presenters were quite at ease while carefully summarizing the mains points raised, whereas others were nervous and tended to wander off the topic. The groups tended to interpret the topics in their own way, depending on their priorities, interests, and levels of knowledge. For example, the group

Figure 2. Community planning in Tóez Caloto

dealing with education discussed how education started with the parents teaching the children respect, passing on their knowledge through
working together on weaving and agricultural tasks, and how this process had been much stricter in the past, with punishments for those who
did not comply. They also talked about the vocational school in Tóez
that had been destroyed in the disaster, famous for the quality of education it offered indigenous students, but to which very few local families
had sent their children. Regarding the future, there were clear ideas
about why they sent their children to their own school in Tóez Caloto,
rather than to the well-established schools in the neighboring town of
Caloto. They hoped the school would produce excellent leaders for the
community and would form the backdrop for founding an indigenous
university. The school, they projected, would serve as a pilot center
for all the indigenous communities in the region. For one community
leader in the group, the overall goal was to achieve a better future for the
individual, the family, and the community.

But other groups interpreted the topics differently from what was
intended by the promotora. For example, the team discussing land use
(*ordenamiento territorial*) was excellent on history, from the conquest
until the present, but said very little about how land has been and is
presently used. This, however, may have been due to the fact that land
use was a new concept in Colombian planning, recently mandated by

the national government. In the case of economy and the environment, the group never came to grips with the topic and seemed to talk around the issues, spending a lot of time romanticizing the past instead of using the past to think about the present and the future.

The second day the groups worked on the problems associated with their particular sector. The group working on economy and environment identified several major problems with the lands bought for them by CNK, such as lack of water, machinery, technology, and credit. While the lands were potentially productive, the previous owners had worked them hard, cultivating sugarcane where there was sufficient water and cattle ranching elsewhere, so that the lands were now in need of heavy fertilization. Because the soils were hard and compacted, they could only be worked effectively with the assistance of a tractor, a plow, and other necessary equipment, none of which the community had. Nevertheless, the group did manage to identify several factors in their favor: they were experienced farmers, they had adapted well to their new environment, and they brought certain culturally relevant experiences with them from Tierradentro.

But what kind of economy did they want for the future? The community had already been approached by several outside investors who wanted to take advantage of the available land and abundant labor. One businessman wanted to produce pineapples, but this would have required a large initial investment by the community. It would also have called for a new type of business relationship, more entrepreneurial, in which the community would have been obliged to meet certain agreed-on criteria regarding quantity, quality, and dates of delivery. To date, the community had shown little interest in this type of arrangement. Severo Atila, the economics student in the group and an ex-governor in his own right, asked if people knew what the word *economy* meant. Various responses were forthcoming: to have food, to have money, to have crops and animals, to store products, to save and have money to cover necessities.

But from his perspective, economics was "the science that studies all the goods [necessary] to satisfy man's needs." These goods included livestock, crops, products, money, land, handicrafts, and the utilization of knowledge, to name the more relevant. In Tóez Caloto, he continued, they had depended to a certain extent at least on what he called a solidarity economy (*economía solidaria*), a system of subsistence production involving both reciprocity and redistribution. The solidarity economy produced enough for people to feed themselves, as well as some money to buy clothes, but not enough to educate their children. He pointed out that people were now obliged to participate in a market economy for which they were ill prepared. There were all sorts of employment possibilities, as a worker, day laborer, individual businessman, or a middleman. Had they taken advantage of the education available to them and their children in Tóez before the disaster, they would not now be looking for employment as laborers, they would not be "slaves of modernity," as he called them. Instead, there would have been some form of "social business" (*empresa social*) or cooperative in which the people would have been members, the middlemen banned. His solution was a form of mixed economy, combining the better elements of both systems, with financing from the cabildo, the state, or even NGOs. But even as he said this, the ex-governor predicted that all vestiges of this solidarity economy would disappear within the next decade. In this, Atilo was remarkably prescient, since Tóez Caloto was in the process of modernizing, of accepting development discourse at face value with its emphasis on infrastructure and a modern, free market economy.

This discussion about the economy in Tóez Caloto was in marked contrast to the proposal for organic agriculture in San José. Although both tended to romanticize the past, the former, with its emphasis on a solidarity economy, tapped into the discourse of the indigenous movement, which supported this type of economy on the grounds that it could foster and strengthen local, indigenous autonomy. In contrast, the focus on organic agriculture in the San José plan originated with the consultants. Ironically in practice, both communities embraced the free market economy, and this was particularly noticeable in the case of Cxayu'ce.

That same day, the groups reported back to the general workshop. A large group had worked on the theme of institutional development, where participants discussed at some length the problems of authority within the community, specifically the diminishing role and prestige of the shamans who historically had been viewed as the spiritual and sometimes the political leaders of their respective communities, by dint of their knowledge, their understanding of Nasa history and culture, their ability to communicate with the gods "above" and "below," and their role in safeguarding the general welfare of the community. This decline in their power was accompanied by a change in the people's way of thinking. According to one of the leaders, "The shamans have lost their credibility and we no longer believe in them. The Indian is losing his way of thinking. He has neither contact nor belief in those gods." They had been replaced by evangelical preachers and Catholic priests with their own discourse who had overcome "our own way of thinking and also our intelligence." The leader deeply regretted this. Had this not happened, they would have been much better off, much stronger, and much smarter. These observations provoked additional comments from other group members, including the fact that the shamans now charged people for their services, whereas previously they had just expected payment in kind.

In presenting their framework, the group concentrated on two major problems: the weakening of authority, and lack of training in the ramifications of customary law. For the first problem, the goal was identified as "autonomy," the community's right to internal self-government, without individual or institutional interference from outsiders. Since authority was lacking, the desired result was expressed as "strengthening traditional authority," which, without the necessary autonomy or at least a degree of autonomy, would be unattainable. The group then followed with a series of quantifiable indicators, some to do with community participation in cabildo meetings and elections, and the others to do with the shamans: the number of rituals of purification they had conducted for the cabildo, the number of people working with the cabildo, and the number of people in the community who used their services. This acceptance of the role of quantification, without any discussion of what the numbers generated might mean (even if they could be generated) and what purpose they might serve, demonstrates the lengths to which the community was prepared to go to produce a plan and thereby prove that it was modern, striving after its own form of indigenous modernity.

The importance attached to the role of the shamans was discussed at some length, since the group was proposing their reinstatement as respected political authorities, in part reflecting the priorities articulated in the indigenous discourse articulated by CRIC and ACIN. This proposal marked an abrupt but dramatic about-face on the part of local leaders. When the new community had been established four years earlier, some of the leaders, who were evangelical, had been strongly opposed to the participation of the shamans. Historically, when communities moved and opened up new lands, the shamans performed certain rituals to determine if the lands were suitable. Each year, when the new members of the cabildo took office, the shaman was supposed to perform a ritual, in which he purified their silver-tipped staffs of office (*varas*). This had not happened in Tóez Caloto, but the proposal under discussion aimed to change this. For individual families, the shaman is also a health specialist, a traditional doctor and healer. But one issue in particular bothered participants, clearly demonstrating just how dependent they had become on a market economy. Why did the two shamans resident in the community charge such different prices for their services? The two were duly summoned to appear and asked to explain their prices. The one who charged more tended to use more medicinal plants and more complex methods and to do more business outside the community, though he claimed to charge local patients less. In contrast, his colleague used simpler methods, his focus was more local, and he cost less. It would appear that they were responding to market demand. Because the former offered more and had a larger clientele, he could charge more. However, there was no discussion about which of them was more effective.

The discussion of the second problem regarding customary law proved to be equally contentious. The 1991 Constitution made special provisions for the incorporation of indigenous customary law into the new system of juridical decentralization through the creation of indigenous special jurisdiction.

> The authorities of indigenous communities will be able to exercise jurisdictional functions within their territory, according to their own norms and procedures, so long as these are not contrary to the Constitution and to the laws of the Republic. The forms of coordination of this special jurisdiction with the national judicial system will be established by law. (República de Colombia 1991, Article 246)

Several issues have complicated this process, but two in particular stand out. The limits of customary law are unclear, and the breadth of its jurisdiction is still being worked out. On a more practical level, many resguardos have not practiced customary law for some time and have forgotten how to practice it correctly. One of the more contentious issues has been corporal punishment, the imposition of which the constitution legitimated at the resguardo level, allowing public whippings and the use of stocks. Depending on the gravity of the infraction, those found guilty can be first whipped and, if this does not deter, later placed in the stocks. The latter, made of wood, are usually some six feet high, and those to be punished are hanged upside down by their ankles for a short time (see figure 3). Both painful and humiliating, these forms of punishment were little used in the decades preceding the new constitution.

The reintroduction of corporal punishment is defended as a form of cultural revitalization, infinitely preferable to long-term imprisonment in Colombian jails, that isolates wrongdoers from their communities and does not allow for their rehabilitation (Gow and Rappaport 2002). But this revitalization has not gone uncontested. During the workshop, people questioned the place of such practices, inherited from the Spanish, in the modern world. If these practices were to be applied, they questioned *how* and under *what* conditions. Carrying out of the sentences in Tierradentro and elsewhere in Cauca in recent years has not been without its problems. Officeholders have used the stocks as a pretext for settling personal grudges. Through ignorance and inexperience on the part of those inflicting the punishment, people are said to have died in the stocks. The punishment, known as a *remedio,* is also supposed to be accompanied by counseling from the shamans. If the shamans are in disrepute, who will provide this essential service? The assembly was asked if they accepted the use of the whip, regarded as a form of purification (*refrescamiento)* and the stocks, with local justice under the mandate of the shaman. While several responded in the negative, there was no further discussion at that time.

The discussion did, however, take place two weeks later, in another general assembly, where the governor was questioned about the stocks. The community had its own set, and it appeared that the governor, in consultation with some of his friends, had used them to punish a teenage girl whom his family had adopted. He did not approve of her personal behavior, and when she did not respond to his suggestions, he decided to teach her a lesson. This was all conducted behind closed doors, but when word got out, people, irrespective of their views regarding the rightness or wrongness of the stocks, were shocked at what they viewed as an abuse of power. In the discussion that ensued, the

Figure 3. The stocks in Juan Tama

women were more opposed to the stocks than the men. One woman argued that it violated a person's civil rights, that there must be other ways of rehabilitating people, such as community service. The younger people were somewhat divided. One man argued that the stocks were a symbol, and their presence showed respect for indigenous law, the cabildos, and the ancestors. Visitors came to Tóez Caloto because they had never seen stocks before; they wanted to see them firsthand and find out how they were used.

But another participant reminded the assembly that they should think about the consequences of punishing young people in this manner, without considering what caused the undesirable behavior in the first place. Did the cabildo only want to punish people, or did it also want to help them to mend their ways? Those in favor of the stocks, however, disagreed about whether the punishment should be public or private. Some argued that if the victim was punished in public, he would be humiliated, even more so if the crowd laughed and made fun of him. The older participants were also divided, reminding the assembly that the stocks came with the Spaniards, who used them to control their black slaves, as well as indigenous peoples: "The stocks do not belong to our culture." One leader pointed out that people were confused about which problems should or could be resolved by resorting to the stocks and that they had few precedents to guide them.

This discussion about shamans and indigenous jurisdiction was also under way in many other indigenous communities, but what is noteworthy about Tóez Caloto is the fact that the leadership, previously strongly opposed to such traditional beliefs and practices, had been obliged to change its opinion in response to political realities. On the one hand, they had to demonstrate to the surrounding Nasa communities that the people of Tóez Caloto, who had relatively recently arrived from Tierradentro, were indeed more Nasa than their neighbors. On the other hand, however, they wished to become members of ACIN, and this meant adopting and accepting the movement discourse regarding the role of shamans and the use of corporal punishment. Similar discussions had been carried out in San José with equally ambiguous conclusions. The ambivalence felt by the communities was demonstrated by the fact that both kept their stocks under lock and key. In Juan Tama, in contrast, where the shamans were relatively numerous and some were widely respected, the stocks were openly flaunted for everyone to see.

On the basis of these workshops and the frameworks prepared by the respective working groups, which had been completed with little outside assistance, ACIN began to play a much more interventionist role. The promotora was replaced by a technician who essentially told the people what to do and the type of information they needed to collect in their surveys. As predicted by the more skeptical, he then took all the information to the ACIN office in the nearby town of Santander, promising to analyze the data and produce the plan (Meneses 2000, 78). Three years later, in 2002, the plan had still not appeared. In the interim, Tóez Caloto had become an active member of ACIN, and the association's involvement provided the community with more political and institutional legitimacy in the region.

Community leaders fully supported the production of the plan, and several were active participants in the workshops. But the support of the community waned over time. Earlier efforts had produced nothing, and according to some community members, there was a long-standing suspicion of most forms of external assistance. More important, however, there were certain deep-seated problems that were not addressed during the planning process. For example, what type of economy did they want and how would it be integrated into the regional economy? How would the local school, the community's most important and most successful project to date, prepare students for finding work in the region without losing their indigenous identity in the process? Most important, it did not deal with the long-term perspective: Who were the people now and who would they like to be in twenty-five years?

Juan Tama: Development Plan as Communal Statement

Although Juan Tama's plan shares certain characteristics with the two just described, it is also radically different, partly because it is a life plan and not just a development plan (Comunidad de Juan Tama 2002).[2] This document was created with very little external assistance, produced with the active participation of the local Nasa population — leaders, high school graduates, school teachers, and parents.[3] CRIC has been active in Juan Tama since 1994, continuing a relationship established with Vitoncó, particularly the section of El Cabuyo, that dates back to the late 1970s. This support has been primarily through CRIC's Bilingual Education Program (Programa de Educacion Bilingüe; PEB), in which Juan Tama has played a pivotal role as a pilot center and model for other indigenous schools in the region. PEB support has taken two forms: technical assistance, in fact, intellectual assistance, with the content of the school program, particularly the curriculum; and the hiring of teachers, all indigenous and some local, paid for by the national government through the La María Accords. While CRIC was not directly involved in the preparation of the plan, the community did benefit from the support of Pacho Rojas, a member of PEB and longtime friend of the community who is praised in the plan "as a tireless and patient adviser working disinterestedly on behalf of the Nasa." Over the years, he has been actively involved in supporting the younger leadership and supporting various development initiatives.

Though different voices speak throughout the document, one way in which this plan differs from the others is that the voice of the community, in this case those individual authors who wrote certain parts of the text, comes across with singular clarity as the authors express their perceptions of the past and the new world in which they find themselves. While ostensibly discussing certain standard topics, such as territory, autonomy, economy, and health, the document is also a clear statement of some basic underlying components of Nasa culture, focusing on history, land, language, and the shamans. To a certain extent, these priorities are also a reflection of the discourse of the indigenous movement. The importance of the cultural hero and founder Juan Tama is acknowledged, particularly since he is said to have been born in Vitoncó, their community of origin. When the shamans of Vitoncó visited Santa Leticia to explore whether it was a suitable place for establishing the new community, they decided that the neighboring archeological site of Moscopán was where Juan Tama rested after creating a seat for himself out of the natural rock (Bolaños et al. 2004, 105):

> The place of concentration of the resettlement is baptized with the name of *JUAN TAMA,* so named by the whole community due to the fact that they thought about his memory, particularly when he says: *"I shall be with you wherever you are . . . I will catch up with you . . ."* and therefore we are subjects, and besides because we have wanted to maintain with pride the name of our *cacique* [leader], who created and strengthened [our] cultural identity, founding defender, legislator of the Nasa people. (Comunidad de Juan Tama 2002, 9; emphasis original)

The land itself is almost as important since it embodies deeply meaningful elements of Nasa culture. It is a territory, a physical and symbolic space that they can occupy and control, a means of sustenance that can feed them and their livestock, and a "mother" who forms the core of their lives.

> For we Páez the land is considered as our MOTHER, not just a piece of flat land or hillside which gives us food. Since we live in her, since we work in her, since we enjoy her and suffer for her, for us she is the root of life. That's why we pamper her and defend her as the root of our customs. The fundamental reason of our present [existence] as indigenous people, she is the base of our subsistence, autonomy. (12)

The role and importance of the shamans in daily and communal life are widely recognized, and Juan Tama is famous for the number who live there, compared with the two in Tóez Caloto, a community with approximately the same population.[4] In Juan Tama, the shaman possesses both knowledge and wisdom, which can be used for either good or for evil.

> He is responsible for controlling and balancing the community, he makes the offerings, turns over the dirt of [i.e., cleanses] the cabildos, the families and the community in general, preventing both cultural illnesses and future ill-

nesses. In this space, you also find the bad shaman (witch), shamans who at the beginning possess good knowledge, but the time comes when the bad spirit accompanies them, he does it above all out of jealousy, to make sure the work [within the community] does not go well. (21)

While the importance attached to shamanic wisdom is part of movement discourse, in the case of Juan Tama it is a lived reality, and the shamans there enjoy a level of importance and prestige not encountered in the new settlements, nor, for that matter, in most communities of Tierradentro. In the case of Cxayu'ce, however, the shamans continued to be important, although none actually lived in the community. Although the situation in Juan Tama is partly a response to the devastation of the disaster of 1994, in which the section of El Cabuyo, the most radical in Vitoncó, was completely destroyed, it is not retrenchment, a falling back on nostalgic values. It is, in fact, a much more dynamic process in which existing values form the base for dealing with and confronting new problems, issues, and challenges.

> Society is the apparatus with which people address the solution to their problems, the realization of their aspirations and the survival of their values. Society is something that can be changed and that has already changed. If a society does not work, the thought and action of its members can correct it through [various] means: organizational, political, cultural, scientific, and economic. (12)

In other words, shamanic wisdom and moral agency are neither incompatible nor mutually exclusive. As articulated in the plan, they are complementary. This dynamic is accompanied by a willingness to learn from other cultures, based on local people's appreciation, understanding, and valorization of their own identity and the potential contribution they can make to the broader goal of liberation.

> To the extent that we recognize and value our own identity, we are in a position to receive and integrate into our life contributions provided by other cultures while at the same time we can contribute with our experiences to the liberation struggles being undertaken by the majority of the Colombian people and by other countries. (26)

This discourse differs from that articulated by the other two communities in its emphasis on the political, in the potential transformation of society. Known as interculturalism (*interculturalidad*), this concept is key to understanding the discourse of both CRIC and PEB, with its focus on the internal, the external, the horizontal, but above all the political: "What we have to emphasize here is that the theories of interculturalism being constructed in the Andean countries are directed towards the construction of a different society and not only a school. That is to say that interculturality is a political project" (Bolaños et al. 2004, 132). The basis for this interculturalism is an appreciation of and pride in their own Nasa culture. In Juan Tama and Cxayu'ce, culture is a given, whereas in Tóez Caloto it is a construct, a (re)invention to meet the demands of the modernizing resguardos of northern Cauca.

This plan also differs from the others in the importance it attaches to education, but education as a political project. Education of the children is given the highest priority — almost 30 percent of the document is devoted to this topic. While education is also important in the other two communities, particularly in Tóez Caloto, only in Juan Tama is it given such prominence in the plan. There are several possible reasons for this. There has been a long-standing interest, especially in the section of El Cabuyo, in alternatives to the formal education controlled by the Catholic Church that long preceded the disaster. Two years after the disaster, El Cabuyo, the largest section in Juan Tama, produced an educational plan for Juan Tama in collaboration with PEB (El Cabuyo/ CRIC 1996), certain aspects of which were implemented by 2000. This proposal provided the basis for the later plan. In the 1996 proposal, education is defined as a lifelong process that provides both meaning and dignity, one that also incorporates certain key concepts, emphasizing a knowledge of history, territory and the environment, harmony with nature, and responsibility to the community. This is also to be an education that emphasizes identity:

> When we know we are part of a social group, when we know very well our way of thinking, and we marvel at who we are, we achieve reaffirmation as both individuals and as community and we can discern what and how to assimilate from external influences and contributions. The territory is not only the space where you find crops or where the town is situated, but also includes the stars, the sea, the tall mountains because the Nasa form part of the great family of the universe; the land is for him the great Mother Earth who must be cared for, loved, and defended; that is why

in the territory where he lives culture is recreated and history is woven. (El Cabuyo/CRIC 1996, 14)

The form of education proposed is based on respect, for culture and for Nasa Yuwe, for society, the individual, nature, and a future that will support an improvement in living conditions, "within the context of human growth and the development of an integrated autonomy" (16). The remainder of the document elaborates on these principles and presents a plan of study for the six years of primary school in four broad areas: mathematics and production, community and nature, man and society, and communication and language, taking as its point of departure a detailed understanding of the child's immediate environment. In kindergarten, for example, the themes to be covered include the family, the community, man and the animals, and the universe. As the students advance through the various grades, these themes are developed in more detail.

To emphasize the importance attached to education, the teachers played an active role in the preparation and writing of the plan (see figure 4). In fact, parts of the document are taken in their entirety, without any formal acknowledgment, from CRIC's overall plan for its pilot bilingual schools, which includes Juan Tama (PEB/CRIC 2000a). Since the teachers were actively involved in the preparation of this overall plan, primarily in the form of a series of ongoing workshops organized by PEB, this is to be expected.

Finally, it may be the only project in Juan Tama around which there is some general consensus that this activity can benefit the whole community. Although glossed over in the plan, Juan Tama has been riven by internal divisions, as a result of which the population dropped by half, and dissatisfied families moved elsewhere, some choosing to return to Vitoncó and others continuing on to other, newer communities. These divisions had their origins in Vitoncó before the disaster, between sections of the resguardo that supported CRIC and those who supported the Catholic Church, between those who supported the MAQL (Quintín Lame Armed Movement) and those who opposed the indigenous guerrillas. Though the exodus removed some of the dissension, internal differences still linger, partly generational between those in charge at the time of the disaster and the younger leaders who have partially replaced them, and partly political between those who support the PEB

Figure 4. Teachers planning in Juan Tama

philosophy and those who do not. The development plan reflects some of these divisions. Some of the proposed projects are designed more to benefit specific interest groups, such as the growers of sugarcane or the owners of milk cows, rather than the community as a whole.

The educational section of the plan provides a brief history of bilingual education in El Cabuyo and later, in Juan Tama, followed by a discussion of the guiding concepts for achieving a sustainable education, taken directly from PEB's overall education plan. Two of these concepts concern work and the economy. Famous historically as warriors, the Nasa are equally famous as hard workers, but for them work is embedded in a social context that includes both the family and the community: "Work is a primordial value, for the indigenous communities. Its socializing and cultural practices fill it with meaning and assign it a creative function in daily reasoning" (Comunidad de Juan Tama 2002, 33). While work may often incorporate the whole family in various subsistence and cash crop activities designed to benefit the household, it may also involve activities designed to benefit neighbors, kin, and the community. Writing about her research on the Nasa conducted in the 1960s, Sutti Ortiz suggests that work also gives value, economic and noneconomic (1979, 208). One of the identifying characteristics of indigenous communities has been various forms of mutual help and reciprocal labor, practices that have been steadily falling into disuse. One of the most immediate effects of the disaster was a resurgence of these forms of cooperation, especially the weekly *minga,* a day set aside for implementing activities meant to benefit the whole community: digging ditches, constructing schools, or clearing trails. The cabildo provides lunch, and there may also be time for discussing any pressing community issues. Each family is obliged to send a representative or a replacement; failure to do so results in a fine. These weekly mingas, practiced in all three communities to a lesser or greater extent, provide a means of strengthening solidarity as well as a forum for the discussion of issues and problems. In this sense, work has value, not only for its economic importance but also for the opportunity it provides for socializing and creative solution of problems.

But when the plan talks about economic growth, the novelty of what Juan Tama is proposing becomes much clearer. Its focus is twofold: "Economic growth only has meaning to the extent that it contributes to satisfying spiritual and economic necessities." While this is not elaborated on in the text, the implication is that economic growth should provide opportunities for people to grow politically and personally. The focus is on a specific type of participation that will provide a critical, responsible, and deliberative attitude benefiting the community. In other words, local people are encouraged to speak up on issues of communal importance. One way to promote this is through some form of economic security. Another way is to encourage people to develop their full potential: "Every person is capable of learning and of reaching something, people have multiple potentials." These concepts express a relatively positive attitude toward individuals and their possibilities, in spite of the empirical evidence to the contrary. For this reason education in Juan Tama is more than the school and the activities associated with it. It is a political project designed to improve the lives of the local inhabitants by encouraging them to exercise their agency on behalf of the community: "Every situation can be improved upon and every explanation can be acted upon." In this sense, the development plan of Juan Tama is a remarkably optimistic document (Comunidad de Juan Tama 2002, 34).

This optimism, however, is in marked contrast to the realities hinted at in various sections of the plan. The final section lists the projects that Juan Tama would like to undertake over the next twenty years, with a one-line description of each. They are a mixture of the mundane and practical on the one hand, and the ambitious and almost visionary on the other. But the most important, with far-reaching implications, is the call for more land to benefit future generations. This request can be justified on three counts. Most significant is the poor quality of the land they have already received. Moreover, CNK has not kept its promise to provide each family with eight hectares of land, and, according to the community's calculations, each family is still owed three hectares (13). Finally, not discussed in the plan, are community hopes to be able to provide land for their children once they become of age, a potential problem for the other communities as well. Over the years, as the children of the new communities reach adulthood and the cabildos have requested more land and more houses, CNK has made clear that it is only responsible for the present generation.

When this need for more land is combined with the poor quality of available land, questions must be raised about the standard of living and quality of life in Juan Tama. When compared with the other two communities, the level of frustration, disappointment, and anger against CNK, particularly in the earlier years, was always higher there. They were somewhat isolated, far from urban centers, as well as from Vitoncó, where they still had livestock and productive lands, as well as many family members. The limited opportunities in Juan Tama had major effects on two groups in the community, children and members of the workforce. The children were most directly affected. Since 1994, there has been a high level of malnutrition, severe and chronic, a problem mentioned in the plan.

> There are health problems according to a study undertaken by the nutritionist, a high level of malnutrition was found among the children that affects their normal development. Two levels of malnutrition were found:
>
> a). Chronic malnutrition in which the child does not reach the height for his age. It is the largest percentage in this community [i.e. the majority suffer from this].
>
> b). Severe malnutrition in which the child does not reach either the height or the weight, and is so extreme that the children do not even reach the weight for the height. Because of malnutrition, the population presents a high level of the disease of tuberculosis, there are many illnesses [caused by] parasites and problems of oral health in the majority of the community. (21)

The Christian Children's Fund (CCF) concentrated the majority of its efforts on children, trying to improve their diets directly through food supplements and technical assistance with agricultural production. Active in El Cabuyo before the disaster, and the sole NGO working continuously in the community, CCF was regarded by the people as their "right hand for the development of the community" (30).

The limited opportunities also affected working-age adults, men and women, who could not find enough work in Juan Tama. Seasonal and permanent migration has been a characteristic of Nasa communities for the past century. Young women would go to the towns and cities and seek employment as domestic servants, whereas young men would find work as unskilled laborers on sugar plantations, coffee farms, or ranches. Some would do this for a few years and return, whereas others would establish themselves permanently elsewhere. But in Juan Tama, this pattern has been more accentuated. In the first two years, while the community was still receiving food from CNK, people of all ages started migrating, sometimes on a short-term basis but also permanently, searching for work elsewhere to supplement their limited incomes, a pattern that has continued until the present. This continuous movement of people has worked against the ongoing well-being of the community by contributing to the impermanence and factionalism that has characterized Juan Tama from the very beginning. Among those who leave are some of the more talented and creative. The most tangible evidence of this continuous movement is the number of unoccupied houses, some temporarily but others permanently, and the number of unfinished houses, some bare shells, others partially completed. No one knows, or no one will say, how many of these houses have been "abandoned," anywhere from 10 to 15 percent of the total, since invariably there is some family member who has a continuing interest in the property. While this problem exists in the other new settlements, it is particularly acute in Juan Tama, and certain parts of the settlement appear to be abandoned, as if the families had packed their bags and moved permanently elsewhere.

But this movement and apparent desertion are nowhere mentioned in the plan, which tends to focus on the world of Juan Tama as it *could* be, rather than the world as it is. Hence, there is an air of unreality, an apparent internal contradiction, something not found in the other planning exercises. Does this mean that the Juan Tama document is basically the work of dreamers, or does it in fact point the way for some form of indigenous transformation?

Being Indigenous, Different, and Legitimate

The process of indigenous planning, as described here, is a response to a combination of both internal and external factors. In all three cases, the original initiative came from within the communities, from the political leadership in Cxayu'ce and Tóez Caloto and from the teachers in Juan Tama. Though mandated in theory, in practice the absence of a development plan did not adversely affect a community's allocation of transferencias, nor its possibilities of seeking and obtaining technical and financial support from sources other than the state. All three communities received various types of assistance long before they produced — or, in the case of Tóez Caloto, tried to produce — their respective plans. The process differed significantly in each case.

In San José and Cxayu'ce, there was heavy reliance on external assistance by planning professionals whose knowledge and understanding of the specific community were superficial. Although the consulting team shared a draft of the plan with the leadership, they did not receive many comments or criticisms, a reflection more of the differences between Nasa orality and mestizo literacy, of deference before the written word, than of any intellectual failings on the part of the community. Their somewhat passive response to the plan may also have indicated a more realistic understanding of the political realities underlying the process. Since the leadership of the community had convinced them that this was something that had to be done, they had complied, on the understanding that once the plan was completed, they could get on with their own affairs. Furthermore, one year's priorities could easily change with next year's leadership.

In the discussions held during and after the workshops in San José, three different visions for the future emerged, one involving land, a second infrastructure, and a third education. Their strategy was to quietly go along with what was proposed while diligently pursuing their successful adaptation to life in Cxayu'ce. This had been achieved partly through their impressive work ethic, as well as their willingness to make the most of the opportunities that displacement had offered them. There is another characteristic, unique perhaps to the San Joseños: their unselfconscious acceptance of the fact that they are Nasa. While the other two communities are self-consciously aware of their Nasaness, albeit for different reasons, for the San Joseños it is not all problematic, a cultural given on which they appear to thrive in their usual understated way.

In Tóez Caloto, external assistance, at least at the beginning, was much lighter, becoming more heavy-handed and top-down over time. The workshops were productive and the discussions lively and at times contentious, dealing with serious issues, such as the type of economy and productive system that people wanted and the role of the shamans and customary law in determining the type of community they wished to establish. There is a certain irony in their choice of topics to debate. Of the three communities, Tóez Caloto has the best resource endowment in terms of quantity and quality of arable land, yet they were unable to agree on the type of economy they wanted.

During the period when the workshops were being held, a local mestizo visited the community looking for families who wanted to work with him; they would provide the land, he would provide all the inputs, the harvest would be divided, with 80 percent for him and the remaining 20 percent to the family. Most peopled balked at the offer, finding the terms of exchange too exploitive. But as this man walked from plot to plot, explaining what the possibilities were, in terms of crops and financial returns, it was evident that he was an "expert" in his own right, something which local people readily acknowledged. Yet the community refused to entertain the possibility of hiring him to advise them on how to work their lands more efficiently. He was an outsider, a mestizo, and hence suspect. There may also have been an element of pride at work, the refusal to collectively admit that they lacked the necessary expertise. Confronted by the same problem, the San Joseños in Cxayu'ce resolved it by going to work for their mestizo neighbors and learning on the job how to cultivate local crops, such as bananas, sugarcane, and coffee. Why couldn't the people of Tóez Caloto have done the same? Perhaps they were no longer interested in being "small" farmers. Perhaps they were content to live with the off-farm opportunities for unskilled labor. While the majority resisted change, a small, politically powerful minority was busy taking full advantage of all the ongoing opportunities within the community, demonstrating on an individual level the rewards of personal initiative and a free-market economy.

The long and contentious discussion over shamans and customary law was also ironic, given that Tóez, their community of origin, was regarded as one of the more "modernizing" communities with little interest in Nasa culture or indigenous politics. Several of the leaders were also evangelicals who, at least in the early years after resettlement, strenuously downplayed the role and importance of the shamans. The dramatic change in their perspective appears to have been political. Tóez Caloto wished to become a member of ACIN, which, like CRIC, has increasingly privileged the shamans and customary law. But there is a deeper, more complex explanation.

The community's attitude to Nasa Yuwe provides a clue. Both the parents and the leadership supported the teaching of Nasa Yuwe in the school, since children's ability to speak it, to say nothing of their interest, was on the decline. But the parents who did speak Nasa Yuwe refused to speak it to their children at home. Since the children lacked the basics to converse, as well as the opportunity to practice, the teachers concluded that the effort was a waste of time. Yet language is one of the key markers of being indigenous. The community was making a conscious, deliberate effort to recover certain parts of its culture, favorably distinguishing itself from its more de-Indianized, "proletarianized" Nasa neighbors. This constructed identity made Tóez Caloto more attractive and more appealing to both its neighbors and to outside agencies (Gow and Rappaport 2002). For Tóez Caloto, the future lies not in the preservation of Nasa culture but in its reinvention, as a means of dealing with modernity on their terms, neither indigenous nor de-Indianized, but as modern Nasa (Gow 1997). However, this reinvention remains at the level of discourse and may never become a lived reality.

The planning process in Juan Tama, like that of Tóez Caloto in its early phases, was generated internally, but in marked contrast to the other two, local voices were not only allowed to speak and be heard but were also documented. Though considerable space is devoted to various aspects of culture, it is accepted as a given, as an integral part of their everyday existence — embedded, understood, and sometimes contested. Underlying this approach is a belief that culture and society are dynamic: if members of a society do not like how they live, they are in a position to change it. For some in Juan Tama, this meant moving on to other places, but for others, such as the schoolteachers and some of the other, younger leaders, this meant accepting the community as *theirs* and thinking of creative ways in which they can improve the situation.

This self-conscious, constructivist view of culture clearly distinguishes

Juan Tama from the other two communities. Not only does it provide the foundation for its major project — elementary education, really a political project around which the community can unite — but also for its strong, in-your-face identity as a Nasa community. This cultural strength and cultural pride have enabled the community to deal with the political and social constraints it has encountered. This has not been the case with its major constraints in the economic realm. In fact, it could be argued that perhaps the lack of economic opportunities in the region has helped strengthen ethnic identity in Juan Tama.

New communities such as those analyzed here can achieve legitimacy in various ways: through the support of the state, acceptance by neighboring communities and local power brokers, willingness to make the most of new opportunities, and a demonstrated "high seriousness." The latter can take various forms, ranging from a well-developed work ethic to maintaining law and order within the community. But it can also take less pragmatic forms, such as the preparation of development plans. While it may well be the case that one does not read the national development plan of a nation to find out more about the country in question, this does not necessarily hold at the community level, where there may well be much less dissimulation since there is much less at stake (Crush 1995). As stated in the introduction, a plan is produced to convince an audience, sometimes internal but more often external, that the community's version of reality is the correct one. In so doing, the community demonstrates that it has reached a certain level of maturity, of legitimacy — that it is, in fact, here to stay. In the following chapter, the most ethnographic in the book, the differences among the three new communities — specifically the ways they choose to deal with education and the local economy, usually privileging the former over the latter — are presented.

4

What do you want your children to be? I want them to be some-
body.—PARENT IN PITAYÓ, a Nasa community, in 2000

Counter-development means shaping and establishing the here-
and-now of modernity.—ALBERTO ARCE AND NORMAN LONG, "Reconfiguring Modernity and Development from an Anthropological
Perspective"

Local Knowledge, Different Dreams:

Planning for the Next Generation

For the resettled Nasa of the three communities, the field of education,
unlike the more restricted field of economic development, may offer
more autonomy and, hence, more potential to experiment, create, and
be original. Indigenous education in its more political form, as practiced in Juan Tama, can question modernity by embracing the past,
questioning the present, and imagining a different future. In contrast,
indigenous education in its more traditional form, as practiced in Tóez
Caloto, can be instrumental in embracing modernity, exploiting the
past, and shifting the terms of identity. This chapter examines how
these two communities view their history, language, identity, manifestations of local knowledge, and key components of their cultures. Where
relevant, additional material is incorporated from the experiences of
Cxayu'ce. Specifically, I am interested in answering the following questions. What do we mean when we talk about indigenous education, and
what part does local knowledge play in it? Does such an education prepare students for coping, surviving, and flourishing in the increasingly
globalized world of the twenty-first century? Finally, to what extent can
the pursuit of indigenous education be a form of creative resistance
to the dominant society or to the dominant development paradigms,
whether conventional or alternative?[1]

Local Knowledge and Counterdevelopment

The discourse of development, both conventional and alternative, enthusiastically embraces the integration of "local knowledge" into the process of planning and implementation, a step that has proved to be increasingly problematic.[2] Proponents argue that this integration can improve the effectiveness of development initiatives and interventions by successfully incorporating local perspectives, local understandings, and local concerns. This assumption underlies the approaches to development planning discussed in the previous chapter while carefully avoiding many of the paradoxes and pitfalls encountered in applying it uncritically. Nevertheless, the phrase "local knowledge" is not without its own problems, given the breadth of its current application. It can refer to "scientific" knowledge about man/woman's relationship to the physical environment. It can refer to "technical" knowledge about the cultivation of crops, the rearing of animals, and the practicalities of everyday life. It can also refer to "political" knowledge about man/woman's place in the existing social and political order. Likewise, it can include "medical" knowledge for explaining and curing human illness. Of course, it can incorporate "philosophical" knowledge to explain the past and the present and to contemplate the future. As Pigg (1997) has forcefully argued, there is a strong tendency on the part of development professionals and their critics to simplify and restrict their understanding and appreciation of local perspectives to such domains as "culture" and "indigenous knowledge," implying that local people do not hold strong opinions about either development or modernity.[3]

But Clammer (2002, 43) has raised broader questions about the nature of the relationship between local knowledge and development planning, and, what, precisely, this relationship is supposed to be. Is it to "discover" this knowledge which local people already have, or to make them aware of just how valuable their knowledge is (but to whom?)? Does it, moreover, open the eyes of those, such as development decision makers, who may be ignorant of the potential of this knowledge? Is it to criticize this knowledge and the practices it generates? While these objectives are not necessarily mutually exclusive, they do raise the possibility of a critical but creative reflection on the part of those who produce and utilize this local knowledge. Nevertheless, Paul Sillitoe (2002) has attempted to define what is meant by the term, as a type of situated knowledge that informs an understanding of the world and which is community-based, embedded in and conditioned by local tradition. Local knowledge is also continually informed by external information, but its distribution is fragmentary, because no one person, authority, or social group knows it all.[4] He argues that studying local knowledge introduces a locally informed perspective into development, challenging "the assumption that development is something that outsiders have a right to impose, and to promote an appreciation of indigenous power structures and know-how" (Sillitoe 2002, 9). Such an approach is inherently subversive, since it raises the possibility of redefining the meaning of development itself, a prospect unlikely to be embraced by more mainstream development organizations, because this could diminish their control.

At the same time, however, the local knowledge "extracted" can be used against the people who "own" or produce it, whether dealing with medicinal properties of plants or histories of resistance against the status quo (Agrawal 1999). While agreeing with Arun Agrawal's concern, Posey (2002) raises another issue, one of direct relevance to the issues discussed in this chapter: What do indigenous people themselves think about their knowledge(s)? He argues that indigenous people view knowledge as emanating from a spiritual, rather than a scientific base, and as a result, the sacred and the secular are inseparable. If this is the case, then the relationship between local knowledge and resignified universal knowledge becomes clearer.

> Spirituality is the highest form of consciousness, and spiritual consciousness is the highest form of awareness. In this sense, traditional knowledge is not *local* knowledge at all, but rather an expression of *universal* knowledge as expressed through the local. . . . The unseen is as much a part of society as that which is seen — the spiritual is as much a part of reality as the material. In fact, there is a complementary relationship between the two, *with the spiritual being more powerful than the material.* (Posey 2002, 28; emphasis original)

If local knowledge is as potentially powerful as both Sillitoe and Posey claim, what relationship, if any, does it have to development as commonly conceived? Put more forcefully, what do shamans, as the acknowledged guardians and fundamental sources of the spiritual components of local knowledge, have to do with bricks and mortar, the basic elements of desired and desirable public works? On one level, the answer is nothing, but that is because we unduly restrict the definition of development. Yet shamans and the local knowledge they monopolize have until recently been regarded as dangerous, first by the Catholic Church and more recently by the guerrillas. Their knowledge signified power, and hence a threat to other institutions who believed that they had a monopoly on knowledge and, hence, on local power.[5]

The acceptance of shamanic wisdom does not entail a blanket endorsement, an essentialization, or "folklorization" of local knowledge. As argued in the preceding chapter, there has been a decline in the prestige and influence of the shamans. At the same time, however, this has been accompanied by the increasing availability of other types of knowledge provided by schools, the mass media, and the indigenous movement, to name the more obvious. To better understand the potential role local knowledge, broadly defined, can play in development, Peters (2000), drawing on the work of Richards (1993) and Fairhead (1993), suggests thinking more in terms of knowledgeable actors producing knowledgeable "performances," rather than local actors drawing on a fount of coherent local knowledge that supposedly can "explain" everything. Addressing the question of how West African farmers resolve the technical problems they encounter, Richards (1993) suggests that performance, creatively responding to the immediate context, rather than planning, using a blueprint based on local knowledge, has more explanatory power. In other words, creatively rethinking local knowledge is more realistic and sustainable over the long run than an uncritical application of what is already known. As analogy, he offers the experience of the concert pianist who, although she practices hard and diligently and carefully plans for the approaching performance, may have a bad night: the acoustics may be awful, the audience may be unresponsive, the performer may feel sick. To survive, the artist must be more than a skilled technician; she must have additional skills on which to draw. In other words she must be creative, able to draw on her knowledge, while at the same time creatively reworking and reinventing it.

The same argument holds for the process of development where there are so many unknowns and where human agency, this individual potential, has a crucial role to play, an argument reinforced by Ortner (1999), based on her own long-term research with the Sherpas of Nepal.

> In the context of questions of power, agency is that which is made or denied, expanded or contracted, in the exercise of power. It is the (sense of) authority to act, or of lack of authority and lack of empowerment. . . . Within the framework of meaning, on the other hand, agency represents the pressures of desires and understandings on cultural constructions, [which assumes] a more active projection of the self toward some desired end. (1999, 146–47)

This commitment to the study of human agency is reflected in the work of Long (1992), who, building on the work of Giddens (1984), has proposed an actor-oriented paradigm that recognizes the central role played by human action and human consciousness, as a counterpoint to more structural approaches that attempt to explain social events primarily in terms of external factors. What is required is the study of "knowledge interfaces," situations in which different, possibly conflicting forms of knowledge intersect and interact, focusing on the interplay of different social constructions of "reality" developed by the various actors and tracing out their social implications (Arce and Long 1992). Planning is an example of such an interface, a form of external intervention which needs to be deconstructed so that it is seen for what it is, "an ongoing, socially constructed and negotiated process" (Long 1992, 35).

The coping skills referred to by Peters and Richards may cover a wide range of categories, ranging from experience and common sense to indigenous theories developed by the performers themselves. Richards cites the work of Harrell-Bond (1986) on refugee resettlement to show the extent to which refugee survival is a skilled social achievement that "demonstrates the need above all to sustain that sense of vision and purpose through which social groups retain their capacity to act in a creative and cohesive manner" (Richards 1993, 74).

While local knowledge can provide the basis for such creativity, it can also serve as a platform for resistance. One way in which this can be achieved is by attempting to "institutionalize" local knowledge within the educational system: from complete control over both teachers and curriculum, as in the case of Juan Tama, to partial control, as in Tóez Caloto. Given the attention that both communities attach to education, it can be argued that this is a form of counterdevelopment, as demonstrated by actions that counter the dominant development discourse and practice. Galjart (1981, 88) defines *counterdevelopment* as "the effort of relatively small, local groups in achieving, in a participatory manner, their development goals, and thus enhancing their members' life chances, in spite of and in opposition to societal mechanisms and processes which influence these chances adversely." Given the importance he attaches to the political dimension, Galjart advocates this more local, more autonomous approach to counter the adverse effects of large development programs that, in his opinion, tend to increase inequality and work against the best interests of the local population. Though his critique of mainstream development is framed in the specific context of economic development, reflecting the fact that he was writing twenty-five years ago, his proposed measures for implementing counterdevelopment are surprisingly contemporary, specifically his focus on mobilization, commitment, and solidarity. For Arce and Long (2000), however, the notion of counterdevelopment can help us understand the processes by which multiple modernities are established, focusing on the "issues of ambiguity, ambivalence and the crossing of cultural boundaries in the constitution of newly assembled localised modernities" (2000, 21). On a more philosophical level, Giroux, discussing the work of Paulo Freire, proposes that education is an optional space for such pursuits. "Education is that terrain where power and politics are given a fundamental expression, where the production of meaning, desire, language, and values engage and respond to the deeper beliefs about what it means to be human, to dream, and to name and struggle for a particular future and form of social life" (Giroux 1988, 110).[6]

CRIC and Its Bilingual Education Program (PEB)

The primary school in Juan Tama has been held up as a model of what other communities can aspire to. All the teachers are Nasa, as are all the students, and they are paid by the Regional Indigenous Council of Cauca (CRIC) with funds received from the national government. They teach according to a Nasa curriculum, based partly on the predisaster experience of their alternative school in Vitoncó and the ongoing assistance from PEB, CRIC's bilingual education program, and also on their daily lived experiences in the classroom and the larger community to which they belong. This program has evolved over the past twenty-five years, learning from its successes and failures, while at the same time developing and operationalizing certain key Nasa concepts and principles. In 1990, a CRIC workshop on curriculum preparation clearly stated that the broader objective of an indigenous system of education was to counter the state system and its imposed values, interests, knowledge, and attitudes. The state system would be replaced by one that would develop indigenous culture through the offices of indigenous teachers capable of creating and sustaining an educational project that would meet the interests and needs of the communities (CRIC 1990). The authors asked, "What sort of person are we going to educate?" The response, a summary of various parents' expectations, embodied a combination of ethnic pride, personal characteristics, and communal responsibilities: "A person proud of being indigenous. An agile, strong, hardworking man who defends and cares for his land in the same way [that he does] for his work and communal life; someone who should be a good leader, *cabildo* member, who respects the traditional authorities and collaborates in strengthening unity" (n.p.). This person would believe in the unity of the universe in which people are integrated into the natural order through agricultural production and various agricultural practices, as part of an ongoing, repetitive process. Any violation of this relationship with nature would become a moral imperative and result in serious consequences for the transgressor.

At a more general level, the authors asked what this program could contribute to the development of communities, specifically the economic aspects that could improve the standard of living, achieve a more equitable distribution of resources, and promote the creation of appropriate technology. At the same time this improved economy was expected to fall within existing communal norms regarding land and labor: "We are not talking about developing an economy of salaried workers, peasants, or small producers, but rather an economy that strengthens communal forms of property and work" (n.p.). Nevertheless, this future envisioned by CRIC had to be balanced against the more practical expectations of the parents.

> When you ask a parent what he expects for his son in school, he tells us that he [the son] should learn to read and write, should learn Spanish well so that he can continue in the official [i.e., state] school, that he have some knowledge of mathematics so that he can conduct business transactions successfully, take charge of the [communal] store, and should know something about agricultural practices or livestock. (n.p.)

This "typical" parent took a purely instrumental view of schooling: school was viewed as a place where children were to be trained how to survive in the larger society, including how to enter the official state school and manage money in an expanding market economy. Only at the end, almost as an aside, was there any mention of the contribution that education might make to improving local agricultural practices. There was no direct mention of expecting the school to inculcate "communal" or "cultural" values. Was this because parents assumed that the school would do this anyway, that such education was really their responsibility, or was it perhaps a realization that the future for their children would increasingly involve a more complex, complicated way of life in which the "community" would play a steadily diminishing role, in both cultural and economic terms? Perhaps it was because parents still had a very incipient notion of what a school should be. Furthermore, it is possible that CRIC had not yet developed a coherent vision of what culture is that could be taken up by the parents. These comments were offered during public evaluations of PEB, and such exercises not only broadened parents' understanding but also helped integrated their voices into educational planning.

CRIC's expectations were very different, in terms of content and methodology. They proposed to replace rote learning with a form of education characterized by dialogue between teachers and pupils, but also, more important, between the children and their parents. In this scheme, the children would talk freely about what they had learned in school and what they had talked about at home, in this way building their self-confidence. According to Aberlardo Ramos, one of the founders of PEB,

> So in this way the parents found out that the children knew about what they had asked about, had expanded upon it, that they could sustain the theme with the community, show and draw maps, that they could show, for example, calculations in mathematics and perhaps some parent could propose to ask the children questions, and the children were sensitized to present themselves and talk in a regular way, confidently, and without fear of being "boxed in" and without fear of making a mistake. (Bolaños et al. 2004, 47–48)

Over time, PEB emphasized the role of culture, contrasting it with the notion of custom (*costumbre*) which was viewed as something static, primordial, to be preserved in a museum. In contrast, culture is seen as something dynamic, as something that generates, a mechanism for survival and not a return to the past, a constructivist rather than essentialist perspective (99). For example, an analysis of *wet uskiwe'nxi,* the concept of culture as conceived by PEB, reveals the following.

> *Wet* is a word that has various meanings, among which the most significant are "agreeable flavors," "well-being or happiness of people or animals" and "harmony." *Uskiwe'nxi* is a compound word formed by *us,* meaning "that which remains or that which has been"; *kiwe,* "land or territory" in the earthly world [i.e., this world], but also in the worlds of above and below which form the three levels of the cosmos; *nxi* functions as a suffix and means "what happens in a process." Taken together, the construction expresses the following concept: "the result of living in harmony with the land." (101)

Hence, the concept of culture is very closely associated with well-being, harmony, and the land, and this analysis helped refocus the program's priorities.

This emphasis on culture has been supported all along by those most actively involved in the school. Don Ángel María Yoinó, shaman, political leader, and one of the founders of the first school in El Cabuyo, Vitoncó, in 1978, reiterated its importance in an interview more than twenty years later.

> Our forefathers were very great thinkers from the very beginning. This [was] so important that they [the communities] were asking: And why don't you take culture into consideration for teaching? Why were they not teaching our elements? [That's what] the elders were saying. I myself was thinking: What are they talking about? But today I understand that we are thinking well. We notice that we have been planning things that are well thought out. And how did we manage to see that? Because we have continued to strengthen ourselves. We see that because we progress with a greater capacity to think. (20)

This capacity was also strengthened by the study of their own language, which in turn strengthened the mechanisms of cultural resistance, personified by the school.

Another important concept that PEB developed and implemented in Juan Tama is interculturalism defined as follows:

Today we understand the concept of interculturalism as beginning with the knowledge of one's own [culture] to continue integrating other types of knowledge from outside. The implementation of interculturalism is purely political, since it seeks to arrive at the creation of horizontal relations of dialogue among different [groups]. That is to say, interculturalism incorporates the relations generated and personally experienced by the valuation and respect for the other, in the search for conditions of equality based on the differences. (123)

Underlying this concept is the acceptance that there is much to be learned from other cultures and other ways of thinking, that Nasa culture in particular or indigenous culture in general is neither static nor primarily inward-looking. Rather there is this welcoming embrace of difference, provided it is something that is not imposed, but can be freely accepted or rejected. From a political perspective, this calls for coalition-building among ethnic groups, peasant organizations, unions, and urban groups. But it also calls for more — for a sharing of common values, a respect for difference, and a willingness to be innovative and creative. One such example is the coalition of groups that successfully elected Taita Floro Tunubalá in 2000 as the first indigenous provincial governor in the history of Cauca and Colombia. The coalition, which included ethnic groups, social movements, peasant organizations, and urban groups, as well as more conservative elements, continued to support the governor during his three years of office.

In an interview, Luz Mery Niquinás, the person in charge of the school in Juan Tama for several years, identified the teachers' major objective as working on interculturalism, identity, and autonomy. Interculturalism can strengthen identity by drawing on ideas from other cultures, and autonomy can provide the political space to make this happen. In short, the practice of interculturalism has potentially radical implications for changing society for the better: "We understand interculturalism as the possibility of dialogue among cultures. *It is a political project which transcends the educational in order in order to think about the construction of societies that are different*" (Bolaños et al. 2004, 119; emphasis added).

Hornberger (2000), based on her research on the intercultural possibilities of bilingual education in Peru and Bolivia, reiterates its creative and revolutionary potential. She tells the story of Julia Pino Quispe, a

Bolivian teacher of English and Quechua, who was assigned to a school in a mining center. On her arrival, she was told to organize the annual celebration of Mother's Day with "dances, funny toys, presents for the mothers, and other activities." But what stood out most vividly in Julia's memory of the event was the way in which one of her students was empowered. This particular student, who had been marginalized by the others because of her peasant background, offered to read a poem in Quechua about someone who had lost her mother and was inconsolable in her grief.

> The poem, of course, made the greatest impression and all were astonished because the form in which she interpreted the poem in Quechua could not have provided more originality nor more sense of life to all those who had the good fortune to be present. After the event, the girl was no longer excluded from any group; on the contrary it served to enable her to value her capacity to be included and it also served as a good example to her classmates. (Hornberger 2000, 191)

Another teacher, Concepción Anta from Peru, told of her experience working in an urban secondary school on the outskirts of the city with students who were poor, using local materials and local natural resources: "What I seek is for all aspects of the student or the person to continue functioning always as an integrated whole . . . where man's lived experience is in conjunction with the life of the animals, the plants, the cliffs, the rivers, the stars, the fields, etc." (192).

For Hornberger, these examples demonstrate the actors' utilization of bricolage, transforming local materials to serve a larger purpose, different from that dictated by social structure. Likewise, this bricolage also contests dominant discourse practices by introducing into the school curriculum language, questions, and content historically excluded. Luykx (1996) makes a similar point in her study of teacher training in Bolivia, arguing that Aymara students use cultural contexts outside of the classroom, such as ceremonial events or student performances, to channel and express their resistance to the dominant ideology. But such resistance is two-edged: while it can be directed against the dominant ideology of the larger society, it can also be directed against the dominant ideology within the indigenous movement. In Juan Tama, the students have learned to be proud of being Nasa, that their culture is dynamic and changing. Though they have learned to appreciate the importance of shamanic knowledge, they have also learned that not all shamans are equally important.

The implementation of the bilingual educational program in Juan Tama has waxed and waned and been the topic of considerable debate and discussion. The teachers, in consultation with CRIC, continued to modify and refine the major components and the specific details based on their experiences in the classroom over the preceding years, combined with suggestions and recommendations from both the parents and the shamans. The plans have also become considerably more detailed and considerably more professional. By 2000, the objective for kindergarten, honed by various commissions, was defined as: "To start the exploration of the relations of interdependence in nature in terms of balance, order, and mutual benefit" (PEB 2000a, n.p.). This was to be explored at various levels, physical and cultural, starting at the level of the individual home and the fireplace, then the house garden, followed by the family plot, and finally the community. In later grades, these levels would be expanded to include the municipality, the region, the province, and finally the nation. It is a Nasa perspective on the world, starting from the inside and steadily and progressively working its way outward. It is also very intercultural, as it expands and progresses from the hearth to the nation.

The educational planning in Juan Tama is radically different from conventional development planning in several ways. It is a process guided by certain clear principles that have to do with children's relationships with their parents, their community, and the larger society, as well as the role of indigenous culture in preparing them for adulthood and citizenship. With its emphasis on interculturalism, the process can sift and winnow ideas from a variety of sources and is not constrained in some philosophical or ideological straightjacket. It is a participatory process in which space and time are there to integrate the voices of all those directly affected by the school. Finally, it is still very much a work in progress, continually being modified, adapted, and changed. For all these reasons, educational planning in Juan Tama is counterdevelopmental.

The Ethnoeducational Center of Tóez Caloto (CET)

While the parents in Juan Tama were interested in their children's education long before the disaster, those in Tóez Caloto only became seriously interested after the disaster, in spite of the fact that they had lived beside a well-respected, well-known vocational high school, established shortly after the end of La Violencia and attended by indigenous students from Tierradentro as well as other parts of Cauca. The disaster totally destroyed the school buildings, and the majority of the teachers, none of whom were local and most of whom were mestizo, chose to accompany the devastated community in its search for new lands. It appears they were motivated partly by a feeling of self-identification with local families since they had all lost everything. When asked why they did this, one teacher, Felipe Morales, responded:

> Well, because I think the ties we had were big and strong because of what we suffered, because what we felt was the same as what those from the community felt, those who lived in the town with us, so we felt that necessity to continue accompanying them here. And since they could help us, as people who were involved in education and they as a group from the community, which had its cabildo and was already a force, then we thought to join this force and continue working here.[7]

The disaster was to serve as a means of bridging the space, cultural and geographic, that had previously separated the teachers from the indigenous community. While land and housing were foremost among the displaced families' priorities, they started talking about building their own school soon after settling on the new lands in 1995, in spite of the fact that schooling was readily available in the nearby town of Caloto. Several factors appear to have played a role in this new interest in education. The presence of a body of committed teachers used to working with indigenous students was certainly one. The fact that the surrounding de-Indianized communities perceived the new arrivals as personifying some elements of Nasaness also played an evolving role. But the changing attitudes of the community leadership was perhaps the most important factor. Jorge Inseca, the leader most responsible for the establishment of the new school that eventually included both primary and secondary, had become involved in the Parent Teacher Association in Tóez before the disaster. He was motivated partly by what he regarded as his own educational shortcomings, but also by the aspirations of his wife, who wished to complete high school, and by their two school-age children. In the process, he became involved in local politics and formed part of the group which, in 1992, managed to elect Abelardo Huetia, also from Tóez, as the first indigenous mayor of the municipality of Páez. This was a major victory, because politics at the municipal level had, until that time, been controlled by mestizos and the traditional political parties. Elected a member of the municipal council, Inseca was able to obtain funds for various projects. By the time of the disaster, he had learned how the local political and administrative system operated and, in the process, how to get things done.

After serving as governor for one year in Tóez Caloto, Inseca decided to dedicate himself to building a school for the community, motivated partly by his embarrassment at the conditions under which education was then being offered. He was also inspired by a vision of the future, a recognition of the chances that they, as parents of schoolchildren, had lost in Tierradentro.

> We need our school in order to favor our education. Education is so important for everything. If there is education for health, then [education] for everything. That's what I say. So as a leader, I aspire to have the school and hope that this school will manage its own curriculum. Let's say we have, for example in our case, [a curriculum] that one wants to manage right now for ethnoeducation, and above all for ecology. You have to give special importance to ecology.[8]

He wanted a school that the community could control, one that could provide the students with skills while at the same time appealing to children from different ethnic and social backgrounds.

> [I] want only development and the school. The problem is there is no leader [here]. That the child should become qualified, that the student should become qualified as a person who can leave for the city and can [also] serve us and perhaps our children. Let's say they can enter to take a leadership position. . . . What one does remains for the children, so I hope that our education is for all those who live near by, be they white, black, mestizo. Whoever wants to become qualified is welcome.[9]

Whereas Inseca proved to be the driving force behind getting the community involved in actively supporting the construction of the school and badgering external agencies for financial support, it was the acting director, Miguel Ángel Achipiz, quieter and more buttoned-down, who, together with some of the other teachers, provided the intellectual leadership. A university graduate, he spoke favorably about his experience teaching in the vocational school in Tóez, where the emphasis was on technical training, public service, and leadership. Although indigenous students were in the majority, there was nothing indigenous about the curriculum, in spite of the fact that there were several indigenous teachers on the staff. According to him, the trauma of the disaster, combined with the first two years of makeshift education in Tóez Caloto, had convinced both parents and community leaders of the need and desire to have their own school with its own curriculum.[10]

Under his leadership, the teachers, in collaboration with the parents and the cabildo, produced the original plans for the new school in the form of three documents: the first for the construction of the buildings (Asociación de Damnificados del Resguardo Indígena de Tóez [ADRIT] 1995), the second for the introduction of a bilingual education program at the primary level (CET 1996), and the third the official project document (CET 1997), which was awarded a prize in 1997 by Ernesto Samper, the president of Colombia.[11] While there is considerable overlap among the three documents, the second is the most interesting because it is the least "official" of the three and contains some interesting ethnographic information. It includes a census conducted in 1995 that indicated that 43 percent of the people spoke only Spanish, 44 percent spoke Spanish and Nasa Yuwe, and 8 percent spoke only Nasa Yuwe (the remaining 5 percent were infants) (CET 1996, 8). Their proposal was motivated partly by the more immediate fear of increasing language loss, but more importantly by their longer term concern that the children growing up in Tóez Caloto were in danger of losing their identity as Nasa, which, like their colleagues in Juan Tama, they summarized in terms of certain characteristics. Although some were more general, such as respect for one's elders, working hard, and condemning laziness and being strong, agile, honest, and faithful, others were more specifically "indigenous." These included exhortations to feel proud of being indigenous; to love, respect, and defend the land; to like working in *mingas;* and to preserve Nasa Yuwe (12).

While this document demonstrates a more spontaneous, participatory, and cultural approach to education and attempts to conserve and strengthen indigenous identity, the first document dealing with the construction of the school relegates these issues to an appendix dealing with the traditions and customs of the Nasa, ostensibly based on "data collected from special people in the community." In spite of this claim to cultural authenticity, the appendix reads just like a textbook. The first section dealing with indigenous government talks about the cabildo, the responsibilities of its members, how the cabildo is elected, and the organization of communal work. Likewise with cultivation techniques, the section starts with land preparation and walks the reader through to harvesting and storage. Also included are descriptions of punishments, such as the *cepo*, as well as descriptions of specialists, such as the shamans, but with no reference whatsoever to their contested role within the community, as reflected in the planning workshops discussed in the previous chapter.[12]

What is striking about the third document, the long-term institutional plan for the school, is the extent to which it attempts to combine and integrate a local-level focus on indigenous identity and values with the larger issues of productivity, citizenship, and nation-building, while in the process pursuing the goal of interculturalism. These concepts are scattered throughout the plan, expressed in the form of various objectives (CET 1997). These include an appreciation of Nasa culture as well as of other cultures, an emphasis on material and scientific advances, and the promotion of a dynamic development process that will promote the integration of Tóez Caloto into the productive sector of the economy. Also important is the achievement of citizenship through creation of a community that "assumes the civic and democratic values of Colombian society." These objectives reflect the reality of Tóez Caloto's present situation: its future and the future of its children are closely tied to the regional economy of Cauca and the modernizing discourse of the Colombian state, factors that will influence the type of identity that its members espouse (Gow and Rappaport 2002). By accepting this discourse, the interculturalism of Tóez Caloto is closer to multiculturalism, with its focus on acceptable differences and civic values. There is nothing here of the interculturalism propounded by Juan Tama and the possibility of organizing society in a different, more realistically participatory way.

The linchpin of cultural recovery in Tóez Caloto was planned to be the widespread use of Nasa Yuwe by the schoolchildren, a desire shared by many indigenous cultures under threat:

> RLS [Reverse Language Shift] appeals to many because it is part of the process of re-establishing local options, local control, local hope and local meaning to life. It basically reveals a humanistic and positive outlook vis-à-vis intragroup life, rather than a mechanistic and fatalistic one. It espouses the right and ability of small cultures to live and to inform life for their own members as well as to contribute thereby to the enrichment of humankind as a whole. (Fishman 1991, 35, cited in Henze and David 1999, 4)

This desire, articulated by the parents on several occasions, was misplaced, because most refused to speak Nasa Yuwe with their children at home. The teachers, on their part, complained that it was very difficult to teach the language virtually from scratch, given the limited amount of time devoted to it in the classroom and the lack of cooperation by the parents at home. Fishman (1999) has emphasized that out-of-school hours and interactions are much more numerous and influential than the in-school hours and interactions. In such a situation, the responsibility for language transmission cannot be abrogated by the parents and totally delegated to the school. It is a guaranteed recipe for failure.

The students themselves had differing views about both their identity and their language, partly determined by age and length of schooling. The older students were less self-consciously Nasa and more interested in the dominant society.[13] One class of sixth-graders had quite clear ideas. There were some twenty-five students, ranging in age from nine to seventeen, with several more boys than girls; all were Nasa, except four who were Afro-Colombian. When asked who they were, they responded they were Nasa; when asked their favorite subject, they responded Nasa Yuwe; and when asked their least favorite, they answered Spanish (though this may have had more to do with the teacher, whom they appeared to dislike, than the language per se). They all intended to continue studying after sixth grade so that they could have a career, and by this they meant some form of off-farm, nonmanual employment. When asked about Tóez, the majority said they had visited the resguardo in Tierradentro and liked what they found there because life was a lot easier. "You plant and things grow. And you can plant whenever you want, whereas here you are much more limited by the seasons." This was an indirect comment on the fact that their families were now fully integrated into a cash economy, that people were continually aware of the need to have money to buy food for the next meal, and that off-farm employment was a necessity if they were to survive. At the same time, however, this nostalgia ignored the economic realities of Tierradentro, with its long history of seasonal and long-term migration. Some of the students said they would like to live in Tierradentro, and others said they would like to live in both places, Tierradentro and Tóez Caloto. A second class of eighth-graders — sixteen students, twelve girls and four boys, ranging in age from fourteen to twenty-seven — when asked who they were identified themselves as students rather than as Nasa and were evenly divided in their preference for Spanish or Nasa Yuwe. When asked why they preferred to study Spanish, they said it would help them speak the language better and make it easier to talk with other Colombians.

One possible explanation for the difference between the two classes, with the sixth-graders demonstrating an apparently stronger Nasa identity, is age. The sixth-graders were considerably younger, and more of their formative years had been spent in Tóez Caloto, where the school and the surrounding de-Indianized Nasa communities strengthened their feeling of Nasaness, something which the community has capitalized on. In contrast, the eighth-graders, the youngest of whom was already eight years old at the time of the disaster, tended to identify more with their peers than their fellow Nasa, a reflection of their earlier years spent in Tierradentro where identity was not an issue.

Another insight into changing student perceptions is provided by public performances. Luykx (1996) suggests that student-produced variety shows, although supervised by teachers, can provide illuminating insights into student humor as well as other aspects of students' ways of viewing the world. Each month during the academic year, the school in Tóez Caloto observes an official ceremony called Raising the Flag, which consists of singing the national and provincial anthems, reciting the pledge of allegiance to the Colombian flag, and presenting performances by the students in the form of poems, short stories, and plays. At one such ceremony in March 2000, a highlight was a series of eight sketches produced by the fourth-graders and their teacher depicting the various regions of Colombia. Each participant wore makeshift regional dress, and each had the opportunity to say a few words into the microphone, a performance that was well received by both students and teachers. This was immediately followed by another act, in which three young girls aged about ten, wearing skirts and tank tops, heavily made

Figure 5. Colombia and its Beauties in Tóez Caloto

up, and each carrying a rose, proceeded to dance under a sign that identified them as "Colombia and Its Beauties" (see figure 5).

The assembled student body hooted and jeered, and the three girls fled. The acting director of the school, a woman, demanded that the students show respect. Once order was restored, the girls returned to continue dancing and shaking their hips, albeit rather self-consciously. The contrast between the two performances, one more folkloric and the other more "modern," was dramatic, as were the very differing responses. While the first played to the school's interests in making the students feel part of a multicultural nation, the second was more visceral and played more directly to the students' interests as young people and their ambivalent feelings about fitting into the multicultural locality where they now lived. Ambivalently, but perhaps successfully, the school was achieving several objectives simultaneously, in ascending order of importance: being indigenous, multicultural, and Colombian.

Juan Tama as Culture Hero or Cultural Artifact?

The story of Juan Tama, culture hero of the Nasa, is well known throughout much of indigenous Cauca, a result of systematic research (Rappaport 1998) and documentation of a widespread oral tradition (CRIC

1996a). Juan Tama is said to have been born in Vitoncó, in the Stream of the Morning Star. Since the shamans had foretold his impending birth, they were waiting for him. After fishing him out of the water, they entrusted him to the care of a virgin nursemaid. So voracious was his appetite that he killed her by sucking her blood. Three more nursemaids met the same fate, as did the cow that replaced them. But with the guidance and council of the shamans and other elders, Juan Tama continued to grow and became a famous leader, responsible for unifying the Nasa against the Spanish and legitimating their authority and autonomy, as well as establishing certain norms and principles that are still quoted today (Guegía Hurtado, Caicedo de Cachimba, and Dorado Zuñiga 1997, 25–26). These are essentially instructions about how to lead a good life and focus on respecting shamanic wisdom, living in harmony with nature, and respecting all forms of life.

At the end of his life, Juan Tama disappeared into a highland lake which is named after him and from whence he can be called by the Nasa should the need arise. Juan Tama Lake is an important pilgrimage site for contemporary Nasa, individuals and families alike, as well as for new cabildo members who go there to be purified and to have their staffs of office "refreshed." But according to the CRIC version of the myth, based on versions provided by the present shamans of Tierradentro, Juan Tama is angry with the behavior of the contemporary Nasa, reflecting a concern expressed in chapter 2, and is scolding his people, at the same time demanding that they change their ways of dealing with each other and with him.

> *What do the shamans think should be done to provide a solution to this situation?*
> According to the thinking and knowledge of the shamans, we must re-cover Nasa memory in order to strengthen the culture and therefore the authority and autonomy characteristic of Páez territory. (CRIC 1996a, 12)

The memory of Juan Tama and what he symbolizes are important for both communities, but the meanings and significance are distinct. For the community named after him, Juan Tama is viewed as a living, guiding presence who provides meaning to everyday existence, as a positive, creative force. In contrast, in Tóez Caloto, Juan Tama is viewed much more critically, as a historical personage whose time has passed, someone who has little to offer contemporary Nasa. These contrasting per-

Figure 6. Mural of Juan Tama (center) holding a scroll depicting key symbols of Nasa culture, the spiral and the crossed staffs of office

ceptions manifested themselves in two public events, a Children's Meeting held in Juan Tama in 1999 and a puppet play about Juan Tama produced a year later in Tóez Caloto.

For the visitor arriving in Juan Tama for the first time, one of the most striking aspects is the colorful murals painted on the outside walls of the Casa del Cabildo (see figure 6), located on a hill which dominates the settlement. The murals, depicting various aspects of Juan Tama's life, were painted by the schoolchildren and their parents under the guidance of the local shamans. At the Children's Meeting organized by the local teachers, the pivotal event was the performance of Don Ángel María Yoinó, the most respected shaman in the community. He told two stories in Nasa Yuwe. The first was funny and somewhat critical of the shamans. A child falls sick and his parents take him to the shaman, who tells them that the only way he can cure their son is for them to slaughter their one and only pig and give it to him. This they dutifully do, and the child is cured. In the second story, Don Ángel recounted part of the myth of Juan Tama, which served as the basis for a whole series of activities undertaken by the schoolchildren from Juan Tama and neighboring communities, including fingerpainting, puppet making, and storytelling.

The most interesting and most creative activity involved a group of ten students, who were hand-picked to work with a couple of volunteers from Cali's Universidad del Valle extension program. These volunteers, teachers themselves, were also musicians, singers, and storytellers in their own right. First, they asked the children what they got out of the Juan Tama story and then used this to put together a sketchy narrative, which the students then acted out. In the story, Juan Tama is associated with water and takes the form of a serpent. As part of the enactment, the students transformed themselves into a snake, a human chain slithering across the grass with each boy holding onto the feet of the boy in front. On the basis of this experience, the students then drew pictures and composed poems about Juan Tama and his exploits and their relevance for his descendants.

The meeting culminated in an impromptu evening concert, attended by the majority of the residents, at which these pictures and poems were on show, arousing a great deal of interest on the part of both children and adults. For example, one picture of Juan Tama was accompanied by the following poem.

> In order that the sun would shine
> So that the earth might be happy
> Juan Tama presented me with:
>> A spring to see the fish
>> A bolt of lighting so as not to be afraid
>> And a star to hear the birds.

While the folk dancing by various student groups also attracted a lot of attention, it was the puppets, built earlier in the day, who brought the house down. At one and the same time, they were funny, critical, and sometimes outrageous. There were five puppets, representing four people and one impressive pig, operated by the teachers and volunteers from Cali. First, there was a monologue in Nasa Yuwe commenting on the day's events, which the audience found very funny. This was followed by a visit from the ghost of one of the mestizo "collaborators" from CRIC who had been unable to attend, offering his excuses and his comments.[14] The final sketch was a reenactment of the pig story told by Don Ángel in the morning in which the gullible family and the rapacious shaman were mercilessly mocked. The child, outrageously dressed in a red-and-white checked nightshirt, shrieked continuously about the pain in his head, his belly, and his penis; the mother was loud-mouthed and abusive, the father obsequious, and the predatory shaman self-consciously pleased at getting his pig. Since there had been little time to practice or rehearse, the performance relied heavily on natural wit and creativity.

At a party later that evening, Don Ángel delivered a passionate, spontaneous speech in Spanish, in which he stoutly defended his pride in being Nasa and the importance of language, history, and culture in maintaining their identity. He referred to both recent historical events and his right to live his life as he saw fit. On another occasion, when asked how his present life in Juan Tama compared with his previous life in Tierradentro, he responded that there was no comparison. "We are in glory here!"

A documentary made of this Children's Meeting and other aspects of daily life in the new settlement, appropriately titled *Being Reborn,* emphasizes the positive role that Don Ángel, among many others, has played in the cultural continuity of the community (PEB/CRIC 2000b). In the documentary, reference is made to the school's *tul,* an extended version of the individual family's house garden. The tul is important not only as a provider of food and medicinal plants but also as a symbol of the Nasa relationship to the land and Mother Earth — one of "harmony and happiness" and, by association, of cultural continuity and long-term sustainability (CRIC 1996b). According to the teachers, the school garden helps integrate the various areas of study, while at the same time it strengthens "a culture, an autonomy to construct their own community education: from an indigenous perspective, with the indigenous community, and for the benefit of indigenous people" (Camayo and Niquinás 1997, 8). For PEB, the tul is also a model of the cosmos, incorporating a variety of intercropped products and animals and their products, as well as the relevant spirits. In this way, the tul simultaneously integrates several key elements, which are practical, educational, cultural, historical, and philosophical. According to the authors of a history of PEB, "Making a tul in the school takes advantage of a vision of the practical that provides continuity between domestic space and school space on the one hand, and, on the other, between the school and the cosmos. All this [learning about plants] is outside the classroom and through experimentation of a space which is similar to [the student's] home"(Bolaños et al. 2004, 114). The tul is a purely Nasa space, interwoven by and generated from the cosmovision. But the school tul is, equally important, a space for intercultural dialogue, where children from other ethnic groups and teachers who are not indigenous can learn by means of Nasa culture and reflect on their own cultures.

In Tóez Caloto, in contrast, there is no tul per se, neither individual nor attached to the school. There are individual house gardens, but they are not tuls. There is a school garden, but its purpose is primarily instrumental: to teach children how to grow crops and to raise animals, as would occur in rural schools throughout Colombia. Furthermore, Tóez Caloto's perceptions of Juan Tama are not only critical but also raise profound questions about his relevance for the contemporary Nasa. In 2000, the community — primarily the schoolchildren, with the teachers, and some of the leaders — wrote a play for puppets entitled *The Owner of the Tall Mountain* in collaboration with William Ruano and Carolina Forgioni, two well-respected mestizo puppeteers from Cali. The local population came up with the ideas and the text, and Ruano and Forgioni helped with building the puppets, the design of the scenery, and the production of the play (Ruano and Forgioni 2000).

In this version of the life of Juan Tama, he disappears into the lake once he has handed down the laws mentioned earlier. With his sudden and unannounced departure, Nasa society begins to disintegrate. At the same time, the *pta'nz* appears ("discord" in Nasa Yuwe, a concept discussed in earlier chapters), a fearsome and filthy spirit, used to hiding in the darkness, who causes all sorts of problems. His first destructive act is to destroy harmony. As a result, there is dissension within the Nasa community, with various groups arguing so strongly over who is more important and more powerful that they decide to form separate cabildos. His second is to destroy the people's beliefs. The pta'nz approaches the leader of one cabildo and tries to persuade him to change his gods if he wants to improve the lives of his people. But the leader responds that he is quite happy with the gods he has and questions the right of the pta'nz to talk to him in this way. The latter then appeals to the leader's vanity.

PTA'NZ: [Calming him down] Good . . . good! It's not necessary that you forget your small gods forever. But . . . you must listen to me, because I am a wise man! I am a messenger from the Great God. All I want to do is to help. Besides, as a leader, the Great God has chosen you.

LEADER: He chose me? And without even knowing me?

PTA'NZ: Yesss! Because the Great God has powers and he's the one who orders all the gods.

LEADER: [To himself] If the Great God orders the others and is more powerful . . . Then he certainly could help! [In a louder voice] I would like to know the Great God, take me to him. (Ruano and Forgioni 2000, 12)

A second leader asks the same question: What do we have to do to better our lives? When the pta'nz tells him they have to learn from others, the leader responds that such a proposal is against the laws handed down by Juan Tama. The leader goes to consult the shaman, but the pta'nz intervenes and neutralizes his powers. The pta'nz then proceeds to congratulate himself on having terminally disrupted Nasa society by weakening two of their major institutions — the shamans and the cabildo — and opening the doors for external intervention and potential control by mestizos.

PTA'NZ: You [the leader] will guide your people with the help of mestizos. With new ideas that teach new crops. You will cultivate and take advantage [of the land] up to the last corner of the mountains and the snowcapped peaks.

The outsiders teach other crops, jor, jor, . . . plant more to gain more, man does not live by bread alone. The mestizo teaches how to make pretty things, pretty clothes and to know other sorts of work and other places. (Ruano and Forgioni 2000, 15)

The final destructive act is the denigration of Nasa Yuwe. The pta'nz convinces the leader that they should forget "that bad old Nasa language," and replace it with other languages so they can read books and understand the truths known only to the mestizos. The damage done, the pta'nz disappears. An old man appears and laments what has happened to the Nasa, as a result of which Mama Kiwe is suffering. The scenery of trees and mountains begins to shake, the lights change color, there is the sound of thunder, and a huge monster covered in scales emerges, the *yu'c ech wala*, the monster who lives in the mountain. Houses are destroyed, and mothers are heard crying. In the final scene, an old man explains what has happened. When the monster saw the Nasa, abandoned and in poverty because they had followed the advice of the pta'nz, and the pain this caused Mama Kiwe, he decided to punish them. They say his anger will continue until the Nasa return to their old lands in Tierradentro. The play concludes with the paradoxical message: "That's why today Tóez lives!" (Ruano and Forgioni 2000, 20).

This conclusion can be interpreted in various ways. One possible reading is that only "pure/authentic" Nasa live in Tierradentro, following the dictates of Juan Tama that the Nasa not fight among themselves and not intermarry with whites. A second possibility is that some Nasa were saved and now live in Tóez Caloto, implying that those who were displaced have been favored over those who chose to remain in Tierradentro. A final possibility is that the Nasa are "returning" to lands long occupied by fellow Nasa. In a sense this is correct, since the Nasa have been living in northern Cauca since the late nineteenth century. As the authors acknowledge, the last part of the play was inspired by a prize-winning short story about the disaster, "The Sixth of June, 1994," written by Hugo Dorado Zuñiga (Guegía Hurtado, Caicedo de Cachimba, and Dorado Zuñiga 1997, 54–55). In the story, the avalanche is the serpent who, like the avenging angel on the day of judgment, destroys everything in his path, except for a mother trying to save her two children from a building that has collapsed and killed her husband. Fearless, she shouts, "Let it come, let the avalanche come, that's it," and the serpent, impressed that her love for her children is greater that her interest in saving her own life, lets her live. But undeterred, the serpent continues on his path of destruction until sated.

> He scrupulously selected the damages and victims in Belalcázar, destroyed all the bridges over the River Páez, drowned more than 1,500 people and finally came to rest in the waters impounded at Betania. *He had defended Nasa territory by frightening the intruders who had hated the Indian from the very beginning and his anger was appeased.* (Guegía Hurtado, Caicedo de Cachimba, and Dorado Zuñiga 1997, 55; emphasis added)

Based on this reading, the conclusion of the play can be read as an acknowledgment of the fact that the Nasa, and the people of Tóez in particular, have been punished for their errant ways, a widely accepted explanation of the disaster, as discussed in chapter 1. But the play itself, taken in its entirety, can also be read as a resounding criticism of Juan Tama and his irrelevance for the contemporary Nasa, as least for those living in northern Cauca.

In a documentary made about creating the play, a process that started in 1996, several community leaders, some of whom played an active role in writing the text and acting in the production, expressed their hope that it would help the community recover what it had lost, while at the same time demonstrating how an indigenous community could survive a natural disaster and deal with the resulting changes (El Grillote 2000). Whether the various audiences who have viewed the play in northern Cauca perceive it in this light is another matter. It was performed various times in Tóez Caloto, which, because of its central location, has now become a popular place for workshops and meetings of various sorts. At one such meeting of governors and council members, it was well received by most (but not all) participants. One exception was Inocencio Ramos, at that time head of PEB, who was highly critical, primarily because he found the play too negative about the state of Nasa culture. He objected to the power enjoyed by the pta'nz at the expense of the shamans who are made to look weak and powerless; he objected to what he regarded as the "disrespect" for Juan Tama and felt the play should have been reviewed by Nasa authorities before being performed publicly; and he objected to the overall theme, particularly when Nasa culture was under threat everywhere.[15]

Given these important differences between Juan Tama and Tóez Caloto, what are the implications for the education of young Nasa and their preparation for the future? Some light is thrown on this question by briefly examining the experience of San José, specifically their fight with local religious authorities to have their children educated and the desire to have their own high school with its own curriculum. There are two schools within the community, one in San José itself, controlled by the Catholic Church based in Belalcázar, and the other in Botatierra, controlled to a certain extent by the community, predominantly evangelical, although the leaders are more influenced by PEB and CRIC than by the Protestant church.

Before the disaster, there were two teachers in the San José school, both paid for by the Church. Since many families left after the disaster, the Church cut back and only supported one teacher. By 2000, however, the number of school-age children had increased to forty-three, too many for one teacher to handle. A request to the Church to provide an additional teacher was rejected on the grounds that this was not their responsibility. An offer of support from PEB was rejected by the "community," in this case by the teacher in charge of the school and his parents, who strongly favored a traditional, Catholic education. The teacher's mother, the daughter of the community leader who had led the displaced families to Cxayu'ce after the disaster, exercised considerable power at the local level.[16] But the elected leadership, in this case the lieutenant governor for the whole community, would not accept this unilateral decision by the teacher and his parents. He continued to badger the Church, pointedly demanding to know if they were prepared to accept the responsibility for denying an education to half the school-age children in the community. At the same time, he solicited the assistance of CRIC, specifically one of its lawyers, who provided the legal basis for requesting Church support. Only when the community threatened to start legal action against the Church did the religious authorities reluctantly capitulate and agree to support a second teacher, one selected by the parents themselves.

Meanwhile in Botatierra, the four teachers there, two of whom worked for PEB and the other two for the province of Cauca, started working with the parents on the preparation of a new curriculum that would replace the existing one provided by the provincial government. As in the case of Juan Tama, it would reflect Nasa values and priorities. At the same time, however, there was a strong move to increase the number of years of schooling available in the community, with the eventual goal of being able to offer a complete secondary education. As in the case of Tóez Caloto, there was already a functioning high school close by in the town of Mosoco, but the younger leaders found this option unappealing. Although the student body was primarily indigenous, the school followed the official curriculum, one which paid little (if any) attention to contemporary indigenous needs, a widespread criticism throughout the province. In addition, the focus of the high school was agriculture, and what, they asked, could it teach the sons and daughters of small farmers? Furthermore, several people indicated that there was very little future for agriculture in San José and only limited potential for livestock. The community had managed to survive since the disaster partly through the increasingly widespread though small-scale cultivation of opium poppies, which, farmers realized, was a bonanza that would not last. Though this had meant that young men no longer needed to migrate in search of seasonal work, it also meant there were a lot more young people around with time on their hands and nothing productive to do. From the perspective of the governor, who was himself a schoolteacher, they would be much better off continuing

161

their education.[17] While the specifics of the proposed curriculum remained unclear, it appeared that as in Juan Tama, culture and interculturalism would be accorded priority.

Education for What?

All three of the new communities are located in areas characterized by
the very real threat of physical violence. The area surrounding Cxayu'ce
is controlled by the National Liberation Army (ELN) and the paramilitaries (see figure 7), that surrounding Juan Tama by the Revolutionary
Armed Forces of Colombia (FARC), and that surrounding Tóez Caloto
is contested by the FARC, the ELN, and the paramilitaries. The last thing
parents want is for their children to join one of the armed groups,
always a possibility since recruiters offer board and lodging, a uniform
and gun, some spending money, and, according to some, the possibility
of a pension. This is why education is so important, but no matter how
good or how bad, education will have little beneficial effect unless there
are employment opportunities for students once they graduate.

While the processes under way in the communities studied have different roots, all have been influenced to a lesser or greater extent by the
attention given to ethnoeducation, in theory a method for teaching in
indigenous communities:

> To train professionals capable of making an impact through strategies of
> education, management, and promotion, who help in the preparation of
> plans, projects and programs for the development of the community or with
> that which it interacts, based on the understanding of the linguistic, cultural
> and historical differences of the distinct groups. (Corrales 1998, 63)

In practice, ethnoeducation programs provide opportunities for rural
teachers, indigenous and mestizo, to obtain a university degree, a process that will help them become more effective teachers. In this way,
ethnoeducation, with its focus on the local, can strengthen indigenous
identity by increasing collective pride and encouraging people to become more involved with their community. At the same time, students
are taught an intercultural approach, how "to integrate critically [ideas]
from the outside without negating their own values" (Becerra 2000).
This is to be achieved by teaching such concepts and topics as cosmovision, myths, rituals, territoriality, diversity, and practices and customs.

Figure 7. ELN graffiti in El Rosario, close to Cxayu'ce: "Because we love life, we fight to the death"

While the PEB program in Juan Tama is an example of this approach in action, CRIC has also worked to "professionalize" many of its teachers who have only a grade school education by helping them obtain their normal school diplomas. Many of those who do succeed have then gone on to pursue their bachelor's degree through CRIC's own ethnoeducation program. There are several other programs under way in the province, some sponsored by the University of Cauca, and others sponsored by the Catholic Church through private, religious universities. Ethnoeducation programs privilege the school and its teachers and begin to make them the center or the focus of life within the community. According to an interview with a teacher in Juan Tama in 1997, "At that time of starting again to reorganize ourselves in the settlement, the school has been like the house where we all meet. From the beginning, the first thing we looked at was what was going to happen with the school, and now a lot of the organizational [activity] is promoted from our school" (Castillo 1998, 138).

A similar process has been under way in certain parts of El Macizo, in the southern part of Cauca, a region characterized by a high level of violence, widespread cultivation of coca, and the bonanza of "easy" money that encouraged nonattendance at school. In the late 1980s local leaders in the municipality of Bolívar, deeply concerned about what was happening to their children, designed an educational and cultural project as a response to these threats. Over time, as more people became involved, the project provided both the space and the context for serious reflection by the community about its own future. Didier Navia, one of the leaders of this process in Lerma and a student of ethnoeducation at the University of Cauca, relates what happened and how people's thinking and actions changed:

> The most important was that people recovered their sense of belonging and identification with the community and its people. What did the people want[?] To directly confront the globalizing model which pulls people out of their local context, which aims to change the thinking of the young. We would like to change the pyramid: not to think from the top down but from the local to the regional to the national. . . . This is how it was, starting with the school and everyday life, how we managed to strengthen values about our own identity. (Corrales and Simmonds 2001, 431–32)

With this thinking as a foundation, the community was able to use the agricultural school as a base for educational activities both within and outside the classroom, as well as a variety of other activities — artistic, cultural, and athletic — something that also holds to a certain extent for the schools discussed here.[18]

With the exception of Cxayu'ce, there is mounting evidence that the other communities cannot or perhaps will not support themselves on the available natural resource base. The most egregious example is Tóez Caloto where, after struggling to obtain potentially productive land, only a few families, primarily the leaders, have taken advantage of the opportunities offered. This has called for significant investment of time and resources that few families appear prepared to make, more for financial than personal reasons since the Nasa are famed for their hard work and industry. The majority has chosen to practice a form of household economy that replicates how they lived in Tierradentro, combining a little agriculture and the raising of livestock with wage labor of various sorts, some of it very unpleasant and physically demanding, such as working as laborers on the neighboring sugar plantations. Young women continue to seek employment in domestic service in the neighboring urban centers of Santander and Cali, and young men to migrate seasonally to harvest coffee, coca, and opium poppies. As in the other two new settlements, some families spend very little time there, and their houses in Tóez Caloto remain shuttered for most of the year.

While the original idea behind the creation of the school in Tóez Caloto was to educate students who would then follow careers that could benefit the community, this only makes sense if there is a vibrant, growing economy that could absorb and provide them with gainful employment. This also assumes that parents will send all their children to school for as long as possible, which has not proven to be the case. The acting director complained that some students were not interested in continuing, sometimes for lack of financial support, and some parents were not interested in having their children continue. In response, some leaders have repeatedly talked of making attendance mandatory. Because there is no way the community can employ all of its own graduates, parents are increasingly asking what purpose all this education will serve, how the community will benefit, and what sorts of jobs they will find on graduation. As one researcher pointedly observes:

> These questions will only be answered when time passes and we can observe the social and cultural life of the resguardo in comparison with today. If cultural resistance today manifests itself through [a form of] education managed by the community, in agreement with their own social and cultural guidelines, that is not static. The educational forms must be constantly revalued according to the guidelines of the state and the resguardo. (Meneses 2000, 75)

In other words, she is discreetly questioning how relevant the education offered is to current needs and how open the school will be to adapting accordingly.

While Tóez Caloto is located less than an hour by road from Cali, it is less than fifteen minutes by bicycle from an industrial park established in 1995 outside Santander, under the Páez Law. The objective of this legislation was to attract national and international investment to the region after the 1994 disaster by offering generous tax breaks. A study conducted by Cauca's Chamber of Commerce five years later argued that the future lay with agroindustry, supported by a more qualified labor force to work in the new enterprises, and a better organized, better trained workforce in rural areas. Furthermore, the report was highly critical of the educational levels of those from northern Cauca who applied for work in the new industries.

Finally, in the selection of candidates whom the companies advance, the low profile of the working competencies shown principally by the young people of the region becomes evident. They presented great gaps in reading and writing, understanding of basic mathematics, oral expression and attitude towards working on a team. To this one should add the lack of knowledge these people show in front of the new realities of the world of work and the new business culture. (Cámara del Comercio del Cauca 2000, 96)

In theory, the law was supposed to benefit those who had been adversely affected by the disaster, but no effort was made to train or employ people who were displaced. In 1999, after a demonstration by the indigenous movement that was reported in the national press, the governor of Cauca mandated the employment of six Nasa, three of them from Tóez Caloto. But there is no indication that the community leadership took any initiative on this or tried to establish some form of ongoing relationship. One young Nasa, Vicente Pinzón, after completing high school in Caloto, did manage to obtain a job there on his own initiative; he sent in his curriculum vitae and waited for a phone call.[19] According to him, employers were looking for high school graduates with some technical training or background, something they would not receive in the school in Tóez Caloto, with its focus on agriculture, livestock, and the environment.

In several conversations and interviews, both Nasa and non-Nasa commented on the difficulty the Nasa have in planning for the medium or longer term, perhaps exacerbated by the importance attached to projects and the need to show quick results, a direct consequence of the one-year tenure of the governor and his council. While it is evident that education does not necessarily fit this pattern — the construction of classrooms does, but the design and implementation of a curriculum does not — how can one effectively and creatively plan in a completely new environment that people are still learning to understand? In such a situation, there is a natural tendency, if not outright temptation, to fall back on the known, on what should be known, whether thinking about history or culture or dealing with work, production, and money. The Nasa also level another criticism at themselves, perhaps more damning, but certainly more paradoxical — that they are scared of new ideas, of doing things wrongly or badly, of being laughed at or ridiculed by others. This comment was made by the lieutenant governor of Tóez

Caloto, a well-respected leader and owner of a small store. Her observation reinforces the comment made by the ex-governor turned economics student regarding the reluctance and outright refusal of the community to seek some effective technical support for assistance with their problems in agriculture. If this is the case, it would explain why Tóez Caloto chose to focus their priorities on education and on being Nasa, while at the same time demonstrating strongly ambivalent feelings about Juan Tama and what he is supposed to stand for.

The economic situation in Juan Tama is more serious because there is less potential for agricultural production, just as there is less unity within the community, yet there is a self-conscious pride in being indigenous. While the same criticisms regarding planning and the acceptance of new ideas may apply in Juan Tama, there is, paradoxically, a more open acceptance of a mestizo education for their children in the neighboring town, just as in Cxayu'ce, in contrast to either Tóez Caloto or San José. Reports indicate that in the early years the mestizo teachers in Santa Leticia worked closely with their counterparts in Juan Tama to achieve a reasonably smooth transition on the part of Nasa students entering the high school for the first time. By 2003, however, Juan Tama was making plans to have its own high school. Unlike in Tóez Caloto, there are few opportunities within the immediate environment of Juan Tama. The most appealing at present is to follow the migratory drift into the adjoining province of Huila, where better land is supposedly readily available.

Cxayu'ce, alone among the three new communities, appears to have developed a viable economy that supports local families. It also has its own school, supported by PEB, but without any of the cultural intensity and aspirations that characterize the others. Like Tóez Caloto, it attracts children from outside the community. Unlike Tóez Caloto, families made a conscious and deliberate effort to befriend their mestizo neighbors and learn from them firsthand about how to do agriculture in their new environment, something they have managed to do successfully. In contrast to Tóez Caloto and Juan Tama, the families have maintained close contact with their community of origin in Tierradentro. Though the children in Cxayu'ce find San José an interesting place to visit, it holds no appeal as a long-term place of residence, a sentiment most likely shared by some but by no means all of the children in the other new settlements. But for the parents in Cxayu'ce, San José still has a strong appeal, for the friends, the lands, the space, the beauty, and the peace. The fact that they now have two worlds in which they can peacefully live is also appealing. But for their children who wish to continue their studies, as some have already done, they will attend the local mestizo high school.

Indigenous Education and Social Inclusion

Although indigenous education has provided local children with an alternative, its most important legacy will be how well it prepares them for their struggle to be recognized as full members of a multicultural society. While the Nasa are not ethnic separatists, they do demand some recognition and acknowledgment of their ethnic distinctiveness on the part of the state. The emphasis on the role of local knowledge — language, history, and culture, as well as a critical appreciation of its relevance for the contemporary context — has provided a crucial basis for the future. But only in the case of Juan Tama can one call this indigenous education counterdevelopmental, a way of resisting the ideological control of the state and proposing a viable alternative to deal with it.

In the case of Tóez Caloto, the tension between indigenous education and counterdevelopment is strongest. The construction of indigenous education has been a deliberate strategy to achieve official recognition by the state, the indigenous movement, and their de-Indianized neighbors. But their "mantle" of indigeneity has not helped them address the economics of development. Their Nasaness has worked against them and, with certain exceptions, they have been unwilling and unable to confront the economic challenges facing them. Their form of counterdevelopment, with its refusal to learn from and cooperate with their neighbors, may well result over the long run in just another community of small farmers dependent on off-farm employment for their survival.

In the case of Cxayu'ce, the people appear to be successfully combining the best of the indigenous and the mestizo. Low-key, nonthreatening, and cooperative, they have made the best of available opportunities. Their school, open to all who wish to enroll their children, and their hard work and willingness to learn have earned them the respect of their neighbors. Having their own school has helped reinforce their identity as Nasa, although this did not necessarily lead to counterdevelopment, except in the form of continued poppy cultivation in San José. Ironically,

Cxayu'ce may have been the most successful of the three communities because it was realistic in its aspirations. As Nasa, they believed and practiced interculturalism and, as a result, experienced few problems with their mestizo neighbors. As displaced people, they took full advantage of all the opportunities that such displacement offered. The community obtained what it had demanded after the disaster: warmer, lower lying lands nearer the capital. This realistic attitude may have its origins in historical factors. San José is a small and geographically isolated community that has successfully retained a traditional ethos. After all, this was the second time within many of the older residents' lifetime that the community had been decimated, first by La Violencia in the 1950s, followed forty years later by the earthquake. This precarious history has been reflected in the community's minor role in the politics of Tierradentro and the activities of the indigenous movement.

Juan Tama is the clearest example of the symbiotic relationship between indigenous education and counterdevelopment, a relationship with direct links to El Cabuyo's educational initiatives in Vitoncó prior to the disaster, where education was already being framed as a political project. While the displaced families, like their neighbors from San José, wanted to be resettled in warmer, lower lying, more accessible land, their large numbers worked against them. As a result, they were resettled on isolated, marginal lands in an area long controlled by the FARC, where the development potential was severely limited. With years of experience resisting and struggling against the Catholic Church in their home resguardo, the resettled families of El Cabuyo continued this struggle against the Nasa Kiwe Corporation (CNK) in Juan Tama, for them the representative of the state and the status quo.

Why CNK would decide to settle them there on such poor land is a question that has never been answered. Did CNK cut a deal with local landowners keen to unload unproductive lands? Was the new community expected to function as a buffer against the guerrillas? Would the geographical isolation temper the community's insistent demands? Whatever the truth of the matter, Juan Tama did not let up in its criticisms of CNK and its policies. Of the three communities, it was the one that resisted most vociferously. It was also the one least influenced by CNK. With little economic potential, the future for their children lay in education, but one firmly rooted in a dynamic appreciation of Nasa culture that would provide the basis for understanding and acceptance by the dominant society. In this way, the practice of interculturalism would make it easier for the children to be accepted on their terms, as Nasa, as students who did not necessarily share all the values of the majority. In this sense the discourse of Juan Tama, though one of resistance and skepticism toward conventional development, can also be viewed as embracing modernity with its promises of pluralism, citizenship, and, most important, a different, but better type of society.

5

I ask the young people to think hard and to fight hard every day
without resting. Let us not forget that the Páez, we always until
now overcame the invaders and this fills us with pride to keep
forging ahead and not to be afraid of death. That is why I ask you
to think and to be brave. If you are really Páez, you must emphasize this value wherever you are; hopefully being indigenous will
not trouble you. Present yourselves as Páez and you will always be
well received.—PADRE ÁLVARO ULCUÉ, quoted in Ezio Roattino, *Álvaro
Ulcué nasa pal: Sangre india para una tierra nueva*

The Nasa of the North and the Tensions of Modernity

The previous two chapters discussed the planning processes in the three
new communities, moving from the general to the more specific, and
demonstrating the differences among the three in terms of priorities,
and their attitudes toward development and modernity. This process
has not occurred in a complete vacuum since there have been other,
longer term projects in Cauca which provide a basis of comparison for
thinking in more general terms about these issues. In this chapter, I
explore the tensions and contradictions encountered by the people of
Toribío, the Nasa of the north, as they consciously create their own
particular, somewhat secular model of development.

In 1998, Toribío was awarded a national prize for producing the best
development plan in Colombia, a culmination of almost two decades of
serious development efforts in the municipality. This plan and its execu-
tion, the Nasa Project, was made possible by Padre Álvaro Ulcué, a
Nasa priest who helped create the project out of a workshop and a
planning document produced in 1980. Following a historical account of
Padre Ulcué's life, I discuss information collected during a workshop
held in Toribío in 1999 as part of a new distance learning degree in
economics and development. The 1980 plan, at least as discourse, is
considerably more radical and more political than the municipal plan

produced eighteen years later, which, to a certain extent, assimilated with the dominant development discourse. In reality, the 1998 plan is more interesting for what it does *not* say, rather than for what it does say. Yet this plan must be understood in the broader and more political context of the ongoing, highly regarded Nasa Project. In other words, there is a marked disjuncture between text and practice. The voices from the workshop, attended by young indigenous leaders from northern Cauca, are more counterdevelopmental and show that thinking about the present and the future integrates the local with the modern, that indigenous modernity can be dynamic, political, and cultural.[1]

An Indigenous Vanguard

The north of Cauca has a long history of political violence, dating from before the time of La Violencia in the 1950s and associated with access to land, political affiliation, and a deteriorating resource base that has resulted in increasing levels of poverty. The violence continues with confrontations among the national military and police, the guerrillas, and the paramilitaries, who are often associated with the military, large landowners, and the drug traffickers. The people of Toribío, a predominantly Nasa municipality in the higher lands overlooking the fertile Cauca Valley with its large cattle ranches and sugar plantations, have always strongly opposed the presence of both the Revolutionary Armed Forces of Colombia (FARC) and the military, resenting the occupation of *resguardo* lands, the assassination of their leaders, the senseless violence and killing, and more recently, the kidnapping of indigenous leaders and the ongoing conflict between the FARC and the state for control of northern Cauca. The region is very poor and produces only 30 percent of its basic food needs, primarily corn, beans, and plantains. Much of the land is given over to small-scale livestock production, and the resulting overgrazing causes serious environmental degradation, as does the clearing of forested areas, which may be used for raising livestock or cultivating coca bushes or opium poppies. This latter activity also competes with the production of food crops on available arable land. Many people are landless or nearly landless and choose to deal with this problem by joining one of the armed groups — the guerrillas, the police, the army, criminal gangs, or the paramilitaries — or by seasonal or permanent migration. Over the years, they have provided the FARC with many recruits.

The people who live in the three resguardos that form the municipality of Toribío, Toribío, San Francisco, and Tacueyó, are regarded by their fellow Nasa as being the most radical, most militant, most political, and best organized group in Cauca — in other words an indigenous vanguard.[2] In the preparation of its prize-winning plan, the municipality received technical assistance from the Association of Indigenous Cabildos of Northern Cauca (ACIN), the regional association of *cabildos,* which was also responsible for producing the final document. Some three hundred pages long, the plan follows a standardized format regarding both structure and content, along the lines described earlier for Tóez Caloto (Municipio de Toribío 1998). The plan consists of nine chapters dealing with topics ranging from health and education to the family and institutional development. Each chapter is structured identically, and the methodology employed follows a linear, logical, modernizing model with its emphasis on describing the present situation, achievements to date, and strengths and weaknesses, concluding with the objectives and expected results. This information is then used to establish priorities, strategies, projects, and a monitoring and evaluation system. This is repeated for each sector. The plan makes for heavy reading, partly because of the standardized format, but also because of what is not treated seriously. History is reduced to a page and a half; culture is included in the chapter dealing with sport and recreation, where it is broadly defined as "all that man has organized or constructed for his existence and understanding between himself and nature" (Municipio de Toribío 1998, 126).

In addition, there is little or no mention of the Nasa Project, which introduced new ways of doing and thinking about development into the area and has served as a model for other Nasa in northern Cauca (1–6). The overall objective of the Nasa Project was to create a new community that would be characterized as "conscientious, united and organized, educated and trained, healthy, happy, without bad habits and without problems, without machine politics [*politiquería*], technified and Christian." This was to be achieved through an integrated approach to development that combined training, education, and consciousness-raising with participation and organization. It included the three components invariably found in development plans: health care, education, and agricultural production. It also included housing and a more radical but not totally unexpected element, evangelization. The motivating spirit behind the whole process would be a Nasa one—participatory, integrated, and liberating—that endures today.

Talking about development texts in general, and development plans in particular, Jonathan Crush (1995) has pointed out that while their structure and form are both stylized and repetitive, the language used, though pedantic and pretentious, is also representational.

> These imagined worlds of development writing and speaking often appear to bear very little resemblance to any common sense reality. To find out about a country, one usually does not read its development plan. In a textual field so laden with evasion, misrepresentation, dissimulation, and just plain humbug, language often seems to be profoundly misleading or, at best, have only limited referential value. (Crush 1995, 4–5)

Toribío's prize-winning plan is no exception, and one can argue that the plan, in fact, does the municipality a great disservice since it flattens and homogenizes what has been a very rich and important historical experience in contemporary indigenous Cauca.

A discussion of the type of plan produced cannot be divorced from the issue of power, since participation in development discourse has come to be seen as "disembedded" from its social, cultural, and political context (Rahnema 1992). Participation, like modernity, is Janus-faced, yet another "resource" to keep the economy alive, so that to participate is to partake in the objectives of the economy. In other words, people are being "empowered" to "participate" in the project of modernity:

> The attempt to empower people through the projects envisaged and implemented by the practitioners of the new orthodoxy is always an attempt, however benevolent, to reshape the personhood of the participants. It is in this sense that we argue that "empowerment" is tantamount to what Foucault calls subjection. (Rahnema 1992, 182)

But this is only partially correct, since it denies a role for human agency. In the process of participatory planning, David Mosse (2001) forcefully argues that there is collusion between the "experts" and the locals. While outsiders' agendas may strongly influence local choices, they do not determine the final selections.

> Arguably, through participatory learning, it is farmers who acquire new "planning knowledge" and learn how to manipulate it, rather than professionals who acquire local perspectives . . . People themselves actively concur in the process of problem definition and planning, manipulating authorized interpretations to serve their own interests. (Mosse 2001, 21)

Collusion between experts and locals is a consequence of subalterity. When Gayatri Spivak (1988) asks whether the subaltern can speak, she is also asking whether the subaltern can plan, questioning the extent to which he or she can speak on behalf of a whole grouping or class. Subalterns who do this effectively are organic intellectuals, "spokespersons for subalterity [who] are taken as token subalterns" (Spivak 1996, 292). As intellectuals, they are no longer subalterns. If they are heard, they are heard on "our" terms, not theirs. For Spivak, then, the subaltern *cannot* plan because in the process he or she stops being subaltern. But what if those locals who speak and plan are seriously and genuinely interested in being heard on "our" terms, while fully aware that the priorities they endorse are only part of *their* model of modernity? These questions will be addressed in the sections that follow.

Padre Ulcué: Nasa, Activist, and Martyr

In November 1984, Padre Álvaro Ulcué, a Nasa, activist, and parish priest in Toribío, was killed by two hired assassins. With the support of the Missionary Sisters of Mother Laura, a Colombian order of nuns, and the Consolata Fathers, a religious order based in Italy, Padre Ulcué had helped create what became the Nasa Project. Over the years, although he was by no means the first leader to be assassinated, he was to become a martyr to the cause of indigenous dignity and justice, immortalized by the progressive Catholic Church as well as by the political left in Cauca. For Padre Ezio Roattino, a Consolata who worked closely with Padre Ulcué and worked in Toribío for many years, he was first and foremost a priest whose religious vocation justified his struggle for social justice on behalf of the Nasa: "Father Álvaro felt very deeply that he was a son of the Church, a militant son. His criticisms were born out of his love for the poor, who are the promised Land of the Church. He wanted a Church that was faithful, committed, and missionary" (Roattino 1986, 55). While bearing witness on behalf of the poor was important, equally important (if not more so) was his Catholicism, his faith in the Catholic Church, and his efforts to convince local people to accept the word of God. For Roattino, Padre Ulcué was both prophet and martyr, his model St. John the Baptist, the patron saint of Toribío, characterized by his poverty and courage: "Nobody bought him with either money or threats. He was the servant of nobody, only of the Word of God. He loved justice and truth more than his own life" (Roattino 1986, 99–100).

For the Regional Indigenous Council of Cauca (CRIC), Padre Ulcué was and still is first and foremost a Nasa who struggled on their behalf and who, on account of his public stands against abuses committed by the state and the local landowners, was murdered. The fact that he was a priest is incidental. Shortly after his death, his followers placed a stone in the place where he died, with the following words of remembrance: "Indian, companion, and priest, assassinated here on the 10th of November, 1984. We have to return here as if you were still here, brother. Know that our struggle on earth will continue" (Roattino 1986, 89). Padre Ulcué was parish priest in Toribío from 1977 until his death.[3] From the time of his arrival there, he made a deliberate and conscious effort to better understand the realities of his parishioners' daily lives. This was achieved through the creation of a group of community animators whose principal responsibility was that of evangelization, in the process of which they were confronted by numerous examples of social injustice in the form of fraud, swindles, physical abuse, personal damages, and threats. The response of Padre Ulcué and the Laurita Sisters was to seek redress from those responsible. Although the latter did not respond directly, in 1979 the criticisms, slanders, and threats against Padre Ulcué began.

On the basis of this experience and his analysis of the situation, Padre Ulcué outlined a series of objectives for his pastoral team in which he incorporated cultural, political, and religious themes. Among the more innovative and threatening were the following:

— Awaken the indigenous conscience in such a way that they themselves are the builders of their own history, through making their own decisions.
— Banish the paternalism that immobilizes and makes life difficult for those who suffer it by making them feel inferior.
— Displace the intermediaries who cheat the Indians and in this way prevent their manipulation.

— Make the Indian feel directly responsible for the construction of a new Church through dialogue and participatory interaction. (Beltrán and Mejía 1989, 154–55)

In this way, he began to articulate and fight for the rights of indigenous people. As a Nasa himself, Padre Ulcué was deeply offended by the practice of paternalism and all its insidious ramifications, since this was a way of belittling people, of denying them their potential as human beings and as political actors. When indigenous people were provided for without having to work, they were being told they were incapable; when they were called "poor little ones" (*pobrecitos*), this was a way of rejecting them, of telling them they were second-class (Beltrán and Mejía 1989, 188).

As the pressures and threats increased against him, the cabildo of Toribío wrote a letter in 1981 to the archbishop in Popayán expressing their concern and support for the work undertaken by Padre Ulcué and the Lauritas. The cabildo also strongly denied the accusations made against them by the local elites, particularly those who were members of Agape, a conservative evangelical group active in the area.

> The rich [local elites] do not understand us, this change that we have started and that is why they hate him, because they do not like to live in this way [he proposes], and it is their money that prevents [the possibility] of some people uniting with others and sharing what they have, and those who know from teaching those who don't, this is what made the parish priest an obstacle for the elites of this region and that's why they reject him and that's why they slander him [saying] that the Padre is a communist, that he is a subversive and even try to kill him, but it's because they do not understand the light of the Gospel. (Beltrán and Mejía 1989, 205)

Padre Ulcué's close identification with the poor enraged the local elites, and he was labeled a communist. This letter was followed shortly afterward by a communication from the three resguardos in which they publicly denounced two local landowners who were threatening the lives of the priest and the nuns. It appears that the landowners were incensed by the social development activities in education, cooperatives, and health that the Church had undertaken, as well as by the fact that CRIC had held its Sixth Assembly in Toribío, right under their very noses.[4]

The landowners appealed directly to the archbishop in Popayán and also pressured the mayor of Toribío to call a meeting of all those most directly involved, including Padre Ulcué, the sisters, the resguardo governors, those in charge of the army and the police, and themselves, the landowners. The meeting was supposed to address the problems of land tenure and public order. When his turn came to speak, Padre Ulcué insisted on reading a copy of the document that the landowners had sent to his superiors, encouraged by the presence of many of those who had signed it. When the landowners attempted to leave, one of the sisters implored, "If you signed the petition, what do you have to fear? We simply ask you to substantiate each one of the accusations that you directed to the Archbishop, without forgetting that clarity and truth support friendship" (Beltrán and Mejía 1989, 207). Though the landowners could offer no proof, the reading of the document did reveal the tactics they practiced to undermine indigenous support in the region, principally slander, defamation, and cooption. Attached to the petition were the signatures of local indigenous people to whom the landowners had promised a little land in return for denouncing Padre Ulcué. Receiving no response, Padre Ulcué explained to those present why he and his pastoral team advised the local people to avoid working for whites who would exploit them and not pay them a reasonable wage. For the same reasons, he advised them not to choose whites as godparents for their children.

Such outspoken behavior did not go unpunished. Early the following year, four of Padre Ulcué's family members were killed and both his parents wounded by the police as they attempted to forcibly remove the participants in a land recovery action close to his home resguardo of Pueblo Nuevo. Both the indigenous people and Christian groups in Cauca and neighboring provinces denounced the government's escalating wave of violence and the persecution of Padre Ulcué. Later that year, when Belisario Betancur assumed the presidency of Colombia, Padre Ulcué and his companions addressed a long letter to him in which they detailed the problems of indigenous people in northern Cauca, and appealed for justice.

> We pray that you hear the desperate, anguished call we make to you, as the voice of those who have no voice, because they are not listened to and when they demand justice, they are unjustly silenced. Only God asks this commitment from you. You in all conscience will know what attitude to take

before him, by means of the indigenous Páez people, regarding this social, human problem which we have quickly laid out for you. (Beltrán and Mejía 1989, 211)

They never received a response. The violence continued, and Padre Ulcué continued to speak out and criticize the abuses perpetuated by the state and the landowners. In November 1984, he was killed by two hired assassins in Santander (see figure 8). His indigenous friends and followers transported his coffin to his home resguardo of Pueblo Nuevo, and the archbishop, accompanied by seventy-five priests, officiated at his burial mass. The presence of both the police and the military was forbidden, and the indigenous authorities were responsible for maintaining law and order through their own civic guard (237). But his death only temporarily slowed down the process of mobilization in the north.[5]

The 1980 Workshop of Padre Ulcué

The 1980 planning workshop gave birth to the Nasa Project, an ambitious program of community development that continues to this day and has served as a model for other resguardos in the north. This workshop lasted a week, and some 150 community members participated.[6] The document that resulted consists of two parts, a report on the actual workshop, some sixty pages long, and a shorter report, twelve pages long, on a planning workshop held earlier. The longer document, the focus of my analysis here, is presented as a cryptic, literal transcription of points discussed in group sessions and observations made during the plenary sessions, a format that is still followed in workshop reports today (Ulcué, Mejía, and Florez 1980). The most interesting part of the proceedings occurred when the participants were divided into three larger groups to discuss the theme "The Nasa Community We Want." The three groups met separately and then reported back to the whole workshop. All three presentations were accompanied by powerful line drawings which were used to stimulate discussion and debate.

In the first drawing, the participants were presented with a densely populated map of the municipality, depicting a variety of activities under way, ranging from agriculture and livestock to dance and music. In the lower left-hand corner, there is an ugly potbellied politician, ignored

Figure 8. Memorial plaque to Padre Ulcué in the church of Toribío: "Reverend Nasa priest / Let us be neither ashamed nor fearful of being Indians / Let us fight for our rights, Alvaro / November 10, 1984 / Indigenous council of Toribío"

and left to his own devices and in the upper right-hand corner, the socially undesirable are being evicted, specifically the military and the members of Agape, the religious proselytizers. Comments from the participants clarify what is happening in the picture. The underlying motif is one of union, of people working together, motivated partly by the church, but also by a more proactive cabildo: "The Agricultural Institute appears and people have been trained. The cabildo concerns itself with the training of the people, the construction of health centers and the preparation of health monitors" (Ulcué et al. 1980, 44). From commentaries such as these, it appears that the large building in the center of the picture represents the cabildo, and the cabildo holds the community together, although the church, rendered here significantly smaller than the Casa del Cabildo, is also accorded an important role. The priority accorded the cabildo is reflected in the explanation provided by the group that prepared the drawing: the creation of a community that is united under a responsible cabildo, a community that is also hardworking and will build on existing organizational structures. The characteristics of "united" and "hardworking" come accompanied by a list of other desirable characteristics, a combination of the personal and the collective, such as happy, healthy, honorable, trained, safe, and Christian. These states are to be achieved through the provision of certain amenities and services presently lacking: happiness through recreational centers; training through schools, workshops, and institutes; and Christianity through evangelization.

The drawing presented by the second group, the one most acceptable to the workshop as a whole, was very different—less natural and more metaphorical. It is dominated by an outstretched left hand emerging from what appears to be a volcano. Arrows connect each of the fingers to specific scenes: a rising sun with a book, presumably a Bible, in the foreground, and a cross in the background; a sick man in bed being attended by a nurse; a unified family contained within the outline of a heart; a couple and their simple house, with the woman standing in front and the man behind; and a productive parcel of land. In the lower center, a group of people are working together. For the most part, the participants' comments tend to state the obvious: the importance of having a Bible in the house to study; that a united community can exploit all its resources; the presence of harmony and love in the family. But the final two comments are different, and more political (Ulcué et al. 1980, 48): "The hand has broken the chain," referring to the desire to break the chain of exploitation and repression discussed in the earlier sessions; and "He who works always has something," emphasizing the importance of work and receiving adequate compensation for that work, a priority raised by the first group in a social rather than an economic context, which is more the meaning implied here.

These themes are elaborated in the explanation provided by the group discussion, which starts with the provocative statement that "the hand has loosened the chain of slavery: we have managed to unite and from this we have dedicated ourselves to work that we controlled" (Ulcué et al. 1980, 48). These activities are explained in relation to the five fingers. The thumb, as the finger that can touch and influence all the others, symbolizes knowledge, both secular (the illuminating rays of the sun) and religious (the Bible with the cross in the background). With the index finger, the emphasis is more practical: the importance of training (the nurse), of having institutions that will provide support so that people can lead healthy lives (the patient is lying in a hospital bed). With the middle finger, the focus is moral: the need for people to change and to stop being so selfish, the importance of good behavior, dialogue, and education in the home, particularly where the children are concerned, and the value of a providing a good example that demonstrates love. With the remaining two fingers, the focus is eminently practical: with the ring finger, the importance of building tidy, comfortable, healthy houses that will last; and, with the little finger, an emphasis on the material wherewithal that will make all this possible, that is, ways to improve the local system of production through the introduction of improved techniques for agriculture, animal husbandry, and natural resource management.

The third and final group chose to focus on unity and peace. Their drawing shows men, women, and children assembling, shaking hands, and being friendly to each other against the backdrop of a large building, roofed with tiles. The comments from the general assembly are more specific:

> Everyone attends the assembly and the governor comes out to greet them. There's strength in numbers.
>
> If we are all united we can build a house like that of the community business. (Ulcué et al. 1980, 50)

But when the group that had prepared the drawing explained to the workshop what they wished to convey, they chose to present it in terms of moral abstractions, such as peace, justice, tranquility, home, and desirable collective characteristics, such as united, happy, and honorable.

While the three drawings are quite distinct, the responses provoked and the explanations offered tend to complement each other and offer a vision of how people in Toribío viewed their future in 1980 and what Padre Ulcué and the nuns regarded as the key components of the process of evangelization that they espoused. A few general observations are in order. There is a strong moral element, ostensibly Christian, but embodying values and priorities that are quite independent of organized religion, that individually and collectively can contribute toward the achievement of social and political harmony. Based on the information provided earlier in the workshop, the participants were angry and frustrated about many aspects of their daily lives. In fact, it is difficult to find any aspects about which they felt positively. Their vision of the future tries to compensate for this, not only on the moral plane but also on the material, specifically the economic, perhaps the Achilles' heel of indigenous society in Cauca.

But the vision is also realistic. In spite of the call for people to free themselves from the chains of slavery and the numerous incidents cited where people had been exploited, abused, and murdered, the tone is generally conciliatory. With the exception of the call for removing the military, there are few references to the state and its role in the past, present, or future. In spite of clearly identified structural constraints, the sentiment expressed by the workshop participants is that these issues have to be addressed internally and it is the responsibility of the people themselves to begin the process of resolving them. Hence there is a strong emphasis on agency.

Equally striking is the fact that there are almost no references to the Nasa as Nasa, apart from passing mention of the problem some participants had in understanding Spanish. For all intents and purposes, the workshop is presented as addressing the concerns of peasants, in essence, small farmers and agricultural laborers, who incidentally happen to be Nasa. The fact that they are indigenous is not accorded any importance. In fact, it is hardly mentioned, but when it is, the discussion is ambivalent, as if the people themselves were ambivalent about their indigenous roots. In one of the sessions, a group discussed bilingual education and in their presentation, rather than present a picture, they chose to present a short sketch.

> Four people, who only speak Spanish, get together to talk about the city and the countryside. Some prefer city life and others the country. Soon an indigenous person who only speaks Páez appears and asks for help because he was sick. Nobody understood him until after a long time they understood that his head was hurting and they gave him an aspirin. Afterwards, the person who spoke only Páez, looks for lodging because it was already very late. As nobody understood him, he had to go away into the woods to sleep like the rabbits. (Ulcué et al. 1980, 33)

At first sight, this would appear to be a story directed against indigenous people, because the Páez (Nasa Yuwe) speaker suffers most, supposedly for his inability to speak Spanish. Another reading would see this as a critique of the four Spanish speakers, who are presumably indigenous but cannot or will not speak Páez. These differing perspectives

Figure 9. The principles underlying the Nasa Project: "Progreso [progress] / Regocijo [delight] / Orden [order] / Yo-nosotros [I-we] / Esperanza [hope] / Camino [way] / Tolerancia [tolerance] / Oportunidad [opportunity] / Naturaleza [nature] / Apoyo [help] / Solidaridad [solidarity] / Alianza [alliance]"

were captured in the comments offered by the group. For some, it was a shame that indigenous people no longer spoke Páez—they should not be ashamed of being Páez and speaking their language in town or anywhere else. For others, the parents were responsible for not teaching their children Páez or for criticizing them when they did. Most revealing was the first remark made by the group: "[The sketch] that had just been presented was very serious and not to be laughed at" (Ulcué et al. 1980, 33). These ambivalent attitudes toward language and being indigenous are precursors to identical debates and discussions twenty years later in Tóez Caloto. But the workshop's focus on certain moral values, as well as human agency, has much more in common with the discourse of Juan Tama. However, the philosophical basis for each approach is quite distinct—progressive Catholicism in Toribío and Nasa cosmovision in Juan Tama. In 1980, then, Toribío was slowly but surely becoming less indigenous, while at the same time collectively taking a stand in favor of a better, more just society.

The results of this workshop were used to establish the Nasa Project, perhaps the oldest, certainly the most famous indigenous development program in Cauca, in which local people, external donors, and the Consolata Fathers have all played continuing and important roles.[7] As mentioned earlier, the overall objective was to create a new community that would be united, trained, technified, and Christian (see figure 9). The first and most important component is consciousness-raising through education and training, and this is pursued primarily through the Center for Education, Training, and Research for the Integrated Development of Communities (CECIDIC). CECIDIC is essentially a local response to the shortcomings in the local educational system, one that historically has done little or nothing to prepare indigenous youth for living productively in their own resguardos. The 1980 workshop discussed many of the educational shortcomings in the region, including the presence of poorly trained, poorly motivated teachers on the one hand, and parents' ambivalent feelings about education on the other. Very few children attended school because they did not think education was important. Furthermore, in the past the landowners said that indigenous people were stupid and therefore should not study (Ulcué et al. 1980, 31–32).

CECIDIC's principal objective is to provide formal and informal educational opportunities to the area as a whole, and this includes families, groups, resguardos, primary schools, and high schools. It is a community space offering educational opportunities for all members. According to Toribío's 1998 development plan:

> It is not only a space for children and young people, it is also a space for the community. It breaks with the old schemes about education being "solely for children and young people," with "a fixed schedule and rules," with "teachers and pupils," in order to create a "vital or existential space," an "integrated educational process," a "community space," that is to say, a full-time community education. (Municipio de Toribío 1998, 60)

Functioning since 1995, CECIDIC cooperates with the local high school as well as offering more practical training in communications, agroforestry, organic farming, fish farming, and smallstock. There is a strong focus on teaching people to better utilize local resources in a sustainable manner. The center, with its impressive infrastructure, also serves as a focal point for a variety of meetings, workshops, and seminars that are held throughout the year. In addition, it is the locus for three distance learning degrees, two offered through the Universidad Pontificia Bolivariana in Medellín, one in social sciences and anthropology and the other in economics and development, and a third in ethnoeducation through the University of Cauca.

The second component of CECIDIC's work is community participation and organization with the objective of actively involving the whole community, not just the leaders. This has led to the creation of youth groups, women's groups, and family groups. The level of participation is impressive. The annual general meeting of the Nasa Project is held there, attracting up to 1,500 people, and this has become one of the defining characteristics of the north: the ability to feed, lodge, and mobilize large numbers of people. The separate meetings held in the three member resguardos to discuss the 1998 development plan each attracted an average of nine hundred community members. This approach has also strengthened local capacity to resist the incursions and abuses of the various armed groups operating in the area. According to local leader Arquimedes Vitonás,

> That conception of leadership and the management of power as a service is a characteristic of Toribío, of Jambaló [a neighboring municipality with its own equivalent of the Nasa Project, the Global Project], of the north of Cauca, [and it] is not so easy for others to accept because in other indige-

nous communities there is authoritarianism on the part of the leader, here it has indeed changed. I think this is one of the things that makes the Nasa Project unique. (Hernández Delgado 2004, 127)

The final component includes various types of environmentally friendly production projects, including a communal fish farming one that produces fish for the community and the children, as well as for the market.

The 1999 Workshop in Toribío

Education at all levels has received the highest priority in Toribío, with increasing emphasis on higher education in the form of distance learning programs sponsored by universities in Antioquia and Cauca. In 1999, CECIDIC organized a series of workshops as part of an introductory course to a new bachelor's degree in economics and development, offered through the Universidad Pontificia Bolivariana in Medellín, and these provided an opportunity to discuss with young indigenous leaders their views about development and the future of their communities. Their views could then be compared with those expressed in the 1998 municipal plan, as well as with those expressed twenty years earlier in Padre Ulcué's workshop. At the workshop in question, the sixty participating students, predominantly Nasa, came from seventeen different resguardos situated in the northern and central parts of the province. They were selected by their respective cabildos on the basis of their experience and leadership potential, with the understanding that they would actively continue to contribute to the progress of their home communities. This particular week-long workshop was the conclusion to an introductory course in economic development, and my role was to discuss my ideas and experiences about development and development planning in Colombia and elsewhere. During the course of our discussions, I raised certain questions about the cabildo and the role of women, issues raised in the 1980 workshop but barely mentioned in the 1998 Development Plan, as well as eliciting participants' views on development, culture, and the relationship between the two (see figure 10). The questions on the cabildo came directly from some earlier work undertaken by Adonías Perdomo, a Nasa intellectual and research colleague introduced in chapter 2, and his colleagues (Escuela de Pensamiento Nasa n.d.).

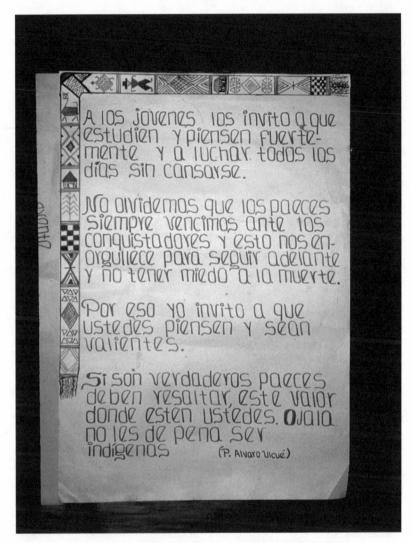

Figure 10. A workshop wall poster with quotations from Padre Ulcué: "I invite the young people to study and think intensively every day without getting tired"; "Do not let us forget that the Páez always overcame the [Spanish] conquerors and this fills us with pride to keep forging ahead and not to fear death"; "That is why I ask you to think and to be brave"; "If you are real Páez you must emphasize this bravery wherever you are. I hope it does not trouble you to be indigenous"

In the 1980 workshop, cabildo members were roundly criticized for their drunkenness, corruption, sale of communal lands, machine politics, and for serving the interests of the large landowners. From the comments offered in the 1980 report, it is evident that the cabildo had little legitimate authority and enjoyed even less respect on the part of the population at large. The Community Action Committee, a community development initiative established by the national government in the 1970s, fared little better. It was viewed as a paternalistic organization whose leaders were just waiting for assistance from the state, an ominous precursor of things to come. Community enterprises and cooperatives fared a little better, since they were viewed as having some potential for improving the local situation (Ulcué et al. 1980, 10–18).

In general terms, the cabildo as institution, one of the defining characteristics of indigenous society, has, at least until recently, proved to be weak and rather ineffective, a perspective widely shared by indigenous society (Perdomo 2005). If anything, the situation has worsened over the past twenty years. Never a strong institution to begin with, it is now saddled with additional responsibilities, the result of the 1991 Constitution on the one hand, and the decentralization policy of the national government on the other. In preparing their development plan in the mid-1990s, the people of Vitoncó, the heartland of Nasa culture in Tierradentro, criticized their cabildo for its top-down, nonparticipatory, secretive approach to decision making and the allocation of community resources such as *transferencias* (FST 1995b). More recently, however, the situation has begun to improve, due partly to the support received from CRIC and the various subregional associations of cabildos.

In the 1999 workshop, there were three questions posed about the cabildo. In the first, groups were asked about the most common difficulties encountered in the internal organization. One major difficulty they identified was the lack of structure and a clear understanding of the duties and responsibilities of the respective council members. There is no such thing as an operating manual for the cabildo and no clearly defined criteria for the selection of the governor and his or her council members. Hence, the governor must rely on precedence, oral tradition, advice from the elders of the community, and personal whims. Expected to lead, he is criticized for not delegating, but he does not have the authority to do so and, even if he had, the community, often singled out for not supporting the cabildo, would not allow it.

This type of structure is inadequate for dealing with the growing demands and complexities of local leadership and responsibility. As the cabildo wrestles with the problem of administering customary law, it is increasingly obliged to venture into uncharted and untested waters: implementation of the existing system of customary law may be incompatible with national legislation and may conflict with people's constitutional rights as Colombian citizens, as discussed in chapter 3. As a result, those elected to office are usually younger and better educated than their predecessors, but often with little administrative or political experience, a reality that does not sit well with the elders.

The second question put to the workshop focused on the most difficult decisions the cabildo has to make. The answers provided dramatically capture the dangers, complexities, and ambiguities of daily life in contemporary Nasa society, at least in northern Cauca:

> The factor of armed groups, whether the guerrillas, the narcos [drug traffickers], the army. Because fundamentally they do not recognize the authority of the cabildo, and think that the solution is using arms.
>
> Decisions involving problems with the shamans.
>
> Making decisions involving the eradication of illegal crops.
>
> Redistribution of resguardo lands.

Whereas the problems of violence in 1980 were restricted primarily to the military and the landowners, they have now become more pervasive and involve more groups. Underlying the comments at the 1980 workshop was the realization that land was an increasingly scarce commodity (as it still is), that some people were prepared to fight for and others just wished to sell, but that access to land was often accompanied by violence.

> When the Indians return to the countryside, they proceed to look for lands which they do not find because the large landowners have taken them. So the companions who return invade the land of their companions and steal. Other times they invade the land in the hands of the large landowners without being too clear [i.e., thinking through the implications] and that's why the repression comes which they are unable to defend themselves against. (Ulcué et al. 1980, 22)

The group discussing cooperatives in 1980 took advantage of the opportunity to criticize the local landowners for killing one of their leaders: "The leader of the cooperative was assassinated in a despicable way by hired killers [*pájaros* — literally "birds"] paid by the large land-owners: we are talking about Compañero Abelino Ul" (Ulcué et al. 1980, 16). This was accompanied by a gruesome drawing showing the bird-like pájaro with a shotgun in his hands, blowing the brains out of the indigenous leader quietly snoozing under a tree, while a pool of blood collects by his body and slowly flows downhill toward his house. The landowners were seen as collaborating closely with the army, and it is the military that came in for the strongest condemnation for their acts of robbery, torture, abuse, and imprisonment. The army was seen as being opposed to the poor in general, be they indigenous people, peasants, students, or workers:

> Another Indian testified: "One time they arrived and surrounded my house. Then they entered and asked us where the arms were but I told them I didn't know about any arms and that I was simply an indigenous person who dedicated himself to working the land. So, what more can we poor peasants do to obtain our daily bread?" (Ulcué et al. 1980, 24)

The current cabildos' relationships with armed groups are delicate, none more so than with the guerrillas. The question that is often asked of cabildos is whether they are with the guerrillas or with the government, in many ways a no-win situation. Increasingly, however, the cabildos have taken a stronger stand against the guerrillas and violence in general. This does not mean that they are opposed to what the guerrillas are struggling for, or at least the principles the guerrillas were originally fighting for. Rather, they are against the increased level of violence, potential or actual, that guerrilla activities entail, including the responses of the state, whether retaliatory or preemptive. They are also against the increasing encroachment of the guerrillas on resguardo lands and cabildo autonomy, as well as the forced drafting of their children, both young men and young women, by the guerrillas. Above all, like the vast majority of Colombians, they desire peace.

In March 1999, the cabildos of northern Cauca issued a document in which they clearly repudiated the activities of the armed groups in the region and argued strongly in favor of the peace process.[8]

> In the past and even in the present, we are victims of a war that is not ours, we do not understand it nor do we support it whatever its justifications. We

suffer the consequences of hunger, the lack of education, health and whole-some pastimes, channels of communication, etc. [All] as a result of the government's internal and external policies. We are accused of belonging to the guerrillas, to the army, to the drug traffickers and now to the paramilitary groups. (Cabildos Indígenas del Norte et al. 1998, 1)[9]

Accordingly, they threatened to expel any community member who voluntarily chose to join an armed group, broadly defined to include the army, the police, the guerrillas, and the paramilitary. The impression given by the workshop participants, however, many of whom were prime membership material for these groups, is that this position is too extreme. They argued that some cabildos enjoy more autonomy and do not feel threatened; some maintain a symbiotic relationship with the guerrillas, of mutual benefit to both parties; and others do feel threatened, usually a result of the permanent presence of guerrillas in the region.

But with the issue of illegal crops, specifically the cultivation of coca, marijuana, and opium poppies, students were more willing to talk, in spite of their leaders' condemnation of this activity on account of its alarming and corrosive social effects. According to the same document,

> We are not in agreement with drug production and drug dealing, because it brings the communities many problems, pushes up the price of local food, weapons arrive, some people are brought down by money, clubs and bars spread, the young believe that this is the only way, there are killings over business deals that have gone wrong.
>
> We do not allow the rental of land for illegal crops, any community member who does either [i.e., rent or cultivate] will lose his land and it will be given to other community members to work for the benefit of the community. (Cabildos Indígenas del Norte et al. 1998, 2)

Reference has already been made to the disruptive social effects that result from such production: increasing levels of violence, consumption of alcohol, and criminal acts, accompanied by decreases in communal participation and food production (Gómez and Ruíz 1997). A collection of indigenous and peasant testimonies on illegal crops, including the opinions of both the Nasa and the Guambiano, expresses some moral concerns: What sort of example are those who produce illegal crops providing their own children (Samper 2000)?

As in other parts of Cauca, the major rationale is financial. According to one student, it is an easier, but more dangerous way of making money: "You pay with your life if you don't deliver!" Compared with the banks and government-sponsored credit programs, it offers a quicker, more effective way of obtaining working capital to finance other, more legitimate activities. "I managed to study thanks to coca," said one diligent student. Frustration with the government's failure to keep its promises has also played a role. Students cited an example from the neighboring resguardo of Jambaló where the cabildo took the initiative and encouraged the voluntary manual eradication of illegal crops on the promise of cash payments from the government. But the government failed to deliver, the cabildo lost face, and the people went back to cultivating coca and poppies. They also questioned why the government criticized them for clearing forest and páramo to plant illegal crops, while remaining silent about the increasing deforestation on the Pacific coast. While students are fully aware of the social problems that ensue, including the increasing local consumption of drugs, there is no explicit moral disapproval. Rather, the cultivation of such crops is viewed as an economic alternative and a financial necessity. One commentator has provocatively suggested that there may also be cultural and political factors at work. Drug addiction affects whites, not indigenous people, although this situation is gradually changing (Ruiz 2000).

The third question addressed the issue of why there are so few women elected to the cabildo. In the 1980 workshop, there was a discussion about the education of women and the constraints they had to contend with: the comments were pointed and directed primarily at the parents, and only secondarily at the men.

Why do we have this problem?

Because we still follow the customs of our forefathers in that a woman should not study because her responsibility is the home and to help her husband in the fields.

Parents treat a daughter as something useless. If the parents do not want education for their sons, what chance is there for their daughters?

Machismo is a problem. The drunk husband beats his wife and frightens the children. Amongst the men, some of us are very irresponsible and when we get drunk we do not work, so the women have to go and work. (Ulcué et al. 1980, 37–38)

In the drawing that prompted the discussion, the upper half shows a barefoot woman dressed in traditional clothing, with a hat on her head and a child on her back, working alone in the fields. The lower half consists of three small pictures. In the first, a woman wearing Western dress, with her hair in a ponytail and carrying a purse, announces that she is going to Cali. In the second, a man and a woman wearing traditional dress are fighting. The husband is punching the woman in the mouth, two children are watching, and a third is shedding large tears. In the final picture, there is a woman wearing trousers and a T-shirt announcing that she has arrived from Cali.

There was sympathy expressed for the woman who leaves for Cali, a result of lack of understanding or decent treatment in the home. The same nonjudgmental opinion was expressed about the fighting couple. The woman has returned from Cali with a child by another man: "In the drawing, you can see that the parents are fighting, the children are watching and there is another child to one side who is assuredly the reason for the fight because he has a different father, a fact that is being thrown in the woman's face" (Ulcué et al. 1980, 38). Rather, it is Cali, the city, that was viewed critically, a potentially dangerous place where women could be easily corrupted: "Many women prostitute themselves in the clubs and when they discover they have a child in their stomach they become frightened and go as far as to have an abortion which is a crime against a defenseless child" (Ulcué et al. 1980, 38). Because the city offered few solutions to women's problems, it was a place to avoid. The discussion included testimony from two women who had been to Cali, both of whom had decided to return home. Hence, while there was strong criticism of the way women were treated, there was equally strong criticism of the only solution proposed, escape to the city.

Trying to explain why there were so few women council members in 1999, some of the student groups reiterated the well-known cultural reasons, such as the prevalence of machismo and the belief that a woman's place is primarily in the home, caring for the family. For some, the communities are responsible through their failure to provide opportunities and their reluctance to promote women and their capabilities. Others blamed the women themselves for being indecisive and insecure, apprehensive about assuming such a responsibility. One group blamed both women and men: "Because as women we do not value ourselves and because men are very macho and doubt the capacities of their wives."

At the 1980 workshop, similar justifications were provided for the treatment of women, and sympathy was expressed for their condition. But twenty years later, although women's voices are openly heard and acknowledged, they are now blamed for being part of the problem, and accused of bringing the problem on themselves (Piñacué 2005).

The questions then shifted to the broader area of development and culture. When asked what development meant to them personally, the groups provided a variety of responses, ranging from the pragmatic to the transcendental. For some the emphasis lies in satisfying the basic needs of the community:

> Development is to overcome and to reach goals that satisfy basic needs.
> It is an integral process by which the communities look for how to satisfy necessities in the economic, political, cultural and social aspects.

For others, the focus is on how to satisfy these needs and priorities through planning and analysis.

> To plan and project the future of the community.
> The capacity to analyze and deal with change.
> Analyze, organize and support.

The most interesting groups, however, looked beyond techniques and pragmatics and gave some thought to what sort of society they would like to live in, one in which there is a social balance between people and their environment; where there is strengthened autonomy, unity, organization, and honesty; and where attention is paid to basic principles: "The way to respond to necessities bearing in mind some fundamental principles regarding the moral aspects, both personal and communal."

When asked what Nasa culture consists of, one group took a broad view: it is their way of thinking and acting as shown by their respective beliefs, rites, customs, and practices. Another group integrated this with the commonly accepted characteristics of indigeneity: "It is the way of living, thinking and behaving within a circumscribed area with an identity, a language, and autonomy." Others, paraphrasing CRIC's three-pronged motto of unity, land, and culture, highlighted the fact that Nasa culture is the result of a historical process that differentiates them from others groups, something which has only been achieved through struggle and resistance. To them, culture is "the historical process which identifies and makes one group different from the others, with its principles such as values and cultural beliefs (unity, land, culture and autonomy). It consists in conserving what is theirs — identity — autonomy — territory — language — organization — cosmovision."

When asked what this culture can contribute to the process of development, one group made the following statement in which they implicitly touched on certain concepts, such as balance, nature, and cosmovision, that are key to understanding their ambivalent and perhaps contradictory views about development and modernity: "Nasa culture can contribute to the process of development only when the balance with nature is maintained because the Indian is always very closely tied to the cosmovision." The fact that they have not lived in balance or harmony with nature for some time is well documented. The desire of some to return to this state of grace, if it ever existed, is reinforced by their wish to (re)create their own local economy, the solidarity economy discussed earlier. Students in the workshop acknowledged the importance of economics and the local economy for development in their respective resguardos. But at the same time, they were fully aware that economics could not be studied in isolation, that it could only be understood in the broader political and cultural context. In an earlier workshop, the participants had clearly stated, "Our economy is a dimension of our culture and our life project: that is why it is so closely linked to the political-organizational dimension and the symbolic part (cosmovision). In order to understand the economy we have and the economy we want, it is essential to know and understand our culture" (CECIDIC 1999a, 8). This expression — "the economy we want" — is key to understanding the role that culture can play in development, at least at a conceptual level.

Another workshop, held in April 1999, was devoted to the local economy, and presentations were given on several local projects, all of which were or would soon be communal enterprises of one sort or another (CECIDIC 1999b). CRIC, one of the original proponents of these organizational forms, also gave a presentation. In the 1970s and 1980s much of the land recovered in the north was organized in communal enterprises with their assistance. Historically, such enterprises have not fared well. In the 1980 workshop, the discussions about community action, cooperatives, and the local marble mine underscored their organizational and financial shortcomings, as well as their dependency on external actors.[10] In the CRIC presentation, the organization admitted that its economic programs have proved problematic, partly because it did not understand the internal dynamics of the local economies. But it also reluctantly recognized that such economies can only be understood within their specific context: "For the indigenous communities there exists a concept of globality in their cosmovision which . . . does not allow the economic to be treated as an independent variable, but [rather as one] that is related to other aspects of their life plan. This concept has recently become stronger thanks to the activities organized to rescue cultural aspects, though obviously not without difficulties owing to external pressures to impose their models" (CRIC 1999a, n.p.). CRIC had learned to its cost that for the Nasa the economy is culturally embedded and cannot be studied in isolation nor, perhaps, accorded the same importance it receives in the dominant society. In fact, the Nasa of the north favor a form of economic solidarity, discussed in some detail in chapter 3 when talking about Tóez Caloto.

In the municipal plan, it is presented as a local production system characterized by solidarity that is expected to contribute to the process of "integral development of the community" through the creation of a series of communal undertakings, such as stores, businesses, and micro-enterprises. It is regarded as a viable alternative to capitalism. A heavily charged indigenous concept, economic solidarity is viewed as more than just an economic and technical option, it is also a political and cultural option. In fact, the chapter dealing with the economy spends several pages describing its cultural dimensions (Municipio de Toribío 1998, 189–98). In the past, the Nasa economy was based on "the cultural use of the soil," meaning that the individual family had usufruct rights to land that was inalienable. This economy was embedded in complicated networks and mechanisms of reciprocity, such as marriage, labor exchange, and gift giving, and redistribution, such as fiestas, communal work, and arrangements with neighbors. The rationale for these mechanisms was both social and cultural, to control personal accumulation and maintain certain community ideals: "All these mechanisms of reciprocity and redistribution make it possible to control the accumulation of profits and maintain equality in the community, the community feeling and the solidarity" (Municipio de Toribío 1998, 192). What makes the use of this concept both remarkable and poignant is the fact that most experiences with such activities over the past twenty years have been predominantly negative.

Conceptually, this desire to (re)invent the economic system, as in the case of Tóez Caloto, is a conscious effort to incorporate some key Nasa values into the realities of a market economy, while at the same time retaining some control over the process, and fostering values such as reciprocity, redistribution, equity, and solidarity. Though several of these mechanisms still exist and new associative forms have been introduced, the north still needs to import 70 percent of its basic food needs. The solution proposed in the 1998 plan and supported by the students is a localized form of indigenous autarky that would stimulate local food production and market products directly to the consumer, within and outside the region. In this way, people would become more involved in the market economy, exerting a little more control over what happens in the region, while maintaining certain cultural values that have helped them survive as Nasa.

Successful, Secular Modernity?

Toribío's development plan is an excellent example, at least from the perspective of the state, of "successful" development planning where, in spite of all the widespread participation, the final document was put together by outsiders — clear proof that indigenous leaders and the local population have accepted and digested the dominant development discourse, presenting only a "partial truth" (Clifford 1986) while flattening, homogenizing, and diluting their own everyday world in the process. It is unclear to what extent the authors "believed" what they had written: the municipality is obliged by law to produce such a plan, because without it they will receive no state funding. While the 1980 planning workshop also relied on external advisers, their presence in the document is much more subdued, allowing more space for local voices. The 1998 document is "authorless," whereas the authors of the 1980 document are named, starting with Padre Ulcué. Although many of the problems raised by these local voices in 1980 — political violence, discrimination against women, overburdened cabildos — have grown progressively worse over the intervening decades, they are hardly mentioned in 1998. In contrast, the students in the 1999 workshop, many of whom come from northern Cauca, openly acknowledged the existence of these problems, as well as others that did not exist in 1980, such as the production of illegal crops, an issue given only passing mention in the development plan, a case of selective ignorance on the part of the advisers and those in charge (Hobart 1993).[11]

The local voice is heard loudly and clearly in Toribío's plan in a section that is not an "official" part of the plan, the introduction written by the Nasa mayor Ezequiel Vitonás, where he makes direct reference to the Nasa Project and its objectives, derived from the 1980 workshop. Discussing the type of society they wished for the future, the 1980 participants concentrated on moral concepts, such as peace, justice, and security, and desirable collective characteristics, such as united, industrious, happy, honorable, and responsible. These principles are reflected in the first objective of the 1998 development plan: creating a new community. The second objective proposes an integrated approach, and the third summarizes the vision proposed by the Nasa Project, one that Vitonás hopes will continue to motivate development in the municipality through a vision that is Nasa, participatory, integrated, and liberating. Little or none of this vision, however, appears in the actual plan, except perhaps in the section dealing with the economy. Yet the comments of some of the students in the 1999 workshop indicate that this vision persists and that some young leaders (and potential leaders) are seriously thinking about the sort of society they would like to help create, reflecting concepts and principles that originate with the Nasa Project.

Whereas the participants in the 1980 workshop expressed ambivalent feelings about being Nasa, there is no mention of this in the 1998 plan. Being Nasa is accepted as a given, or is at least taken for granted, yet there is little indication of what this means in contemporary Toribío. For the authors of the plan, a defining cultural characteristic of the Nasa of the north is the concept of the solidarity economy. This view is also widely shared by the students in the 1999 workshop, in spite of all the empirical evidence to the contrary regarding the nonviability of the local economy. (In the 1980 workshop, there is no mention of the solidarity economy.) While there is a tendency to essentialize this "traditional" economy, their development "message" is clear: the desire to exert some control over their lopsided, impoverished local production and marketing system, and at the same time recover certain key social values already lost. Wendell Berry (2002) has suggested that this idea of a local economy rests on two intertwined principles: neighborhood and subsistence:

> In a viable neighborhood, neighbors ask themselves what they can do or provide for one another, and they find answers that they and their place can afford. This, and nothing else, is the *practice* of neighborhood. . . . But a viable neighborhood is a community; and a viable community is made up of neighbors who cherish and protect what they have in common. This is the principle of subsistence. A viable community, like a viable farm, protects its own production capacities. (Berry 2002, 209–10)

According to the 1998 plan, CECIDIC is to play an important role in the creation/recovery of this economy, within its broader "mission" of "creating space for non-formal education, oriented towards preparing people to be protagonists in the process of integrated development of the community. It has to be an educational space for life, and not merely for show" (Municipio de Toribío 1998, 61). What the plan does not mention is that the center provides practical training in a variety of activities, such as agroforestry, organic farming, fish farming, and small-stock, all of which can be undertaken on either an individual or a communal basis to produce goods for which there is considerable local demand. These activities, less dependent on "modern" inputs, can also slow down the process of environmental degradation. It is worthwhile mentioning that for an increasing number of indigenous youth talking about the local economy implies working to implement a system of organic production that not only conserves the land and the soil (*La Madre Tierra*) but also provides more nutritious food for their families.

But for the young leaders in the 1999 workshop, the type of economy they would like to establish can only be understood in the broader context of politics and Nasa culture, topics hardly touched on in the municipal plan. Underlying their approach is a quest for harmony with nature and their fellow men in the face of discord (*pta'nz* in Nasa Yuwe), a key Nasa concept striven after (if not fully realized) in places such as Juan Tama. Yet the culture they embrace is significantly different from that practiced in either Cxayu'ce or Juan Tama and has much more in common with that evolving in Tóez Caloto, a hybrid steadily incorporating more elements from the dominant mainstream culture at the expense of the indigenous. For the Nasa of the north, their politics rather than their culture provides them with some collective identity, forged from a long history of oppression on the one hand and successful resistance on the other, reinforced and strengthened by the widespread activities of the Nasa Project, particularly in the areas of education, training, and production. It is no exaggeration to say the Nasa Project is a modernizing project designed to prepare people for admission into and acceptance by the larger society. The project has been only partially successful in achieving this goal on account of enduring opposition by both local elites and the guerrillas.

Yet what the Nasa of the north exemplify is another form of indigenous modernity, more secular and more political, but continuously evolving, with its own built-in tensions. The workshops in 1980 and 1999 directly confront the enduring political problems, all discretely ignored in the official 1998 plan, a characteristic shared with most official development plans. The exercises in 1980 and 1998 have little to say about culture, yet the participants in the 1999 workshop articulate clear visions of the important role they believe that indigenous culture can play in their future. On the one hand, it can be argued this is indigenous nostalgia, a form of cultural myopia that refuses to face contemporary realities. On the other hand, this interest in their admittedly recovered indigenous culture can provide a basis for dealing with the demands and challenges of modernity.

The justification for the solidarity economy draws on the past, and the ways in which it is seen to embody certain key values, such as reciprocity and redistribution, and is characterized by hard work and an ethic of austerity that limits personal accumulation and consumption. By adapting this model to the demands of the market economy through some form of mixed enterprise, the Nasa will be able to maintain, and perhaps even strengthen, these key values. But in the process, if successful, they will undoubtedly change in ways they cannot predict. For this reason there are political and cultural tensions in the north. The Nasa of the north are indeed a model, but a model of what? They are proposing an alternative, indigenous modernity, one in which certain of the basic tenets of modernity are questioned, specifically the individualizing role of modern economics. Underlying this questioning is the continuing struggle for social justice, a topic elaborated on in the next chapter.

6

When I asked one of the leaders of the Regional Indigenous Council of Cauca (CRIC) when the resistance movement had started, he answered me as if it were obvious: "Five hundred years ago."
—JUANITA LEÓN, *No somos machos, pero somos muchos: Cinco crónicas de resistencia civil en Colombia*

Most people I encounter in warzones work to create a healthy society. While the usurious and abusive do exist, they do not predominate. In a society bereft of the normal institutions that supposedly regulate society and moral norms, people, for the most part engage in humane world-building. . . . Why in the midst of a violent breakdown of order, do *most* people *not* respond with disorder and discord, but with vibrant ways of re-creation?—CAROLYN NORDSTROM, *A Different Kind of War Story*

Beyond Development:

The Continuing Struggle for Peace, Justice, and Inclusion

In chapters 3 and 4, I presented and analyzed the process of planning for development by comparing and contrasting the different experiences of the three new communities: the more secular, modernizing approach of Tóez Caloto; the more agnostic, entrepreneurial approach of Cxayu'ce; and the more radical, cultural approach of Juan Tama. I also argued that some of the differences in the ways in which they responded to the new opportunities could be explained by each community's unique historical past in Tierradentro. In the last chapter, I addressed the deeper planning and development experience of Toribío, demonstrating some similarities with that of Tóez Caloto but emphasizing the inherent tension between the past and the present, between discourse and practice, and between youth and the established leadership. There is a continuity between the discourse of Padre Ulcué and his fellow planners in 1980 and that of the young Nasa leaders almost twenty years later in the ways they address the larger issues facing indigenous society, issues not addressed in Toribío's prize-winning development plan. This more liberating discourse is found in the Nasa Project, treated as something separate and distinct by the official plan.

Juan Tama, the Nasa Project, and the younger Nasa leaders share a common characteristic: pride in being Nasa and a determination and commitment to defend that identity. This pride is neither ethnic chauvinism nor ethnic separatism. It is a form of cultural politics. For those of the north it is the political dimension, while for those of Juan Tama it is the cultural dimension that provides the foundation for contesting and opposing the demands of the state. They do not speak as inappropriate others, but rather as others who wish to speak on behalf of all others similarly persecuted, marginalized, and excluded. This radicalism has not evolved in a vacuum and can only be understood by closely examining Cauca's political history over the past century and the ways indigenous people, and later the indigenous movement, defended their interests against the demands of various groups. These demands were articulated by the national and provincial governments, together with their allies, the economic and political elites of Cauca, as well as by the guerrillas, primarily but not exclusively the Revolutionary Armed Forces of Colombia (FARC). The communities I have described all continue to participate in this process to a lesser or greater extent.

A point of departure for understanding the historical precedents is La María: Territory for Living Together, Dialogue, and Negotiation, established in 1999 as an alternative political space. In this chapter, I examine the extent to which La María can be described as the site of a subaltern counterpublic and argue that what has been created there builds on and is inspired by earlier acts of resistance, which it uses as a basis for imagining and justifying the continuing struggle for peace, justice, and inclusion, a struggle now framed in the discourse of ethnic pluralism through the strengthening of civil society. In the process, I also show how the goals and strategies have changed and become more sophisticated. In the first section, I present the example of La Quintinada, a movement to recover indigenous lands in the early twentieth century, which has served as an example and an inspiration for both the Regional Indigenous Council of Cauca (CRIC) and the Quintín Lame Armed Movement (MAQL). Motivated by a strong feeling of social injustice, the movement was proactive and accompanied by a certain amount of political violence that terrified the local elites. In the second section, I deal with the MAQL, the major political and intellectual precursor of La María, in this case a movement established to protect the lives of indigenous leaders against the violence of the state and the FARC. In theory under the control of the *cabildos,* the MAQL also worked closely to strengthen and reinforce their local capacities. I shall discuss the contributions made by the three indigenous representatives to the Constitutional Assembly in 1991, called primarily at the initiative of the April 19th Movement (M-19) but also supported by the MAQL. In the third section, I focus on La María itself, specifically on two of the workshops held there and their relationship to Cauca's Alternate Plan for the development period 2001–2003. In the final section, I analyze the ways in which La María has broadened its multiethnic base, while at the same time maintaining its role as a counterpublic site. In brief, while La María is a social movement with its roots in indigenous Cauca's struggle for land, its appeal and objectives are much broader as it seeks to represent a much broader constituency of the marginalized, dispossessed, and voiceless, the basis for which could be a more just form of development.

Resistance and an Indigenous Public Voice

In June 1999, CRIC, together with some 12,000 of its supporters, successfully blocked the Pan-American Highway, the main artery connecting northern and southern Colombia, for a period of eleven days. This was in protest against the government's continuing failure to fulfill its earlier promises to the indigenous people of Cauca regarding health care and education. The protestors took their stand at a place called La María, some thirty kilometers north of Popayán (Espinosa 2005). They had two major concerns. The first was that the national government recognize CRIC as a traditional authority, akin to a cabildo, responsible for negotiating on behalf of the indigenous population in the province. At the time, the government argued that since indigenous organizations such as CRIC did not adequately represent the interests of the *resguardos,* they were better represented by their traditional authorities, the cabildos (Jackson 2002). The second concern was that the government address the deteriorating social, cultural, and economic conditions in which indigenous people found themselves (CRIC 1999c). There had been earlier large-scale mobilizations protesting essentially the same issues, to which the government had often responded in a similar way — by sending a high-level member of the government, usually a minister, to negotiate directly and publicly with the leadership of CRIC. The long-term effects, however, had been minimal. But the closing of the highway in 1999 was different. It involved more people, and it lasted longer. The demands included a proposal to establish an indigenous territory where the local population and other marginal groups, all ostensibly part of civil society, could meet and talk, under the oversight of the human rights community. The objective was to have their voices heard in the peace process initiated a year earlier. One participant defined La María as an indigenous "safe area," an alternative to San Vicente de Caguán where the official peace process between the Colombian government and the FARC was then under way.

During the mobilization in 1999, the leaders were responsible for establishing and maintaining a tent camp — really a small, temporary town — and providing the necessary services, ranging from law and order to drinking water and health care. The individual delegations were responsible for providing their own food and fuel, as well as additional community members to replace them after a designated time. This often entailed complicated logistical arrangements with their home resguardos. They were also responsible for contributing volunteers to the civic guard, the young men and women responsible for maintaining order around the clock. The consumption of alcohol was strictly controlled and the use of drugs banned. People found selling drugs were asked to leave the camp. Guerrillas were also banned from the site. At the time of the mobilization, the FARC attacked the nearby town of Caldono and wished to take advantage of the situation to move their own forces unobtrusively. They were run out of the camp by the civic guard, armed only with their staffs of office.

Negotiations with the government representatives at La María were open and democratic, with indigenous leaders encouraging broad participation. Resguardo delegates, meeting on the bluff overlooking the highway, communicated the issues on the table directly to their resguardo members blocking the highway below, who, once they had discussed them among themselves, informed the delegates of their decisions. Participants included not only men but also women and children, who, when it appeared that attempts might be made to open the highway by force, served as shock troops, as the first line of defense. While the overall mood of the people was serious, they also demonstrated a certain degree of optimistic realism — optimistic about their continuing capacity to mobilize, but realistic about what they could expect from the government.

Although closing the highway did not lead to any immediate improvement in the situation of Cauca's indigenous population, it did contribute to the establishment of La María later that year to mark the five hundredth anniversary of the Spanish invasion of the Americas. At the founding meeting, the objective was clearly stated: create a political space where civil society could make its voice heard in the peace process then underway with the FARC and in the decision-making about Colombia's future development — specifically, the restructuring of the state and the necessary social, political, and economic reforms (CRIC n.d.2). What this future development might look like in Cauca and the neighboring provinces was to be elaborated on later. This was also an appeal to create a "multiethnic and pluricultural nation," enshrined as a fundamental principle in Article 7 of the 1991 Constitution (República de Colombia 1991). At the same time, however, it was a strongly worded criticism of the state and the elites who supported it for the way they had progressively marginalized both the indigenous and nonindigenous population, thereby severely restricting their meaningful participation in the political process. From the very beginning, La María was designed to have a broad popular appeal by reaching out to Afro-Colombians, as well as peasants and urban dwellers (CRIC/FST 1999).

The proof of CRIC's commitment to this multicultural goal was tested shortly afterward. In November 1999, there was another mobilization, this time organized by the Committee for the Integration of the Colombian Massif (CIMA), which closed the Pan-American Highway north and south of Popayán for twenty-five days, virtually cutting off the city from the outside world (Herrera 2003; Zambrano 2001). This mobilization was broad-based and involved the participation of upwards of fifty thousand people, including various popular sectors in Popayán, who later regarded this event as one of the more dramatic in the city's recent history. The reasons for closing the highway were the same: the failure of the national government to honor its promises regarding heath, education, and infrastructure, in this case to El Macizo, the most abandoned region, located in the southern part of the province. The government finally agreed to the protestors' demands and signed an agreement, the components of which were slowly implemented over the ensuing years. CRIC lent its support and various indigenous groups actively participated, which was the first time that CRIC had directly supported a nonindigenous struggle. This mobilization successfully withstood the threats and intimidation posed by the government. In the process, the participants became aware that they were creating and living a form of solidarity that crossed both ethnic and class lines.

> At the same time, the presence of the demonstrators made clear that this type of mobilization creates ties of belonging and solidarity among all of them, stimulates forms of political socialization and sociability which permit the reproduction of the meaning of their action, thereby assigning it impact and coherence, and helps with the development and consolidation of collective identities. (Zambrano 2001, 261–62)

This active participation on the part of CRIC helped strengthen the appeal of La María and considerably broadened its base of organizational support.

Since its inception, La María has played host to a series of workshops and meetings, many, but not all, organized by CRIC: workshops for women and other specific groups, the quadrennial congress of CRIC (CRIC 2001); meetings of the Indigenous Social Alliance (ASI), a political party established after the demobilization of the MAQL in 1991; and as a staging ground for organized, peaceful marches to protest the assassination of indigenous leaders. The fact that the peace process collapsed in January 2002 did not affect La María, because its importance and credibility were already established. By summer 2002, efforts launched by the governor's office were made to replicate the experience in other parts of Cauca, both rural and urban.

But what precisely *is* La María? From one perspective, it is part of a social movement, broadly defined. Space and place have become key concepts in contemporary anthropology, yet how to relate them to the study of social movements is problematic since such movements are often and intentionally *not* place-specific. While La María is a specific site, it is also an alternative political space. Arturo Escobar (2001) has proposed that the study of place-based practices in such realms as culture, ecology, and economics can provide important sources of alternative visions and strategies for reconstructing local and regional worlds. Research on social movements in Latin America has viewed them through the optic of cultural politics and has attempted to re-define not only social and political power but also the more profound process of contesting, negotiating, and formulating key principles and concepts. "When movements deploy alternative conceptions of woman, nature, race, economy, democracy, or citizenship that unsettle domi-nant cultural meanings, they enact a cultural politics" (Alvarez, Dag-nino, and Escobar 1998, 7).

The events enacted at La María all focus on pressing social and politi-cal and developmental issues that it would be difficult, if not outright dangerous, to address elsewhere, at least in a public forum. For this reason, Nancy Fraser proposes that we think of multiple publics, what she terms subaltern counterpublics, as arenas where subaltern groups invent and circulate counterdiscourses and "formulate oppositional in-terpretations of their identities, interests, and needs" (1997, 81).[1] Such arenas are not enclaves, since they seek to disseminate their discourse to other, broader publics. Nevertheless, in stratified societies such as Co-lombia, these subaltern counterpublics can play a dual role. "On the one hand, they function as spaces of withdrawal and regroupment; on the other hand, they also function as bases and training grounds for agita-tional activities directed towards wider publics. It is precisely in the dialectic between these two functions that their *emancipatory potential resides*" (Fraser 1997, 82; emphasis added). If this is the case for La María, it has to be shown how these dual roles relate to each other and to the larger society, as well as how they have evolved over time. In addition, it is open to question whether a counterpublic, continuously articulating counterdiscourses, can survive and be effective over the long term without permanently alienating the dominant society or, al-ternatively, moderating its position to become more inclusive. The emanicipatory potential that Fraser posits requires a certain degree of compromise, as well as a willingness to be part of the larger society, while the terms of that engagement may well remain contentious and contested. Implicit in the discourse of the counterpublic is the struggle for inclusion, rather than exclusion, of not only indigenous groups but of all marginal groups, irrespective of their ethnicity. Liberation move-ments can emerge out of such social and cultural circumstances, collec-tive efforts to end the economic, political, and social structures that enforce subordination and the cultural practices and beliefs that perpetuate discrimination and marginalization (Flacks 2004). This is a radical proposition that can only be examined in an historical context, but one well grounded in ethnography. It is also a framework that forces us to de-essentialize what we think an indigenous movement is.

Quintín Lame: The Indigenous Advocate

At the turn of the twentieth century, when the political map of Colombia was redrawn and Gran Cauca was dissected into a series of states within the more centralized Colombian nation, Popayán and its ruling elite lost a great deal of territory, as well as the political authority and prestige they had enjoyed during the colonial era. As a result, the Caucan elites turned inward, increasing their exploitation of the indigenous and peasant populations and their encroachment on indigenous lands (Rappaport 1998, 112), passing laws that were to facilitate this process (Castillo, 22). Decree 74 of 1889 consisted of 178 articles designed to speed up the elimination of resguardos by singling out those considered "vacant," deemed underpopulated and, hence, with land to spare, that the population was then encouraged to dispose of. A later law, Law 55 of 1905, went even further by authorizing the regional authorities to order the partition of those resguardos they deemed underpopulated. In such cases, the land was sold in public auctions. This combination of discriminatory legislation, encroaching haciendas, and advancing colonists severely threatened the livelihoods and future of the indigenous population. As their land base steadily eroded, many indigenous people became landless or nearly landless and were obliged to work as hacienda sharecroppers. In return for usufruct of a piece of land on the hacienda, they had to provide service in the form of several days of labor each week for the hacienda owner.

From 1910 onward there were increasing confrontations between the elites of Cauca and the growing landless indigenous population fighting to maintain or to reestablish the resguardos (Rappaport 1998, 113). This movement, which came to be called La Quintinada, was led by Manuel Quintín Lame, a landless Nasa whose family had migrated from Tierradentro to Polindara, near Popayán. His major collaborator was José Gonzalo Sánchez from the Guambiano-Coconuco area of Totoró. Both men had spent considerable time outside of their communities, were literate, and claimed familiarity with Colombian institutions and Colombian history (Rappaport 1998, 114). Although they were to lead a multiethnic movement of indigenous groups from Cauca and the neighboring provinces of Tolima and Huila, my focus here is primarily on their activities in Cauca and their organizational activities with the Nasa.

It was not only the loss of land and the increasing impoverishment of the people that motivated Quintín Lame. Like the MAQL some seventy years later, he was also incensed by the conditions of semi-slavery in which they were forced to live and work, and the loss of human dignity that this entailed.[2] Lame's demands covered five points, which reverberated throughout the indigenous movement for the rest of the century. When CRIC was established in 1971, its proposed program covered essentially the same points:

> Defense of the resguardos and militant opposition to the laws authorizing their division and redistribution;
>
> Consolidation of the cabildo as the center of political authority and the base for organizing;
>
> Recovery of lands lost to the large landowners and the rejection of titles not based on royal decrees;
>
> Liberation of the sharecroppers, through refusal to pay rent, or any other form of personal tribute; and
>
> Affirmation of indigenous cultural values, and a rejection of the racial and cultural discrimination to which the Colombian Indians have been subjected. (Castillo 1971, xviii)[3]

Of the five demands articulated, three are still highly relevant a century later, specifically the resguardo, the cabildo, and indigenous culture; a large number of the haciendas have been incorporated into resguardos, and sharecropping has virtually disappeared. If anything, culture has become more important with the passage of the years, as demonstrated by the increasing value attached to local control of education, the respect shown the shamans, and the role of customary law in the resguardos. Lame and his followers, the Lamistas, sought to achieve their goals by various means: through political organization, preparation of legal documents, interviews with the press, and, at least for a time, participation in national elections. The extent to which they also supported the use of arms is open to question, although they were in favor of armed struggle.[4]

According to information that he provided, Lame was elected "Chief, Representative and General Defender" by the cabildos of Pitayó, Jambaló, Toribío, Puracé, Poblazón, Cajibío, and Paniguardo in 1910. In the years that followed, he organized intensively throughout Cauca, mobilizing indigenous people against the break-up of the resguardos, while at the same time articulating his strong opposition to "civilization" as personified by the elites in Popayán, the hacienda owners, mestizo settlers, and the business practices of middlemen (Castillo 1971). In a book completed in 1939, he roundly denounced the aristocrats and what they did to the cabildos:

> That garden of human nature has told me not to be afraid of saying the truth to anyone, regardless of how white he might be, like those who threw me in the dungeons in Popayán for an entire year incommunicado with iron shackles, without having been heard or convicted in a trial. This was done by a gang of aristocrats from Popayán, for which reason Popayán is today in ruins, because of the injustice against the Indian councils! The Law of Compensation [the coming indigenous millennium] is drawing near, gentlemen! (Castillo 1987, 151)[5]

His message resonated with the indigenous population and encouraged them to resist the oppression and exploitation by utilizing the well-tested "weapons of the weak" (Scott 1985). Landowners accused the people of cattle rustling, slaughtering livestock for domestic consumption, distilling liquor, refusing to comply with labor obligations, and collecting dues for the Lamistas. Particularly troubling were reports of *boleteo*, personal threats to the lives of landowners and their foremen, with the objective of getting them to leave the area (Castillo 1987, 33). In a 1971 interview conducted by Gonzalo Castillo, one of the Lamista militants recalled, "Quintín said to us that we needed to arm each other until the entire population of the sector was armed to the last man, to oppose the division of the resguardos. He told the women to guard respect for themselves [i.e., defend their honor], resorting if necessary to kitchen knives! I have never seen or heard any man like him!" (151).

In 1911 the authorities responded by authorizing the landowners to arm their workers, register them as rural policemen, and organize them in squads. They were supported by the priests and missionaries of the region. As insecurity increased, the governor of Cauca accused Lame of being a "subversive," an "arsonist, " and "the instigator of a racial war." By 1915, he had authorized municipal mayors to organize "commissions" to search and capture Lame (33). That same year, Lame was captured in the chapel of the hacienda San Isidro where he had land and where, at the invitation of the priest, he had been participating in religious exercises in preparation for Holy Week. He put up a fierce struggle, and there was a bloody confrontation between his followers and the police. Kept prisoner in Puracé, he was released after a month when no formal charges were laid (34). Two months later he was captured again near the El Cofre River and jailed for a year with his legs in shackles and chained to an iron bar weighing twenty-eight pounds. In his book, Lame recounts, "I had been held incommunicado since the day I was captured on the El Cofre Bridge because of a treason on May 9 of 1915. And on May 9 of 1916 the blacksmith came in hastily, armed with hammer and chisel and said: 'Señor Lame, I have come to take off the bar between your feet. Congratulations!'" (103).

But Lame could also be effectively elusive, and the authorities were prone to overreact on the basis of very skimpy evidence, sometimes little more than hearsay. In February 1915, the mayor of Belalcázar in Tierradentro reported to the governor's office in Popayán that there were rumors that Lame intended to attack and destroy the houses of the whites. The provincial prefect had warned him and two other mayors to keep close watch on the indigenous population and make sure they had no contact with Lame, who was intent on "stirring up the Indians and burning towns." A few days later, the mayor received word from his colleague in Inzá that Lame had entered Mosoco, a neighboring town, with a force of three hundred men. He ordered the citizens to defend the bridges and other strategic points in Belalcázar, although it seemed unclear how solid the evidence was for supposing that Lame was about to occupy the town. The secretary of government describes the aftermath in his annual report of 1916:

> Anyway, the second day dawned; everyone sleepless and wet because it was raining. Everyone was convinced that there had not been any danger. And finally, on the 13th, the governor of the province informed us that Lame was peacefully minding his own business in the hacienda of San Isidro. This news

given by the chief executive calmed spirits, and put an end to all the gossip. The commissions which had been sent out beforehand returned and reported that the Indians were unconcerned and involved in their fields and work, and demonstrated that they had no indication of Lame's intents. (Castrillón Arboleda 1973, 123)[6]

But in November 1916, a serious confrontation did occur in Inzá. In his report to the governor, the secretary reported that Lame had attacked the town with his followers, leaving some dead and wounded. This version was substantiated by Father David González, a priest who worked in the area and who also wrote a book about the Nasa (González n.d., 103–4).[7] Lame's version of what happened was very different. According to him, the police had attacked while Indian children were being baptized in the church, killing seven people and wounding eight, including women and children. Years later, Lame accused the priests in writing and held them directly responsible for the massacre: "One of the priests led the militia units which had been after us, and incited them to kill Indians, since the Indians were not Christians. [Later on] the same priest had the Indians who fell prisoners hanged from trees to make them confess my whereabouts" (Lame 1922, 1).[8] An official report from the secretary of government not only substantiated this intervention on the part of the Catholic Church but also publicly acknowledged the collaboration of Don Pio Collo, a local indigenous leader opposed to the politics of Lame (Castillo 1987, 35).

In a telegram to Bogotá requesting reinforcements, the governor of Cauca stressed the gravity of the situation and the fact that the "white race" (i.e., mestizos) was under threat. The government complied by sending troops, and Lame and many of his followers were apprehended the following year and imprisoned for four years. His capture was made possible by the treachery of José María López, a mestizo peasant who had gained his confidence. In an interview in 1971, his daughter, Tulia López, explained why her father had betrayed Lame and what became of him and his family as a result:

Lame wanted the rich to disappear; [he] wanted to eat their cattle, take away their lands . . . the rich in Popayán were in despair and all of them (the Arboledas, the Angulos, the Valencias) offered to give my father money . . . but you know if the money is not received first, afterwards one gets nothing. They did not give anything . . . instead my father earned for himself the hatred of the Indians and, with his ten children, had to flee the area because the Indians threatened to burn his house. (Castillo 1987, 169).[9]

When he was released from jail in 1921, Lame left Cauca to continue the struggle in Huila and Tolima.

The importance and enduring appeal of Lame are based on a combination of personal factors, particularly his charisma and mystique, and political factors, principally his focus on justice. His personal charisma and the way he presented himself in public were most in evidence during his teaching *mingas,* political meetings named after the traditional Andean communal work parties. According to an eye-witness account, it was his supporters who would organize these meetings. People would be instructed to assemble in a particular place, and members of his inner group would arrive first, loaded down with papers and a copy of the legal code. Others would be posted as lookouts, to warn of the approach of government authorities. The meeting would begin with Lame, standing on a box, ceremoniously greeting all those present. They would then all start to sing the national anthem, when he would suddenly raise his hands and ask for silence and start his speech in a solemn and stately tone with the following words.

> Everything that the National Anthem says is a lie, because liberty has not arrived among the Indians. I come to defend the dispossessed, weak, ignorant tribes, abandoned by the "whites" who govern us with no [legal] right and who have taken the lands of America that Jesus Christ Our Lord gave us so we would work them and defend them. I am writing a law to take to the government of Bogotá asking that it order the return of our lands to us, that the whites have. We Indians do not have to pay rent because Colombia is one big homestead that the King of Spain could not grant to the white conquerors who came to rob us and murder us. (Castillo 1973, 91–92)[10]

He would continue to talk in this way for some time, after which he would read articles from the legal code or from the Colombian constitution that dealt with lands and liberty. According to those who heard him, his way of speaking was not fluent, but he had a powerful and authoritative voice, and his vocabulary was rich in imagery, much of it drawn from nature. Like the MAQL with its guerrilla schools and La María with its workshops, Lame believed strongly in the importance of training, education, and knowledge for indigenous people as an important component in the process of collective liberation. Like Padre Álvaro Ulcué more than sixty years later, Lame was not afraid to speak truth to power, even when it entailed risking his own safety, and throughout his life he demonstrated both moral and political courage.

In his organizing, mingas, appeals to the national government, writings, and later activities in Huila and Tolima, Lame focused on several enduring themes, including defending the resguardos, strengthening the cabildos, and encouraging activism and militancy on the part of the dispossessed, all of which can be subsumed under his quest for justice and human dignity for indigenous people.[11] In 1939, Lame completed the writing of a book-length manuscript, *Los pensamientos del indio que se educó dentro de las selvas* (*The Thoughts of the Indian Educated in the Colombian Forests*), which was finally published in 1971 in Bogotá as *En defensa de mi raza* (*In Defense of My Race*). Of Lame's book Gonzalo Castillo writes, "The style is rustic but the message is clear, revealing a human experience of remarkable depth and expressing a religious conviction and a moral protest from within a distinctive cultural perspective, a social experience of oppression, and a keen sense of historic solidarity with what he calls 'the Indian race'" (Castillo 1987, 3).[12]

Whereas Lame's book is a combination of personal biography, historical interpretation, and religious thought, it can also be read as a treatise on indigenous political action, outlining indigenous rights and ways of achieving them (Rappaport 1998, 121). In his analysis of Lame's book, Castillo (1987, 46–47) discusses his vehement denunciation of injustice and argues that Lame's major concern (at least in the book) was not so much the redress of particular grievances but the moral denunciation of a society that denied Indians their humanity. The denial justified society's inhumanity. His personal experience of this helped fire his own militancy when, like Padre Ulcué, members of his immediate family were affected. On one particular occasion, returning to his father's house in San Isidro, he found his father, his brother, and two other Indian tenants hanging by their wrists from the ceiling for failing to pay rent to the hacendado. He cut them down, deeply offended by this violation of human dignity, and resolved to seek redress.[13]

Throughout Lame's book there are criticisms directed at whites and the ways they chose to treat Indians, and Lame warns his readers not to trust them. From his perspective, such relations are always characterized by attitudes of domination, contempt, and hatred (Castillo 1987, 49).

He reserves his strongest criticism and condemnation for the Colombian system of justice and its representatives. Judges are described as "frightful and vindictive" and lawyers as "false" (50), and people are warned to place no faith in due process.

> Hear, you Indians! The elements of proof are three: the first is confession, the second is the testimony of witnesses, and the third is written documents. But be careful not to make the confession of anything . . . [because] there are many prosecutors around who threaten the ignorant with torture, with the dungeon, and with exile, with sentences of twenty years, etc. . . . . There are many judges and prosecutors who say "Don't deny it, don't deny it! Because there are testimonies that say it was you who did it." But what they want is to become famous by means outside the law, outside reason and justice. (114–15)

For Lame, such behavior on the part of whites was a direct consequence of their desire to dominate, their identity as whites determined by the nonidentity of Indians (52). Any attempt to change this relationship was viewed with deep mistrust, if not outright fear, because such changes could have profound social and political consequences. While those in power in Cauca were genuinely afraid of Lame and La Quintinada, they appear to have been astute enough to realize that they were better off with Lame alive than with him dead.

Lame believed that his systematic persecution, which placed him in jail 108 times, stemmed from his advocacy, particularly his organizing, mobilizing, and educational activities, on behalf of indigenous people:

> After 447 years [i.e., the time elapsed from the Spanish invasion of 1492 to the 1939 completion of his manuscript] it has not disappeared, because the Indian is always under the white man's boot like a slave; and the Indian who defends his right is persecuted like a fugitive robber by the non-Indian. This enemy seeks a thousand ways to smash materially, morally, and socially the indigene when he has come close to the garden of science. (124–25)

But in spite of his strong critique and condemnation, Lame did believe in the importance of standing up and confronting the system of legal injustice. This was one of the practical objectives of his advocacy. While this strategy may appear paradoxical (66), it has a certain logic and appeal that has been repeated over the years by the indigenous movement in Cauca, as demonstrated by its relationship to and expectations of the state. Lame recognized that the national government, particularly the Supreme Court, had acted justly on a number of occasions, overruling the decisions of lower courts, including at least two in which he was absolved (122). Lame felt a dual loyalty, to both his people and his country, as Castillo pointedly explains: "Thus, Lame sees himself as a citizen of two worlds: on the one hand, he is first and foremost the apostle and advocate of the Indians, and on the other, he is bound in loyalty to the national society based on the moral bond of 'justice'" (64).[14] This dual loyalty has continued as an important if somewhat paradoxical component of contemporary indigenous resistance, but with one crucial difference. Lame's hatred of whites has been considerably diluted, whether dealing with CRIC, the MAQL, or La María where select sympathetic whites have played, and indeed continue to play, important advisory roles.

The Quintines and the Defense of the Poor and Exploited

Among the more committed and engaged supporters of La María were several indigenous and mestizo Quintines, members of the MAQL, who have continued to be politically active since their demobilization in 1991. The MAQL emerged in the early 1980s as a local response to the increasing persecution and assassination of local leaders by local landowners, their hired killers, and the FARC. As a result, the more radical elements within the indigenous movement felt they had no choice but to form small, mobile self-defense units if they wished to survive at all. According to Francisco Gembuel, an indigenous leader and activist, "These groups of guerrillas regarded themselves as lords of the land and did not allow others to do anything, there were some encounters in '78, I think, in '82 and '83, until '85, with serious problems in the resguardos of Toribío and San Francisco and some in Jambaló, where the self-defense units created by FARC started to kill the leaders of CRIC."[15] As the level of violence continued and several more indigenous leaders were assassinated, the Quintines became more proactive.

In 1984, two events in northern Cauca precipitated their entrance into the public arena. The first was the successful recovery of López Adentro, a large sugar plantation worked by the resident tenant farmers, a mixture of indigenous people, Afro-Colombians, and peasants (Espinosa 1996). An earlier action by the sharecroppers had been countered by a military rout, resulting in increased militancy. Much more than land was at stake, as discussed in some detail in the previous chapter. The indigenous movement was simultaneously angered by the assassination of Padre Álvaro Ulcué, a radical indigenous priest who had insistently and courageously, yet peacefully stood up for the rights of indigenous people and spoken out forcefully against the abuses of the large landowners. Although several different people were identified as possible assassins, including police and soldiers reputedly hired by a local landowner, no one was ever charged with his murder (Peñaranda 1998, 74). Over time, Padre Ulcué became identified as a martyr for the Catholic Church and for the indigenous movement (Roattino 1986).

In deciding how to respond, the Quintines agreed to collaborate on a joint action with the Ricardo Franco guerrillas, also active in the area. This was a splinter group from the FARC, established in 1984, which became infamous in 1986 for the massacre of 172 of its own members in Tacueyó, on the grounds that they were government spies. On January 4, 1985, at 4:30 in the afternoon, four hundred armed men occupied Santander, the second city of Cauca, located on the Pan-American Highway between Popayán and Cali. While four groups blocked the highway and the major exits from the city, the major force marched on the center of the town and attacked the police station. The station, as a very tangible, physical representation of the state and its apparatus, is a favorite target of armed groups. One can gauge the level of armed activity in a region by the level of fortification of the police station and its degree of accessibility. If the guerrillas manage to drive out the police, then the town becomes a de facto guerrilla town, even if the guerrillas are not obviously present.

Another group went through the city, painting graffiti on the walls and shouting slogans against the army and the killers of Padre Ulcué. At the same time, however, this group was said to be searching, unsuccessfully as it turned out, for specific people named on a list drawn up by the Quintines, including several policemen (Peñaranda 1998, 82). The assault on the police station was unsuccessful, in spite of the numerical superiority of the guerrillas, and the MAQL leadership blamed the failure on the inexperience of Ricardo Franco, as well as their possible complicity with the authorities in Santander. For many of the Quintines, however, this experience was, quite literally, baptism by fire. According to one participant, Alfonso Peña, "It was a very tough situation, because wherever we moved there was lead [i.e., shots], they were shooting at us from the houses. For us it was the first experience, it was the first fight I had ever been in in my life, so the first thing one thinks about is death, but in spite of everything it went all right."[16]

The propaganda left by the Quintines consisted of fliers, explaining who they were, under the title *Comando Quintin Lame: For the Defense of Indigenous Rights* (Peñaranda 1998, 83–85). What becomes clear on a close reading of the text of these broadsides is that initially the Quintines viewed themselves as more than a self-defense unit, organized solely to defend the lives of the leaders of the indigenous movement. They also took a more general stand in favor of human rights, dignity, and autonomy for all indigenous people and against capitalist oppression in general.

Why fight?

We fight for the fundamental human rights of indigenous communities, such as land, culture, organization. In the same way for the dignity of all indigenous people.

We defend the autonomy of the indigenous movement, which should not subordinate itself to any outside organization. For us the communities are the maximum authority and we place all of our capacities and strengths at their disposal.

We also participate in the struggles of others who are exploited and oppressed by defeating capitalist slavery and constructing a more just country for all. Popular organizations, armed groups, are our brothers, and shoulder to shoulder we shall fight with them to overcome our enemies. (Peñaranda 1998, 84)

In this document, the Quintines addressed both indigenous and universal demands. The emphasis on the indigenous reflects the influence of CRIC and the indigenous movement, but the focus on the universal introduces a new element that only took root after the Constitutional Assembly. This new element may have resulted from the multiethnic composition of the MAQL membership. Though many were indigenous, others were not. Their first leader, Luis Ángel Monroy, was Afro-Colombian; two of the most important political advisers, Pablo Tattay and Henry Caballero, were mestizos; and there were also several non-indigenous combatants, national and international. In the first paragraph the objectives are indigenous demands and indigenous dignity, reiterating the ideology articulated by CRIC since its creation. In the second, the objective is the defense of indigenous autonomy; on the one hand, freedom from external intervention, a perennial issue that endures to the present, while on the other, the unquestioning acceptance of the authority of the cabildo. In practice, the promise to work closely with and strengthen the communities was to become the Achilles heel of the Quintines since this severely limited what they could do and constrained them both geographically and politically. But the final objective presents a broader, more universal panorama — close identification with the oppressed wherever they are, while at the same time fighting against capitalism and for the creation of a more equitable society.

The introduction of the name of Quintín Lame established some historical continuity in the ongoing struggle of the Nasa, the major ethnic group involved in the Quintines, that dated back to the time of Juan Tama, their culture hero of the eighteenth century. The Quintines felt honored to take his name and follow his example. At that time, however, Quintín Lame was not exactly a household name, partly because his work in Cauca covered only a decade in the early part of the twentieth century. According to their military commander, Gildardo Peña:

> In 1982 we held a meeting with all the support groups, and the objective was to choose the name with which we were going to baptize the group. At that time there was discussion, they talked about Juan Tama, the Cacica Gaitana, but finally we considered that Quintín's was the most relevant [fresco]. At that time he was totally unknown in the communities, even among the leaders there were many people who did not know who Quintín Lame was, in addition in some places we had to talk to them a little about Quintín Lame, who he had been, why he had fought.[17]

The fact that he was a conservative, while the Nasa are generally liberal, also contributed to his neglect. Nevertheless, the top leadership was quite clear why Quintín Lame should be their model and example. As outlined in their manifesto, Lame pursued legal means of redress as well as armed insurrection, which at the time had a traumatic effect on the landowners and political elites of Cauca. This was particularly the case with the armed occupation of towns in the 1910s. Gildardo Peña explains:

But the armed part also had an important influence, like the occupation of Paniquitá, the occupation of Inzá and other towns where he, by means of force, made it understood that in Cauca it was not easy to strike a blow against that class of large landowners, for that reason we believe that for us, yes it is much more significant to have the name of Quintín Lame because it is something which attracts, something which has an impact on the armed struggle.[18]

For the Quintines, the focus was on the life and political resistance of Lame, rather than on his advice to make full use of the courts and existing legislation (Rappaport 2004).

With their new recruits, both men and women, the Quintines pursued two lines of action. The first was military training and the second was political training that in practice appears to have been considerably broader and more practical. Guerrilla schools, like the meetings organized by Quintín Lame some seventy years earlier and the workshops later organized at La María, were basically a form of popular education, teaching participants about their history and their rights, their problems and how to address them, but also providing practical information they could use on their return to their home resguardos. Many of the recruits regarded this training as one of the major benefits of having belonged to the MAQL. According to Efraín, a participant in a 1993 workshop for the demobilized Quintines:

> If you stay only in the community, you don't know many things, but if you perhaps leave on a short trip or for other reasons, you learn many things that you see are necessary. For example, I learned many things, I learned how to meet people, I learned to stop being shy, I was a young person, far too shy and didn't even know how to run a meeting and other events and there I learned things, I learned to do things for the community, I knew about some rights that the communities had, how to redress them, for me the change was very important. (Peñaranda 1998, 111)

Many like Efraín were in their teens and "raw" in the purest sense of the word: little or no education, little experience of the world beyond their home communities, no military experience, and politically unsophisticated. As there was a continuous turnover in the membership with people leaving for various reasons to return to their communities, training, retention, and recruitment were perennial issues.

In practice, there was a permanent core of some sixty to eighty guerrillas, with another hundred "floating" combatants at any given time. Potential members were selected by their home communities, and sometimes included those regarded as a social nuisance, in the hope that this form of "obligatory military service" would help straighten them out. Interviews conducted with the Quintines when they demobilized in 1991 indicate that many of the ex-combatants had been motivated to join by feelings of social injustice to which they had been subjected. Compared with other guerrilla groups operating in Cauca, they preferred the Quintines because they were committed to the indigenous cause, their military profile was low-key, but principally because they were more flexible; it was easy to join and easy to leave, and they were also able to maintain close contact with their families (Peñaranda 1998, 106). But the leadership regarded this flexibility and informality as both a challenge and a major constraint.

In addition to the training, the most valuable, long-term benefit of being a Quintín was the opportunity to meet other people and travel to other parts of the province and thereby acquire direct, firsthand experience of the problems in other communities, thereby making their "imagined community" of Nasa more tangible and directly experienced (Anderson 1991). Equally important was the spirit of leadership inculcated by their guerrilla teachers, and the fact that many became leaders in their own communities. According to Henry Caballero, one of the nonindigenous political leaders of the Quintines and one of the forces behind the creation of La María, one of the ideals was and continues to be the belief in "popular power" and the creation of parallel institutions to those of the state in such domains as the economy, government, justice, and education, with the latter defined as "education that will recover history, culture and the resources and necessities of each community and its surroundings" (Caballero n.d.). Such locally controlled institutions could offer serious alternatives to the dominant discourses of the state. In practice, the Quintines chose to participate directly in the electoral process through ASI, their own political party established after the demobilization in 1991. In the subsequent years, they have successfully elected mayors, state representatives, a national senator, and, most important, the first indigenous governor in the history of Colombia, Floro Tunubalá, a member of the Guambiano ethnic group, from

2001 to 2003.

Unlike the other armed groups in the region, the Quintines made it clear from the very beginning that they were not interested in taking power. Rather, they saw their role as primarily, though not exclusively, defending and strengthening the indigenous communities.[19] One way in which they served was by helping the community leadership resolve internal problems of order, often associated with robbery, theft, or violence. When a community member accused of some serious infraction did not follow the cabildo's judgment and orders, the Quintines would be called in. The accused was given three opportunities to change his behavior. Failure to do so meant that "revolutionary justice was applied in order to create a certain fear in the other thieves who would then correct themselves, forgetting about these activities."[20] In return for the services provided by the Quintines, the community would treat them well and provide food and intelligence, on the understanding that there was to be no fighting in the area. Should the army appear, the Quintines were expected to move on, quickly and quietly. But some Quintines, particularly the military leadership responsible for implementing activities in the field, found this role of policeman both limiting and frustrating. From their perspective, the Quintines' agenda should have been more ambitious, although the specifics of what this might have looked like remain unclear. According to Gildardo Peña, "In the long term, that's what it was, to become community policemen but deep down there was nothing else. I myself was one of those who thought most [about this]: What are we doing here, carrying arms up and down? As if there was no future and the [political] leadership had a very small vision."[21]

The decision by the political leadership of the Quintines to demobilize in 1991 was based on several interrelated factors (Ibeas 1999, 221–25; Peñaranda 1998, 174–79). First, there was an increase in the level of violence in northern Cauca, a result of the growing paramilitary presence financed by drug traffickers and supported by the military. Better armed and more experienced, they posed a serious and deadly threat to any groups who opposed them. The fact that the M-19, the Quintines' sole ally in the region, had already demobilized made them all the more vulnerable. Second, in spite of the efforts of the Quintines, the incidence of rustling, robbery, and theft within the communities did not decrease on a permanent basis. This continuing lawlessness was sometimes aided and abetted by the more recalcitrant Quintines. Third, there was growing opposition on the part of other social organizations, because the activities of the Quintines provided an excuse for increasing repression on the part of the state and its right-wing allies.

As a result, the indigenous movement, the communities themselves, the leaders of CRIC, and other organizations such as the Indigenous Authorities of the Southwest (AISO, later Indigenous Authorities of Colombia, AICO), responded by publicly denouncing all violence and rejecting any external interference in the affairs of the communities. In the Declaration of Vitoncó, signed by sixteen resguardos in April 1985, their leaders clearly and forcefully articulated four non-negotiable principles, including respect for local autonomy and the nonintervention of any armed groups in the internal affairs of the communities. In sum, there was an internal contradiction involved in the MAQL strategy. To be effective, the Quintines needed a force of around two hundred guerrillas, for which they had neither the human nor the economic resources to support. In practice, they could field between fifty and sixty combatants at any one time, which meant that the communities were always vulnerable. Even if they had been able to support a larger force, the political consequences would have been very serious, since they lacked widespread indigenous support.

As a result of the demobilization, the Quintines gained the right to send a representative to the Constitutional Assembly, established under the government of César Gaviria to write a new constitution, which was completed in 1991. Commentators agree that the participation of a Quintín, together with that of the other two indigenous representatives, one from AICO, and the other from the National Indigenous Organization of Colombia (ONIC), had both substantive and symbolic value (Fajardo et al. 1999; Peñaranda 1998). Their key achievement was the institutionalization of indigenous people as a group, with special rights in Colombian society (Van Cott 2000). On the substantive front, the MAQL delegate, Alfonso Peña, presented a proposal for constitutional reform, which included several important themes, such as the multiethnic and multicultural character of the state, the protection of civil rights and social guarantees, and the rights of ethnic groups.[22] Equally important, perhaps, was the symbolic value of indigenous participation: it reaffirmed the pluralism of the Constitutional Assembly and reinforced its image as a place of peace (Peñaranda 1998, 220).

The legacy left by the Quintines is mixed. Commentators, such as

Ricardo Peñaranda (1998) and Juan Ibeas (1999), drawing on the work of Eduardo Pizarro (1996), concur that the Quintines can be viewed as "societal" guerrillas on account of their focus on local demands and local priorities, the creation of a strong local base with shared interests and recognized reciprocal obligations, and the geographical and political limitations on their activities. In fact, Ibeas (1999, 211) goes so far as to classify the Quintines as a type of partisan, an "indigenous combatant of agricultural origin who forms part of his own collectivity and his sociocultural surroundings." This characterization helps distinguish the Quintines from other guerrilla groups, which he classifies as either military, with their emphasis on the violent overthrow of the regime, or political, identified closely with an established political party. Although this distinction provides the Quintines with a certain advantage over the others in terms of flexibility and a certain freedom of action, in practice it was relative since they still had to respond to the cabildos and the cabildos were ultimately in charge.

The roots of the Quintines were planted in the late 1970s with the creation of the first embryonic self-defense unit, inspired partly by fear for the lives of their leaders but also by a strong sense of social injustice and moral outrage.[23] This assertion of agency provided meaning for their decision and subsequent acts: "Participation per se expressed moral outrage, asserted a claim to dignity, and gave grounds for pride" (Wood 2001, 268). It was moral outrage over the fate of the families in López Adentro and the murder of Padre Ulcué that prompted their first military interventions. This was also the case in their defense of community autonomy. But in their daily relationships with the communities, it appears that this moral outrage translated into a sense of moral authority, which they were called on to exercise on behalf of an impartial sense of justice that communities were willing to accept. But there was also a certain moral and political vision, articulated in the fliers distributed during the occupation of Santander in 1984, and later legitimated in the new constitution, with the importance attached to dignity, rights, and pluralism.

But the Quintines also have considerable symbolic importance. Their occupation of Santander in 1984, albeit for only a few hours, was an important event with historical precedents of similar indigenous uprisings earlier in the century. Their demobilization in 1991, conducted under international supervision and captured on video, is another. It

attracted a crowd of more than two thousand people, primarily indigenous, and the scenes from the event are included in many documen-
taries produced by CRIC and FST, established by the Quintines after
their demobilization. What is striking about these scenes is the extent to
which they validate the conclusions articulated by Alfonso Peña, regarding the recovery of indigenous pride. Both the crowd and the ex-
combatants are happy. As the guerrillas hand over their arms, they are
smiling into the camera. There is a festive air about the whole process,
and there is obviously something to celebrate. This is not the surrender
of a ragtag army; rather it is, if not a celebration at least an official
recognition of the Quintines and what they stood for, as demonstrated
by the terms they negotiated with the government and the fact that they
were represented by their own delegate at the Constitutional Assembly.

While a similar moral outrage characterized La Quintinada, there was
no productive or creative way to channel it. Although Quintín Lame believed in the potential of the national government and the Supreme
Court to change things for the better, this was an act of faith on his part,
rather than a considered decision by his followers. Although the MAQL
was more focused, there was a nagging, underlying feeling, particularly
on the part of the combatants, the vast majority of whom were indigenous, that they wanted to be involved on a larger stage that would
include more than just their fellow indigenous colleagues, that their solidarity and their struggle was much larger than just indigenous Cauca.
Participation in the Constitutional Assembly, the creation of their own
political party, and the election of their own representatives to the National Congress in Bogotá could potentially provide this opportunity.
The seeds planted by the Quintines in the 1980s were to bear fruit in La
María at the beginning of new millennium.

La María

The creation of La María has contributed to the establishment of a
viable civil society in Cauca. Though the concept of civil society has
been overutilized and overgeneralized over the past decade so that it can
incorporate almost any organizational form that falls on the spectrum
between the household and the state, it is important to accept and
understand that civil society can work either for or against the best
interests of the poor, the marginalized, and the excluded (Howell and

Pearce 2001). From the perspective of the right, a stronger civil society will enable the poor to participate more effectively in the project of modernity, on terms determined by the state where political stability is as important (if not more so) than political freedom and where the acceptable levels of peaceful opposition and dissent are carefully controlled. In this scenario, civil society can serve to check the excesses of government, without undermining or questioning the basic tenets under which the state operates, thus supposedly serving the common interests of society.

In contrast, the perspective of the left envisages civil society as the basis of a strengthened public sphere that can be the source of new and constructive thinking about the state, as well as a realm wherein dominant values and practices are contested. This happens when political space opens up and alternative candidates can freely run for public office, with all the necessary civil and political guarantees. But how can such a public sphere be established or strengthened where there is a long history of repression and ongoing political violence? It can only grow out of the courageous engagement of people at all levels of society: "This requires that people engage in collective action, build trust and confidence in their own capacities and the actions of others, and develop the ability to oppose and negotiate and ally themselves with other groups within civil society and with government as required" (Uvin 2004, 105). This collective action can take the form of a social movement, one that is dynamic and can build alliances and coalitions with other groups and other movements with similar or at least complementary interests. Social movements are often viewed as short-lived and ephemeral or long-lived and ossified. La María is neither: it is a beginning that continues to endure.

La María is strategically located on a bluff overlooking the Pan-American Highway on land donated by the Guambiano resguardo of the same name. The site consists of a complex of buildings: a large structure — a hangar-like building with a stage, tin roof, and open sides, which can accommodate several thousand people — and several smaller structures, including a dormitory, a communal kitchen, a community store, and a few houses. The place only comes to life when there are events, otherwise it is virtually deserted and has an abandoned air about it. Not surprisingly, the majority of events held there have been meetings of various sorts. One of the first to be held there in 2000 was a workshop entitled "From Silence to the Spoken Word." Held every weekend over a six-week period during January and February, it attracted over 250 participants, most of whom were under thirty, and some of whom were nonindigenous, from neighboring communities and from El Macizo, the Colombian Massif (La María 2000a). The objective of the seminar was to educate participants about the history and context within which the ongoing peace process had evolved by bringing in guest speakers from various parts of Colombia, as well as from neighboring Ecuador, to talk about a variety of topics. Subjects included the social agreements signed with CRIC and CIMA the previous year; the regional and national socioeconomic situation; the problems confronting indigenous groups elsewhere in Colombia; agrarian reform; human rights, justice, and economic, social, and cultural rights; and ways in which people could become directly involved in the peace process. Like the political schools of the Quintines more than a decade earlier, the primary objective was to educate people about what was happening in contemporary Colombia and encourage them to make their voices heard by the two sides involved in the peace process, the government and the guerrillas.

On a typical weekend, Saturday would be spent listening to and questioning the invited speakers, often well-known and well-respected leaders who talked about human rights, social inequity, and the peace process. The roster also included indigenous speakers from ONIC and the recent successful, large-scale indigenous mobilization in Ecuador. The audience would listen respectfully and attentively and, when the time came, respond with thoughtful comments and observations. The quality of the speakers varied considerably from those who tended to be dry and factual to those more obviously engaged and charismatic and to whom the participants responded more enthusiastically. The next day, Sunday, would be spent working in groups, discussing questions based on the speakers' presentations, selected partly by the audience and partly by the organizers (see figure 11). The groups, which brought together a wide cross-section of society, including teenagers, young adults, indigenous leaders, and elders, discussed a variety of topics and themes. While there were questions to do with the development of Colombia, there were others to do with the future of Colombian society and how Colombians were ever going to be able to live peacefully with one another:

Figure 11. Participants at La María working inside

— How to have an effect on the discussions about the distribution of the national budget and the other international loans and Plan Colombia?

— This territory is for living together, dialogue, and negotiation. What are we going to negotiate, and with whom?

— In a peace process can one accept "forgiving and forgetting?" If one does not, can one still reach an agreement between the parties?

The discussions were sometimes drawn out and tedious, but they could also be spirited, provocative, and challenging. The quality and intensity depended to a large extent on the person elected to chair the session: if she had some understanding of the issues at hand, then she could guide the discussion and also call on the more opinionated to speak out. For some, this was the first time they had participated in such an event where they were expected to participate in groups with people whom they perhaps did not already know and to discuss issues that transcended the local. But most participants were prepared to speak up when called on, achieving the overarching objective of this workshop in particular and La María in general to give voice to those previously silent and provide them with a public forum where they would be heard. In both the group and plenary discussions, all those who chose to speak were treated with the same respect and patience, irrespective of their age, gender, or ethnicity. Although there were outsiders from the Universidad San Buenaventura in Cali involved in the organization of the workshop, it was CRIC, with the assistance of FST and the Quintines, who exercised the overall leadership and responsibility.

The participants themselves reflected a mixture of interests determined partly by their degree of political activism but also by their geographical proximity to La María. They included representatives from several indigenous groups, Guambiano, Nasa, Coconuqueño, Totoreño, and Yanacona as well as Afro-Colombians; small-scale farmers; and mestizos, among them students and high school teachers. The students and teachers tended to be more radical, more critical, and better informed than the other participants. For this more radical group, specifically some students from Cali, the influence of the United States, whether in its support for Plan Colombia or its close relationships with the country's political and economic elites, was viewed as an important, if not crucial factor in explaining the present situation. Equally critical of the Colombian state, they were also skeptical about the effectiveness of initiatives such as La María, which they viewed as little more than a palliative. But this criticism went even further: respect for human rights was criticized as an imposition by the United States and hence not to be taken seriously or respected. This prompted a spirited defense of human rights by Henry Caballero, who argued that respect for human rights was one of the elements associated with democracy and that groups had been obliged to struggle for years before the national government acknowledged their importance and passed the necessary legislation guaranteeing their rights. While the participants accepted the right of the students to express their differing opinions, they did not appear to take them very seriously, since the students failed to either appreciate or understand the practices and potential dangers of everyday life in rural Cauca.

At the final meeting of the workshop, participants discussed ways in which they could disseminate what they had learned among the members of their own resguardos, as well as what to do in the future. They agreed to establish working groups, involving both indigenous and nonindigenous participants from the provinces of Cauca, Nariño, and the southern part of Valle, to deal with the unfulfilled social agreements; political violence; the lack of economic, social, and cultural rights; and agrarian reform. These groups later completed their work and their proposals were presented in Caguán to the FARC, though there is no record of the guerrillas' response. Subsequent discussions with the FARC, however, indicated that the guerrillas had no plans for treating indigenous people and other subaltern counterpublics any differently. In fact, they made it quite clear that indigenous people would not receive preferential treatment and would be treated just like any other Colombian citizens.

During the workshop some of the participants returned to their home communities at night, but many chose to bring blankets with them and sleep over in the makeshift dormitory. The meals were eaten communally, with participants dutifully lining up three times a day to be fed by a team of local volunteers. During the weekends, there were also cultural activities provided by participating groups, which included music, dancing, and even a puppet show depicting the life of Juan Tama (described in chapter 4) written and performed by the teachers and schoolchildren from Tóez Caloto. There were also cultural events during the workshop itself, specifically performances by groups of musicians and dancers, mostly young, spirited, and very enthusiastic (see figure 12).

The parallels with the closure of the highway in June of the previous year were striking, particularly the respect and reciprocity between the leaders and participants, and among the participants themselves. People were willing to pitch in and contribute to the overall undertaking, and a heightened level of trust was created. In La María everyone felt secure, in contrast to the outside, a difference driven forcefully home during the workshop. One weekend, during a discussion of the problems encountered in implementing customary law, word reached the participants that a well-respected indigenous leader who had recently stepped down as governor of his resguardo had just been murdered by some members of his own community in retaliation for action he had taken against them for dealing in drugs. Workshop participants were outraged that such acts of violence should occur within their own communities, and recur, continuously undermining the social fabric of indigenous society.

Because La María was regarded as a form of safe haven, certain types of behavior were unacceptable. While the FARC was and still is active in the area, the guerrillas did not accept the invitation, at least publicly, to participate in any of the events there, though they were fully aware of what was happening. They were not allowed to enter the area carrying arms. During the preceding years, local families had engaged in intense

Figure 12. The faces of the future

discussions with the guerrillas as they tried to recruit their sons, and sometimes their daughters, to join their forces, offering a uniform, a gun, food and lodging, and some financial renumeration, a tempting proposition for those with few employment alternatives. Local inhabitants who were known to have looted trucks "detained" by the guerrillas were fined. Excessive drinking was also severely sanctioned.

A second workshop, held in November 2000, was called "The Encounter of Social Organizations" and attracted some 1,500 participants from various parts of Colombia, as well as from overseas, for its two-day session. The principal objective was to discuss the relevance, focus, and alternatives to Plan Colombia, the U.S. government's program for the eradication of coca and opium poppies, organized primarily through support for the Colombian military and the provision of matériel for widespread fumigation (La María 2000b). A month earlier, Floro Tunubalá, a local leader, politician, teacher, and a member the Guambiano ethnic group, had been elected governor of Cauca, the first indigenous governor in the history of Colombia. His election had been made possible by the efforts of the Social Alternative Block, a coalition of progressive political groups, popular organizations, and social movements highly critical of the retiring governor and his administration, all determined to offer an alternative to his handpicked successor. In his speech of welcome to this workshop, the governor-elect expressed his hopes that the conclusions reached by the participants would help the incoming administration create new policies, clearly distinct from those that the national government had been pursuing in Cauca. He also invited all the participants to attend his forthcoming inauguration and take advantage of the unique moment in Cauca's history, not only because of his election but also because of the immense voter turnout. Speaking of the voters' effort, Tunubalá said:

> That indicates that deep down the people of Cauca have a different way of thinking at this very difficult time, so beaten by the different armed groups, therefore to invite you so that we can reflect upon these problems [of illegal crops] with a clear head and that with this clear head we can look at the destiny of Cauca and we can prepare a policy where all the social organizations can participate with hopes in an immediate future in which Cauca will offer a different scenario for social and economic development. (La María 2000b, 22–23)

Here, the governor-elect was capitalizing on his broad base of popular support across the various ethnic groups and social classes, rural and urban, found in Cauca, with the hope that together they could agree on and create a new way of addressing the province's problems and envisioning its future.

The Alternate Plan for Cauca

Although La María exists in people's memories as a place where they have directly confronted the state and in their imaginations as a space where they can demonstrate their autonomy and demand to be respected and taken seriously, its reality is based on "happenings," such as those discussed here, events that are out of the ordinary, a response to events in the larger society that are increasingly life-threatening, such as abandonment by the state, exclusion from the peace process, and, latterly, violation by Plan Colombia. These crises served as catalysts and contexts for the creation of solidarity, and the spaces that were opened provide opportunities for those previously excluded to provide an alternative vision of civil society, one in which they would be participants and actors. The November 2000 workshop offered some clues as to what this alternative vision might consist of and laid the groundwork for what was to become Minga for Cauca, the province's development

233

plan for the period 2001–2003 (Departamento del Cauca 2001). While the events at La María captured the concerns and voices of the marginal, those excluded from the political process, the development plan articulates some of the same priorities, this time produced by those who were now part of the process.

The plan provides a brief vision of what a more peaceful, just, and inclusive Cauca would entail. While its most immediate roots were in evidence during the November 1999 workshop that officially created La María, its longer term roots have been nurtured over the decades by the thoughts and actions of those who have resisted and sought to change the status quo. There has been a growing demand for autonomy and economic solidarity, accompanied by an increasing realization that indigenous people cannot achieve this on their own. If Cauca is to change for the better, this will only happen through a concerted, peaceful effort by people and groups from all walks of like, increasingly dissatisfied with present conditions.

In the text of the plan are embedded certain key concepts, all of which fall under the general rubric of sustainable development with a core of "integrated human development." In this framework, the human is privileged over the economic, with an emphasis on quality of life, social equity, harmony, and stewardship for future generations. Environmental sustainability is viewed as a means for conserving life, not as an end in itself. Demand for imported goods would be lowered; locally produced, environmentally benign products would be offered in their place; and patterns of Northern-style consumption eliminated. This restructured economic system would generate a surplus that would be used to benefit the whole collectivity within a system of economic democracy. This anticapitalist proposal is rooted in indigenous nostalgia about the production systems of the past and clearly stated in other contemporary indigenous development plans discussed in earlier chapters.

Throughout the plan, reference is made to groups rarely highlighted in development texts—children, women, young people, the handicapped—further underlying its inclusive appeal. In addition, culture is emphasized as a force that can contribute to improved mutual understanding between groups and the collective resolution of regional problems. Indigenous culture is singled out for its potential contribution: "Indigenous culture, which guards in its heart the fundamental principles for the strengthening of social capital, will be the basis for a teaching process through which to spread the application of the principles of identity, governability and 'associativeness,' the major ingredients for constructing collective synergy" (Departamento del Cauca 2001, n.p.). This statement characterizes contemporary indigenous culture as the basis for strengthening social capital and disseminating certain key principles, all of which can serve to counter the feelings of neglect and exclusion. Identity can instill pride, governability implies the acceptance of the rule of law, and "associativeness" refers to the more positive aspects of social capital and the potential to come together and work out common solutions.

In the plan, there is a chapter entitled "Strategies of Harmony and Peace," a direct response to the war in Cauca, with a section, "Alternate Plan to Plan Colombia," that sketches out a framework for dealing directly with the problems associated with the chemical spraying and eradication of illegal crops. It proposes manual eradication accompanied by the introduction of alternative crops, both of which call for state support and are practical and viable. This framework and its accompanying principles — the environment, local knowledge, and cultural processes — offer different ways of thinking about development, modernity, and the future. The Alternate Plan is presented as a process for the reconstruction of Cauca, based on cultural identity and environmental sustainability, and incorporating the development plans produced by resguardos and municipalities. People's relationship to their immediate physical environment is highlighted, and they are viewed as part of it, not separate from it.

During the governorship of Tunubalá, this Alternate Plan, while still a work in process, expanded and became part, in theory at least, of a regional plan incorporating five neighboring provinces. The objective was more regional autonomy with the authority to negotiate directly with the various armed groups active in the region (Jaramillo 2005). But when Álvaro Uribe assumed the presidency of Colombia in August 2002, his government would have nothing to do with this plan, in contrast to the Europeans, who had no qualms about financing certain parts of it. In an interview in 2001, at the end of a very dangerous first year in office, Tunubalá clearly stated how the Alternate Plan differed from previous state development plans (Jaramillo 2001). It was a political and organizational process that captured the diversity of opinion and thought expressed by the various groups in the province — indigenous

235

people, peasants, intellectuals, academics, and workers. This process also made possible his election and his selection of cabinet members who would implement the plan. Finally, it was a direct challenge to the policy espoused by the national government and Plan Colombia with its emphasis on the forced eradication of illegal crops, a policy that continues to bedevil Cauca.

These key concepts, the practice of which is radical, provocative, and articulated by an increasingly vocal counterpublic, embody the ideal of "communitas," first employed by Victor Turner in his studies of ritual (1969) and Christian pilgrimages (Turner and Turner 1978). Communitas can best be understood in relationship to structure and the ensuing tension between the two:

> Structure, or all that which holds people apart, defines their differences, and constrains their actions, is one pole of a charged field, for which the opposite pole is communitas, or anti-structure, the egalitarian "sentiment for humanity" of which David Hume speaks, representing the desire for a total, unmediated relationship between person and person. (Turner 1974, 274)

The bonds of communitas are antistructural because they are undifferentiated, egalitarian, direct, extant, nonrational, existential relationships. While communitas is spontaneous, immediate, and concrete, it is part of the "serious life" and tends to bypass structural relationships (Turner and Turner 1978, 250). Of the three types of communitas identified by Turner (1969, chap. 3), existential, normative, and ideological, the latter most closely approximates the experiences of La María and the principles of Cauca's development plans: "The formulation of remembered attributes of the communitas experience in the form of a utopian blueprint for the reform of society" (Turner 1978, 252). The solidarity that people are nostalgic for and reminisce about is another form of this communitas, articulated through the discourse of a counterpublic that has used La María as a base for overcoming the barriers of exclusion.

The Alternate Plan presented one way to think about how Cauca as a province might be reformed, and La María has continued to serve as a staging ground for principled stands and broader reforms that implicate the country as a whole. In September 2004, CRIC, in collaboration with popular organizations and other social movements, organized a peaceful march from La María to Cali, primarily to protest the ongoing violence and repression but also to raise other issues dealing with proposed changes to the national constitution, as well as the ongoing negotiations over the proposed free trade agreement between the United States and Colombia and its Andean neighbors. The march lasted four days and mobilized sixty thousand participants, many indigenous, and many who were not. The march was peaceful, with the indigenous civil guard responsible for successfully maintaining law and order. It attracted both national and international attention, partly because it was multicultural and partly because the indigenous movement was viewed as the only entity with the organizational capability and political courage to mount such an undertaking. The full title for the march embodies how far the resistance of Quintín Lame, Padre Ulcué, CRIC, and the Quintines had come in a little less than a century, and how much broader and all encompassing it had become: Minga for Life, Justice, Happiness, Autonomy and Liberty, Mobilization against the Project of Death, and in Favor of a Life Plan for the Towns and Communities.[24]

From Partisans to Citizens

In their discourse as a guerrilla force, the Quintines claimed that they were fighting on behalf of indigenous rights, as well as indigenous dignity, just as Quintín Lame had done earlier. CRIC has peacefully struggled for the same goals, under the banner of unity, land, and culture. With their demobilization, the Quintines, in close collaboration with CRIC, continued this fight in different fora — the Constitutional Assembly, the work of FST, the creation of La María, the election of the governor of Cauca, and the continuing social mobilizations. In the process, the movement tried to expand its constituency within Cauca to include both Afro-Colombians and peasants, building on the Quintines' earlier discourse of pluralism, while at the same time appropriating selected components of the civil society discourse of inclusion. This growing appeal and increasing political sophistication have been accompanied by some serious challenges presented by a national government, which in spite of the agreements signed, refused to honor its commitments. Yet even with these setbacks, the movement continued to petition the government when all the evidence indicated that their efforts were futile, at least in practical terms. Analyzing a similar situation that confronted the coca producers of Putumayo in 1996, María Clemencia Ramírez (2001b) argues that a mass mobilization of this type demonstrates a politics of recognition through which the national government is obliged to compensate for its enduring absence and neglect by appearing in person to negotiate directly with the leadership. The highly publicized negotiations completed, the state then retreats, leaving the situation unchanged and the mobilized increasingly marginalized. But in the case of Putumayo, the mobilized also demanded that the government treat them as human beings, as Colombian citizens. By insisting on direct negotiations and the signing of agreements, the marginalized were not only exercising their rights as citizens but also participating in a system of participatory democracy promoted by the state. In other words, as active members of Colombian civil society, they were arguing for an end to their marginalization and the promotion of their inclusion, which only the state can grant.

In the case of indigenous Cauca, and other groups such as Afro-Colombians and peasants, such inclusion has been only partial. But this does not answer the enduring enigma of why, after decades of protest and government neglect, the indigenous movement continues to mobilize on behalf of their rights as citizens. Albert Hirschman (1984) has suggested that people who have participated in earlier, more radical movements that generally failed to achieve their objectives, often because of official repression, do not necessarily lose their desire for social change nor their faith in collective action. He refers to this enduring, paradoxical phenomenon as social energy, capable of reappearing under certain conditions, but perhaps in a somewhat different form, aided, in the case of Cauca, by the social and political space offered by the new constitution. There is abundant evidence from elsewhere in Latin America of such continuities, not only from one era to another but also across social movements (Edelman 2001). Discussing a similar phenomenon in Mexico, Jonathan Fox (1997) asks why civic failure leads to powerlessness and frustration in some cases, whereas in others it is creatively reworked into social energy. Repression can cut both ways: it can lead to a downward spiral of demobilization or, alternatively, it can facilitate collective action. He suggests that political ideas and culture may make the difference, in the process privileging the thoughts and actions of those most directly involved.

La María filled this role by providing the political space not only to organize and strengthen collective solidarity among the various participating groups but also to serve as a forum for spreading ideas throughout the province, one counterpublic responsible for reaching a wider (counter)public. This was clearly demonstrated by the workshop in 2000 with 1,500 participants dedicated to exploring alternatives to Plan Colombia, later to appear in Cauca's triennial development plan. Fraser (1997) talks about the liberating potential of such counterpublics. In the case of Cauca, some of this potential has been realized by La María and its followers, but with an added twist. The struggle was (and still is) also a fight for recognition, respect, and dignity, the desire to be accepted by the larger society and to permit indigenous ideas to transform not only indigenous society but the dominant society as well. But this struggle has been only partially successful, since this acceptance has not been accompanied by major changes on the part of the state nor by other major actors, such as the guerrillas.

The state, for example, has done little to protect the indigenous movement and its leaders from the continuing armed attacks of the armed groups of the left, of the paramilitaries, or the military, for that matter. In spring 2005, the FARC renewed its attacks on the Nasa of the north, attacking and laying siege to several resguardos, including Toribío and Tacueyó. They were finally repelled, until the next such attack, by the peaceful resistance of the local population and the military occupation of the zone, supported by helicopters provided by Plan Colombia. For La María to effectively survive as a counterpublic and be able to contribute to ongoing debates and actions about the province's — and the country's —future, it has tried to become more inclusive by confronting issues that potentially affect all Colombians, not just those who happen to be indigenous. The political space offered by La María helped open up a wider, broader, more inclusive political space in the province under the leadership of its first indigenous governor. This victory clearly demonstrated the potential of the counterpublic, of the effort made by the Quintines and the indigenous movement to evolve from partisans to pluralists into citizens determined to participate in the political process but also dedicated to changing it to become both more inclusive and more responsive. This called for the forging of a culturally informed *mundus imaginalis moralis*—a moral imaginary—that reinforces and strengthens an indigenous presence in the region but also engages the moral promises of the Enlightenment, complementing the discourse of human rights with those of economic, social, and cultural rights.

239

I want us to keep in mind at least two audiences for our work. There are, first of all, the students, for whom studying [social] movements ought to be a moral enterprise. This is a field rich with the stories about human possibility, about moments of transcendence, about the times when ordinary people have changed the world.—RICHARD FLACKS, "Knowledge for What? Thoughts on the State of Social Movement Studies"

Countering Development:

Indigenous Modernity and the Moral Imagination

The struggle for social justice is more than political and cultural: it is also philosophical. James Jasper (1997) proposes that the incorporation of culture into the study of social movements is often highly cognitive, with little attention devoted to either emotions or moral visions. He suggestively argues that collective action is a fertile arena for new understandings of the world and new patterns for action: "Learning—which is difficult for perfectly rational or perfectly irrational human beings—lies at the heart of social movements. *Far from being the opposite of rationality, culture, including emotions, defines rationality*" (98; emphasis added).[1] Furthermore, culture itself is inherently dynamic and subject to continuous and continuing change. In the processes described in the previous chapters, culture has played differing and sometimes ambiguous roles. In the resettled communities, people have chosen to accept it, manipulate it, or flaunt it. In the movements of resistance, culture has evolved from one based on a particular identity to one embracing many identities and sharing certain key values and beliefs. As Arjun Appadurai (2004, 59) has argued, "It is in culture that ideas of the future, as much as ideas about the past, are embedded and nurtured." While the disaster of 1994 and the continuing armed conflict have between them caused considerable pain and suffering for the people of Cauca, indigenous and nonindigenous alike, they have also paradoxically provided unthought-of and perhaps unheard-of possibilities and opportunities. It is during precisely these traumatic events, these moments of total crisis, that people have the opportunity to remake themselves, their culture, and perhaps their society.

Throughout the book, I have discussed how persistent and courageous the Nasa have been in various situations and contexts, as well as the extent to which they have been creative and imaginative. Their continuing principled stand against the political violence of the state and the armed groups of the left and the right bears this out, as does their willingness and capability to maintain order without resort to arms. Their persistence in establishing their own system of education, as well as the reinvention of the importance of the shamans and the role of customary law, bear witness to their creativity. Furthermore, they have also been moral. In the preceding chapter I argued that much of the indigenous resistance in Cauca has been fired up by a strong sense of justice. This fight has been only partially successful, if judged solely in legal or material terms, so why do people continue to struggle? The politics of recognition offers a partial explanation, since the struggle has also been about citizenship, pressuring the state to fulfill its responsibilities to all Colombians.

Kevin Hetherington (1998) has suggested that the success or failure of new social movements, particularly those directed at changing society, or at least certain parts of it, cannot be viewed solely in instrumental political terms. He writes, "Alternative criteria include a sense of group belonging, communitas and solidarity, personal achievement through being involved, converting skeptics to a cause, and highlighting the alternative values expressed by a group. . . . Therefore, political action and the performance of identity are inextricably intertwined" (146). In Cauca, the success of the indigenous movement has been built on resistance to the earlier persecution by the state and local landowners, as well as the continuing persecution and assassination of their leaders. This persecution was perhaps most severe during the late 1980s when those in power identified the Regional Indigenous Council of Cauca (CRIC) with the Quintín Lame Armed Movement (MAQL), and the elected leadership was either imprisoned or forced to go into hiding. In the case of the Quintines, it can be argued that they have been more successful as demobilized guerrillas (*reinsertados*) than as active combatants with the creation of their own foundation, the Sun and Land Foundation (FST), the founding of La María, and the establishment of the Indigenous Social Alliance (ASI), their own political party.

In this conclusion, I pull together several strands that have tied the preceding chapters together — specifically the roles of planning and culture, and the resulting communitas. I also, however, wish to incorporate the idea of the moral imagination, creatively manifested in other conflict-ridden countries, as a bridge to the larger themes underlying much of this book: the quest for citizenship and the recognition and observance of human rights. I argue that this is a different and more productive way of thinking about development. From this perspective, development is less integration into the project of modernity and more a creative form of resistance, a form of counterdevelopment, more explicitly critical of modernity, which can contribute to a radical politics of inclusive citizenship.

Planning as a Subversive Act

Planning is often regarded as one of the necessary evils of development, a task that has to be completed to satisfy bureaucratic requirements, thereby severely curtailing if not outright eliminating any tendencies toward creativity or spontaneity. Yet planning, in the broader sense of thinking about ways to deal with present injustices, can also be subversive if the actions undertaken threaten the underpinnings of the status quo. The processes described in chapter 6, La Quintinada, the Quintines, and La María, as well as the responses to the 1994 disaster, can all be viewed from this perspective. They have long-term implications and effects that seek to enlarge the political space and shift the political balance from the local to the regional to the national. These processes serve as a model of what people can achieve when they work together. They provide a glimpse of the possible. Though the disaster did not create the need for development planning, it did provide the context for a more creative vision of what planning could accomplish, an opportunity to subvert conventional ideas about development, often in unpredictable and unforeseen ways.

Planning at the community level has been Janus-faced. On the one hand, it is a process that fulfills the requirements of the modern bureaucratic state, providing a category of information that can justify the release of resources, usually financial, to implement certain specified activities. The information requested usually falls within certain carefully specified parameters that define what is acceptable; plans falling outside these limits are deemed unacceptable. Hence, communities learn the rules of the game and usually propose the types of activities that they know the state, or other entities with control over resources, will approve. As a result, there is little room for either originality or creativity. On the other hand, given the increasing importance attached to participation and empowerment in conventional development discourse, planning opens a potential Pandora's box, since it provides a window of opportunity previously closed to all but the politically powerful. This tension between the acceptable and the unacceptable, between the bureaucratic and the creative, is exemplified by the planning process in San José and Cxayu'ce where the two major issues were (and still are) land and education. While neither appeared in the official community plan, since neither fit the accepted "bricks and mortar" definition of development, both figured prominently in the everyday lives of the people, forming an unwritten addendum to the written development plan.

One way to deal with this paradox is for a community to plan for one activity, but use the resources provided to support another activity, in hopes that the discrepancy will pass unnoticed, not an uncommon occurrence in the field of development. Another way is to have two distinct types of planning, one for the state and its priorities, and another for the community and its priorities. The latter offers the opportunity to subvert the status quo because it is the community that initiates the process by privileging local knowledge. While critics have argued that local knowledge merely reflects the interests of local power and that subalterns cannot plan because in the process they lose their subaltern perspective (Spivak 1988), others have viewed local knowledge as fluid and dynamic, continually informed by external events and information, but fragmentary in its distribution (Sillitoe 2002). Planning for education offers such an opportunity. While this process was still in the embryonic stages in San José and Cxayu'ce, both Tóez Caloto and Juan Tama had not only produced their own educational plans but also implemented them in their own schools. Teachers were, of course, active participants in both places, as were the members of CRIC in the case of Juan Tama. But there were significant differences between the two processes' responses to external and internal factors.

The process in Juan Tama was more creative and original, drawing largely on Nasa concepts; it was also more realistic, accepting the fact that if students wished to continue their education, they would have to do so as Nasa in the neighboring mestizo school. As a result, teachers from both schools were actively involved in trying to make this transition and integration as smooth and as equitable as possible. It also says something about the faith and confidence of the teachers and their parents. They obviously felt that their students had the necessary training and self-confidence to survive in the world beyond the community. The same process could be observed in the CRIC school in Cxayu'ce, indigenous but surrounded by mestizo peasants, where students, once they had completed primary, could continue their secondary education in the neighboring mestizo town. This process is also very much part of the intercultural and pluralistic vision of CRIC, the Quintines, La María, and the government of Floro Tunubalá with its emphasis on mutual learning, respect, and collaboration.

Tóez Caloto shared Juan Tama's desire to control the substance of its children's education, but it did not enjoy the same autonomy. As a public school entirely dependent on state funds and supervised by a state-run educational administration, there were limits on the extent to which it could experiment with the curriculum. In addition, Tóez Caloto had a different and perhaps grander agenda: to (re)cover that which they had "lost" culturally in Tierradentro, thereby convincing their indigenous, Afro-Colombian, and peasant neighbors that they were "authentic" Nasa. In this way, they hoped to create a political space for themselves in northern Cauca. But they lacked the vision of Juan Tama and CRIC: their recovered authenticity was a passport to a modernizing ideology that did not permit them to look inside indigenous culture and inside themselves to create an original curriculum (or an original development plan, for that matter).

In the process of demonstrating their "Nasaness," parents in Tóez Caloto (and to a lesser extent teachers) were simultaneously subverting or transforming indigenous culture, as exemplified in their fixation on having Nasa Yuwe taught in school to reluctant students whose own parents were unwilling to teach them the language or even speak it to them at home. This ambivalent attitude indicates that parents did not regard fluency in Nasa Yuwe as important, which was reflected in the differing responses of the students when asked which language they preferred. Hence, the teaching of Nasa Yuwe was primarily for external consumption, for the benefit of neighboring communities and the larger context of the indigenous movement. In this way, language became a commodity to be marketed. But this ambivalence was more fully demonstrated in the puppet play. Their production of the story of Juan Tama, in which teachers and students played a crucial role, was creative and imaginary, but it was highly critical of one of the core elements of Nasa culture: unquestioning acceptance of the role and importance of Juan Tama in Nasa history and the strengthening of indigenous identity. From their perspective, his actions were responsible for the present situation of the Nasa. In essence, the play argued that Juan Tama and his message were irrelevant for the contemporary Nasa, specifically those living in Tóez Caloto and, by implication, those living elsewhere in northern Cauca, in places such as Toribío. In short, they viewed culture in an essentialized way, in contrast to Juan Tama, where culture is fluid and malleable, making it strong enough to interact with appropriate dominant cultural forms.

The discussions in Tóez Caloto during the planning workshops, concerning the proper role of the shamans and the importance to be attached to customary law with its implied blessing of corporal punishment, were more political than cultural. In the earlier years, local leaders had indicated their disdain for such practices and refused to allow the shamans to have any official role in community affairs. Over time, however, they changed their opinions to reflect the perspective endorsed by the indigenous movement as a whole. In this, they were very much in a minority in the community, where the role and importance of the shamans had been steadily decreasing. Once again, this can be seen as a deliberate attempt, in spite of all the internal evidence to the contrary, to demonstrate to their neighbors just how indigenous they are, without making an effort to revitalize a lived culture.

The Nasa of the north, specifically those living in Toribío, were proposed as a potential model because they have the longest direct experiences of planning activities and are also the most politically sophisticated. But as a model of what: indigenous modernity or peasant survival? What is most striking, and perhaps most disturbing, about Toribío's experiences, when comparing the plan of 1980 with that of 1998, is the different way in which politics and culture are viewed. The 1980 document is radical and subversive in its discussion of political violence, discrimination against women, and overburdened *cabildos,* and in its call to people to resolve their problems on their own, to exercise their autonomy and their agency. However, there is little or no mention of culture per se, perhaps not surprising in a workshop sponsored by representatives of the Catholic Church, and the discussion of identity is presciently ambivalent. In the prize-winning 1998 plan, politics has disappeared, culture has, for the most part, been relegated to the domain of sport and recreation, and identity is not an issue. Nevertheless, this sanitized document also contains its own imaginary: its dream of a solidarity economy, a moral community built on regional self-sufficiency, reciprocity, and mutual respect. This imaginary is potentially subversive, since it seeks to have some control over the market while at the same time introducing some moral order into it. Yet the values put forward are essentially peasant values, those shared by small farmers throughout the region. Like the people of Tóez Caloto, their colleagues in Toribío may also be subverting indigenous culture, whatever remains of it in the north.

In Juan Tama, in contrast, people view economic growth as a means of providing security, as well as the opportunity for them to grow spiritually and politically. They also stress the social and cultural importance of work, of physical labor, as a distinguishing characteristic of the Nasa. This is demonstrated by the fact that they have managed to make the land more productive by nurturing it, rather than dominating it. At the same time, however, there is a realization and acceptance that the economy per se is unpredictable, more precarious than in the other communities. When Don Ángel, the leader and shaman, boasts that they are living in glory in Juan Tama, he is talking in cultural rather than economic terms.

Communitas and Culture

Extraordinary events create communitas among those most directly affected, a process replicated in other liminal situations. Social movements can also create this aura of solidarity and responsibility, as shown by the events described at La María, and the histories of the Quintines and La Quintinada. The same holds true for disasters, where people will do extraordinary things on behalf of their fellow women and men. But does this communitas extend beyond such events and touch the everyday lives of ordinary people? The most dramatic example of a continuing communitas created by the disaster is Tóez Caloto, a fragmented community back in Tierradentro. While the totality of the disaster forced them to cooperate and help each other, this solidarity continued afterward, as shown by their efforts to secure more land, establish a health clinic, and build their own school.

But this solidarity also had its limits, since it could be both exclusive and conservative. The community as a whole was very critical of those families who, for various reasons, decided to return to Tierradentro. On the one hand, they were accused of being feckless and failing to take advantage of the opportunities offered to them in the form of land, housing, and education. On the other hand, they were the victims of self-righteous moral opprobrium, suspected of returning to Tierradentro essentially to work full-time on cultivating opium poppies. There was a widespread belief, one not necessarily shared by all the families in Tóez Caloto, that Juan Tama had sent the disaster as both a warning and punishment to the Nasa for deserting their old ways and ignoring the principles that he had laid down. Prior to the disaster, it was common knowledge that Tóez was one of the centers of poppy production. The discourse of exclusion was also self-serving, because many families in Tóez Caloto, (as well as in Cxayu'ce), returned to their home communities in Tierradentro to tend their poppy plots.

Solidarity could also work against the better interests of the community, as shown by the unwillingness of Tóez Caloto to realistically address, as a community, the crucial problems of agricultural production and productivity, the basis for some form of economic viability. While the people of Cxayu'ce were only too willing to learn how to cultivate from their new mestizo neighbors, most of the families of Tóez Caloto were not, although knowledgeable neighbors did approach them offering their services, albeit for a fee. The leaders of Tóez Caloto had fought long and hard to obtain these productive lands, winning the admiration of many for their persistence and tenacity, only to fall short when it came to devising ways to work them productively. At times, it appeared as if the formal and informal leaders in the community were the only ones able to or interested in taking advantage of these opportunities.

Ironically, one of the original arguments made by the Nasa Kiwe Corporation (CNK) for not buying such productive land was that the Nasa lacked the necessary technical experience to work it effectively. 247

Although this reservation proved to be correct, it does not capture the community's ambivalent feelings about wholeheartedly embracing the market economy of northern Cauca. Addressing the lack of technical expertise would have required external assistance, something which could have jeopardized the community's well-developed sense of autonomy and their desire to serve as a model for neighboring communities. Another, perhaps more realistic explanation is that the majority of people in Tóez Caloto were just not that interested in being economically successful, realizing the gravity of the risks involved. By accepting that radical changes would be demanded in their present behavior if they were, say, to start producing for specialized urban markets, they were well aware they might finish up losing their land if things did not work out as planned.

In the case of Juan Tama, the disaster contributed nothing to overall communitas in the short term. The various sectors involved in the exodus brought their old political and religious differences with them, and it appeared that the disaster only exacerbated these fractures, strengthening the feeling of communitas only within individual sections and eventually providing them with the necessary cohesion to leave and establish their own new communities. Yet in spite of the fact that half of the original population of Juan Tama left, the factionalism and political in-fighting continued. Several factors, however, helped overcome these debilitating characteristics. First was their ongoing struggle with CNK over what they regarded as their due in terms of land and housing. This type of griping was also found in Tóez Caloto and Cxayu'ce, but it was particularly pronounced in Juan Tama, where it was almost an obsession, only alleviated when CNK finally delivered on its original promises.

A second contributing factor was their isolation in a frontier-like no-man's-land located between two provinces, where there was a long-standing, well-known Revolutionary Armed Forces of Colombia (FARC) presence and they were the only indigenous people in the area, surrounded by mestizo neighbors, most of whom were small farmers like themselves. The police station in the local town of Santa Leticia had been closed down years before, so the guerrillas could come and go as they wished. The Nasa, however, appear to have worked out an acceptable modus vivendi with both sets of neighbors. Coming as they did from Vitoncó, the heartland of Nasa culture and the home of Juan

Tama, they had no doubts about their Nasaness and took pride in boasting that they were Nasa to their neighbors.

A third factor that evidently helped to create solidarity was the establishment of the CRIC-supported school. While the school had existed in Vitoncó before the disaster, it had been obliged to compete with the Church-affiliated school. This struggle continued in Juan Tama, until CRIC won out and the Catholic school withdrew, with its teachers accompanying the families who left to the new settlement in Itaibe. Though the disaster made this victory possible, it did not eliminate all the criticism and dissent within the community. It did, however, provide a center around which the community could focus its considerable energy and imagination. In Juan Tama, culture has provided a powerful base to inspire their educational philosophy and reinforce their indigenous identity, not as ethnic separatists but as indigenous citizens who wish to embrace modernity, but on their terms. In Tóez Caloto, in contrast, culture, in the guise of separatism, has been reinvented as a way to make modernity's embrace that much easier.

The situation in Cxayu'ce is distinct. Both Juan Tama and Tóez Caloto had such contentious relationships with their communities of origin in Tierradentro that they wished to separate themselves completely and form new, independent *resguardos,* something Tóez Caloto achieved in 2005. Cxayu'ce, in contrast, has maintained a close relationship with San José, though this did prevent it from also becoming an independent resguardo in 2004. There is a strong feeling of communitas that already existed in San José prior to the disaster. Although much smaller than the other two new communities, three families dominate the politics and economy, just as they did before the disaster. But the major difference is that this is the second time in forty years that San José has been destroyed, a reality that weighs heavily on the minds and memories of the older community members. The occurrence of two disasters within living memory gave rise to ambivalent feelings about Tierradentro as a physical rather than a cultural home. As a geographical location, San José had suffered politically and environmentally. But as a cultural location, embodying much of importance to the Nasa, it still exerted a key attraction. A second significant difference is that Cxayu'ce has a viable economic base. After the disaster, the leaders of San José, like their counterparts in Tóez Caloto, were adamant about obtaining lower ly-

ing, warmer lands near the provincial capital. In this they were successful, accepting from the very beginning the absolute necessity to learn
about new crops and new technologies from their mestizo neighbors.
Nevertheless, they did not try to enter the market with products requir-
ing complex inputs and radical reorganization of their labor inputs, the
choice facing Tóez Caloto. They remained small farmers, but ones willing to take advantage of any opportunities that might arise.

Culturally and politically, the people of Cxayu'ce have more in common with Juan Tama than with Tóez Caloto, but without the simmering
frustrations and pretensions of the other two and without their cultural
self-consciousness. They have few qualms about being indigenous, nor
are they trying to prove anything to their neighbors, who view them
as hard-working and industrious. The fact that the primary school is
open to all has helped the process. The access to new, productive land
tapped into a long-standing but never clearly articulated frustration with
a steadily deteriorating natural resource base in Tierradentro. The disaster offered one clear-cut, simple way of dealing with this problem, while
at the same time allowing people to get the best of both worlds — the
"old" in Tierradentro and the "new" in Cxayu'ce.

Indigenous Modernity and the Moral Imagination

In her powerful, provocative ethnography of the civil war in Mozam-
bique, Carolyn Nordstrom (1997) offers many examples of how, once
the peace accords were signed and began to be implemented, individuals and communities created new worlds that neither the international
community nor national leaders knew about, were interested in, or
cared to support. For example, international assistance was provided for
health care in the form of clinics and hospitals, but not for the shamans
who were trying to educate people away from a mentality of violence
and war. The same ignorance and benign neglect characterized education and local systems of justice. Nordstrom wrestles with this question
of how local people manage to survive under appalling social, economic, and political conditions, how they go about creating a world in
which they can live in relative harmony. She proposes the concept of
mundus imaginalis, the creative imaginary, "that realm of the imagination [which] mediates between sense and intellect, matter and mind,

inside (self) and outside (self-in-world), the given and the possible"
(Nordstrom 1997, 202).[2] The imagination is the main source of auto-
poiesis (self-production) amplifying Arturo Escobar's point that social movements can be characterized as autopoietic since they are self-
producing and self-organizing entities (Escobar 1995b, 224).

Nordstrom provides an example of this in an interview with a group of
older women, who detail a community's responses for those who return
after having suffered as a result of the civil war. One participant stated:

> When people come back to our community . . . one of the most important
> things they need is calm — to have the violence taken out of them. We ask
> that everyone who arrives here be taken to a Curandeira [shaman] or Curan-
> deiro for treatment. The importance of the Curandeira lies not only in her or
> his ability to treat the diseases and physical ravages of war, but in their ability
> to take the violence out of a person and to reintegrate them back into a
> healthy lifestyle. (Nordstrom 1997, 210)

This offer is open to everyone: "They do this with soldiers too. If someone finds a soldier wandering alone, we take him and bring him to a
Curandeiro. They remind the person how to be part of their family, to
work their *machamba* [farm] to get along, to be part of the community"
(210). It is the community and its resident specialists who creatively
work to reintegrate those who return, irrespective of which side they
were on and what they may have done during the conflict, including
those who may have instigated violence against the community itself.
There are several related themes here, such as responsibility, compassion, and forgiveness, all reinforced by the moral authority of the community, particularly that of the women.

Nordstrom's research also indicated that most people in areas of conflict work to create a healthy society. While fully acknowledging that the
new communities created were not free from injustice, she sees the
majority working for the common good (212). Hence, she argues that
the creative imagination also contains a fundamental ethics, a *mundus
imaginalis moralis,* a moral imagination that allows people to empathize
with the plight of others.[3] Michael Ignatieff (2001a) reinforces this
point, arguing that without this empathy, there cannot be any solidarity
worthy of the name. But Nordstrom is also careful not to fall into the
trap of blinkered idealism.

> To say people's creativity is endowed with an ethical imagination is not to say that people create worlds free of abuse and contestation. . . . There is no reason to conclude that, while people created new communities in war-torn Mozambique, they created communities free from injustice. Certainly theft, murder, oppression, domestic violence, sexual abuse, incest, and interpersonal aggression existed in the communities being rebuilt in Mozambique during the war. . . . Every community [I visited] (and here I mean civil community) generated systems and institutions for dealing with exactly these problems. (Nordstrom 1997, 214)

The exercise of moral imagination calls for empathy with the plight of others, of being aware of their specific needs and problems, while at the same time having some clear idea of what is right and what is wrong, along with "a set of images of one's own obligations for achieving through practical action better conditions for all concerned" (Fernandez and Huber 2001, 263). This moral element was behind the founding of CRIC, the establishment of the Quintines, and the creation of La María. Though all three may be viewed as direct responses to external threats to personal security and livelihood, they also contributed to what people hoped would be the creation of something different, better, and more moral — the achievement of harmony, balance, and peace. The Nasa quest for justice has not been exclusive, restricted solely to their own ethnic group. Rather, it has been inclusive, directed at benefiting all who have been exploited and discriminated against, demonstrated most clearly in the events at La María, CRIC's support for the Committee for the Integration of the Colombian Massif's (CIMA) month-long blockade of the Pan-American Highway, as well as the march to Cali in 2004. Where participants have been able to successfully control their own immediate environment, they have been able to put their moral imagination to practical use in the ways that they have related to each other as well as to the representatives of external institutions and organizations, such as the state or the various armed groups. But the experiences of the communities studied also provide insights into how the moral imagination can generate a process of countermodernity.

Trends and practices that operate in opposition to the mainstream, such as counterdevelopment and counterpublics, fit in well with the larger story of ongoing resistance. Yet this resistance to the state is not in opposition to it; rather, it is the demand to be recognized as indigenous and be treated as citizens: to become a vital part of it. The key words are *recognition, respect,* and, by implication, *inclusion.* While the quest for justice is a demand for respect and dignity, it is also a request that the state be more inclusive, more democratic, that it treat *all* of its citizens better and allow *all* of them to contribute to the national well-being. The future desired by the Nasa, at least in the communities described here, has to a certain extent been influenced by both positive and negative external factors, but there is a strong core of ideas of local origin. Over the past century, and even longer, the Nasa, and other indigenous groups in Cauca, such as the Guambiano, have struggled to control and, where necessary, recover their land base, while at the same time they have maintained their dignity and demanded respect from the dominant society. By securing their land, they hoped to maintain their autonomy, because without land and control over it, there could be no indigenous community. But even in such a relatively isolated place as Tierradentro, outside influences could not be kept at bay. While it is key to understand how people have responded to these influences, also important is the extent to which it is possible to generalize from this experience to the larger world of the poor, the marginal, and the indigenous.

The ongoing struggle for citizenship in Cauca shares certain characteristics with similar struggles in other parts of the world. In a recent volume, Naila Kabeer (2005) identifies four key values shared by those striving for full citizenship. The first is justice, but more as a sense of fairness than retribution, with the expectation that the state should act fairly and impartially toward its citizens. The second is recognition "of the intrinsic worth of all human beings" (4). The third value she identifies is self-determination, the ability to exercise some degree of control over one's life, whether individual or collective. The final value is solidarity, which she defines as "the capacity to identify with others and to act in unity with them in their claims for justice and recognition" (7). All four values have characterized the indigenous struggle in Cauca and continue to do so, sometimes under different names. Instead of *self-determination,* the preferred term is *autonomy.* The nostalgia for economic solidarity espoused by Toribío is another manifestation of this. Underlying the desire for recognition is the quest for dignity and respect.

But the quest for citizenship is also a quest for human rights, and the 253 two are closely related. The Universal Declaration of Human Rights adopted by the United Nations in 1948 established a code of moral conduct for how we should treat each other as human beings, specifically how the state is expected to treat its citizens (Friedman 1992). For some, human rights are socially constructed and inseparable from the mentality of the Enlightenment and, hence, the product of a particular society at a particular time: Europe in the aftermath of World War II. As a result, for some the UN declaration is yet another "cunning exercise in Western moral imagination" (Ignatieff 2001b, 102). For others, however, the discourse of human rights is full of rules that are actually the products of the historical processes of industrialization, urbanization, and the communications and information revolutions, but which are replicable everywhere, even if they occurred first in the West (Franck 2001). Nevertheless, as attention to human rights has increased, so has criticism, directed particularly at its purported universalism (Nyambu-Musembi 2005). Human rights discourse arouses strong opposition precisely because it challenges the control exercised by entrenched power on behalf of the powerless. It is in this sense that the exercise of human rights can be subversive, radical, and dangerous: "Rights are universal because they define the universal interests of the powerless—namely, that power be exercised over them in ways that respect their autonomy as agents. In this sense, human rights represent a revolutionary creed, since they make a radical demand of all human groups that they serve the interests of the individuals who compose them" (Ignatieff 2001b, 109).

Historically, the focus has been on civil and political rights, the first-generation rights, which include the right to life, freedom from torture and arbitrary arrest, and freedom of speech, religion, and association. These rights are often described as negative rights, because they proscribe state actions that violate human dignity. Economic, social, and cultural rights, the second-generation rights, which have received less attention, encompass the right to education, the right to an adequate standard of living, and the right to organize. These are regarded as positive rights since they require that the state pursue an active role in their achievement (Uvin 2004, 14). The indigenous movement in Cauca has been struggling for the realization of both sets of rights, but also for *communal* rights, which is what many people have opposed to the individual human rights of the UN declaration.

Historically, the discourses of human rights and of development have remained separate and distinct. Peter Uvin (2004) has forcefully argued that this should not be. For him, the real potential of human rights lies in its ability to change the ways people perceive themselves and their relationship to the state and nonstate actors. To this should be added the awareness and recognition that violations are neither inevitable nor natural, but arise from deliberate decisions and policies. As a result, people can demand explanations and accountability, which, in the case of Colombia, often entails considerable physical danger (Kirk 2003). Since development discourse and practice have traditionally shied away from such encounters, Uvin proposes that the development enterprise look at poverty through the lens of human rights, in the process becoming more principled and more courageous. This would mean thinking more in terms of policy, inequality, exclusion, and discrimination. In the specific example of education, Uvin argues:

> The realization of the right to education depends on focusing on issues of discrimination and access to education, especially at the primary school level; of taking into account the degree to which local communities can exercise the right in guiding education and in providing support for their children's education. It is not necessarily about buildings but about the resources and policies to enable all children to enjoy the rights, regardless of their geographic location, their gender, race, language or ethnic origin. (Uvin 2004, 130)[4]

The experiences of CRIC and its Bilingual Education Program (PEB) bear this out since the right to education is about much more than bricks and mortar. It is also about the right to determine the substance of that education and how it should be taught, as well as about forging a new philosophy of society built through community participation in local schools.

On a broader canvas, the experiences of the Nasa communities presented here, embedded as they are in the ongoing history of indigenous resistance, provide a cogent and powerful example of the capability and potential of ordinary men and women to stand up and demand that they be treated with respect. In the process, they have obliged the state and other nonstate actors who fear their independence and their moral strength to take them seriously and accede to some of their demands. While the state and other actors have not always kept their promises and fulfilled their obligations, the people described here have never given up the struggle. With each stand and every confrontation, they have continued to state their case, earn broader public acceptance on the national and international levels, and slowly win over their enemies. In the context of contemporary Colombia, this is a major achievement and an example of what is possible when ordinary men and women engage in collective action to achieve their rights and contribute to the common good.

What the Future Holds

Most recently, Richard Wilson (2006) has rather cryptically stated that the loose human rights framework offers little in the way of context or vision of the "common good." Simply put, they list things that governments cannot do to their citizens, combined with things they must do. Though the various human rights covenants share certain basic principles, they do not provide the basis for a fully worked-out moral political philosophy. Nevertheless, all societies have aspirations for the future and notions of the good life, or about health and happiness (Appadurai 2004). While the specifics may differ from country to country, such aspirations are a part of culture, people's ways of thinking, being, and acting, increasingly in the political realm (Chatterjee 2004). As I have argued, the discourse of human rights is part of a larger struggle for full citizenship, perhaps not always clearly articulated as such, but one in which human rights can play a pivotal role. For the Nasa, citizenship can be viewed as an integral part of their desire for a different type of modernity, a counterdevelopment that is also a form of critical modernity. Richard Peet and Elaine Hartwick (1999, chap. 7) argue that the principles on which modernity is based—democracy, emancipation, development, and progress—have been corrupted and debased by the social and political systems in which they are embedded. They propose a more critical approach that retains a belief in the potential of development but distrusts all elites, favoring the view of oppressed peoples, and supporting the creation of alliances of the oppressed majority to counter the power of the exploiting minority. "Critical modernism should focus on the question of development, understood as the social use of economic progress, as a central theme of our age. . . . Development seen as material transformation for the world's hungry people is an ethical and practical necessity, one just as pressing as the natural constraints on growth" (Peet and Hartwick 1999, 199).

This is part of what indigenous modernity is about, and I would like to propose that the indigenous experience in Cauca, while unique in certain respects, also shares some characteristics with other movements and processes involving the poor and the marginalized. Sam Hickey and Giles Mohan (2005), drawing on a variety of case studies of participatory approaches to development, suggest that the more successful have pursued a more political but also more universal agenda. On the one hand, they have privileged politics, not by supporting specific political parties but in their advocacy for social movements that question and perhaps threaten the political status quo and existing power relationships. On the other hand, such approaches have broadened the definition of development, a responsibility that governments must fulfill, but often only when they are pressured to do so. Once acknowledged as such, development by definition must be inclusive, available to all, and not restricted to certain favored groups or interests. Nevertheless, this quest must be weighed against a stance of critical modernity which views most development initiatives of the state with a well-justified skepticism. This is why Hickey and Mohan call for a radical politics of inclusive citizenship, a hope and a vision for the future.

When proposing such strategies, however, the *longue durée* is imperative. The 1991 Constitution mandated a more inclusive politics, and the indigenous movement responded by becoming more radical in its tactics and more pressing in its demands. The blocking of the Pan-American Highway in 1999, first by the indigenous movement and later by CIMA, as well as the creation of La María, achieved long-lasting political and symbolic significance. Yet the extent to which the situation has changed for the better in social, political, or economic terms is questionable.

In May 2006, CRIC organized a three-day summit meeting at La María to discuss the proposed free trade agreement with the United States, the need for land reform, and the failure of the national government to fulfill its earlier commitments.[5] The organizers also emphasized the importance of defending human rights and negotiating a peaceful solution to the ongoing civil war through active citizen participation. Some twenty thousand people attended, many representing social organizations active in Cauca and neighboring provinces. The summit just happened to coincide with a ministerial visit to Popayán, specifically the ministers of Defense and the Interior, to discuss security arrangements for the upcoming presidential elections. The understanding was that the ministers would come to La María and dialogue directly with the organizations gathered there. The meeting did not materialize and the government sent in one thousand soldiers and police, already present to intimidate the participants, to clear the area and end the mobilization. This was the first time there had been violence of any sort at La María, an alternative political space, a place of peace established precisely for the realizations of such types of public dialogue. With the help of helicopters, tear gas, and armored vehicles, the government cleared the participants from the area, killing one young man in the process and leaving a scene of devastation behind them. Some of the younger participants, as in other troubled parts of the developing world, defended themselves with sticks and stones, but to no avail.

The government justified its response on the grounds that some of the participants had chosen to close the Pan-American Highway, an act that terrified the political and economic elites of Cauca with its reminder of the financial losses they claimed to have sustained in 1999. In addition, the FARC was said to be offering its active support, a charge regularly leveled at any social mobilization critical of the government. Bloodied but undaunted, the leadership of CRIC responded by condemning the violence and the infringement of human rights and proposing that a national inquiry be conducted to document what had really happened. They also reiterated their demands for a national debate on free trade, perhaps leading to a referendum, and the need for agrarian reform, as well as the fulfillment of previously signed agreements and the provision of guarantees of respect and free association for the mobilized communities. Furthermore, they protested directly to the American embassy in Bogotá, arguing that the soldiers and police supported by Plan Colombia, which has provided support for drug eradication efforts and the training of counterinsurgency forces, were being used to violate the human rights of civilians, citizens of Colombia peacefully protesting against the current policies and practices of their government.

While there are some eerie parallels with the discourse of 1999, there are important differences, reflected in the demands made by the mobilizations mounted during the intervening years. The audience is no longer national but international. Present were representatives of CNN, the UN, and the European Union, among others. The proposals are no longer just regional, and some affect the whole country. The demands are both political and moral: what can be done and what should be done. In this way, La María has become a lightning rod, prodding the rest of the country to resurrect their moral imaginations and exercise their rights as concerned citizens. This will call for courage, conviction, perseverance, and the strong belief that this generation has the responsibility to make Colombia a better place for the next generation.

Notes

Introduction: Beyond the Developmental Gaze

All illustrations are by the author, as are translations unless otherwise indicated.

1. I am obliged to Joanne Rappaport for bringing Trinh's work to my attention.
2. "The concept of structural violence draws our attention to unequal life
   chances, usually caused by great inequality, injustice, discrimination, and
   exclusion and needlessly limiting people's physical, social, and psychologi-
   cal well-being" (Uvin 1998, 105).

1. More Than an Engaged Fieldnote

1. This expression was coined by June Nash (1976), based on her experience
   doing research in the politically charged environment of tin mining in
   Bolivia: "In Bolivia it was not possible to choose the role of an impartial
   observer and still work in the tin mining community of Oruro, where I had
   gone to study ideology and social change. . . . The polarisation of the class
   struggle made it necessary to take sides or to be cast by them on one side or
   the other. In a revolutionary situation, no neutrals are allowed" (Nash
   1976, 150, cited in Sluka 1995, 286).
2. The anthropology of development focuses on the study of the problems
   and processes of development, whereas development anthropology focuses
   on the practicalities of doing development.
3. Taussig (2004, 9) points out, correctly in my opinion, that the word *delin-
   cuente* covers a wide range of criminal activities ranging from pickpocketing
   to murder and proposes that the closest translation would be "murderous
   thug."
4. The New People's Army is the armed wing of the Communist Party of the
   Philippines.

5. This section draws on Gow (2002, 305–6).

6. While the best anthropologists have always done this, some have been more committed to this principle than others. One interesting predecessor to Vasco was Marcel Griaule, best known for his work with the Dogon of Mali, whom he visited on a regular basis in the process of documenting various aspects of their culture. In 1947 he conducted a legendary series of interviews with the Dogon sage Ogotemmeli. Apparently acting on instructions from the elders, Ogotemmeli instructed Griaule in the wisdom of the Dogon, *la parole claire,* the highest, most complete stage of initiatory knowledge (Griaule 1965 [1948]). Though Griaule's repeated visits helped deepen his understanding of indigenous knowledge, specifically the cosmology of the Dogon, there was also a radical transformation in his manner of doing research: the ethnographer, who cross-examines his informants following an agenda which he has established, becomes a student while his informants, the Dogon intellectuals, become his learned interlocutors, who carefully control the type and quality of information available to him (Clifford 1983).

7. The Guambiano followed the same methodology in the preparation of their Life Plan (*Plan de Vida*). The first of its kind in Cauca, for a long time it served as a model for other resguardos (Cabildo, Taitas, and Comisión de Trabajo del Pueblo Guambiano 1994).

8. And, I should add, my most astute critic, buttressed by more than thirty years of involvement in Colombia.

9. In admitting this, I am fully aware that I do not always manage to practice what I preach.

2. Disaster and Diaspora

1. Employed for many years at the World Bank, Cernea has perhaps contributed more than any other social scientist (at least publicly) to making the case for the positive contributions that social science can offer for improving development.

2. Most of Neiman's information about the Lisbon earthquake comes from the excellent book by Kendrick (1957).

3. Interview recorded in the 1994 documentary *The Waters Have Given Birth* (FST 1994).

4. This theme is explored in more detail in chapter 4, in the discussion of a puppet play about Juan Tama produced in Tóez Caloto.

5. The principal ethnographies on the Nasa of Tierradentro have been written by Arcila Vélez (1989), Bernal Villa (1953, 1954a, 1954b, 1955), Gómez and Ruíz (1997), Ortiz (1979), Rappaport (1998, 2005a), and Sevilla Casas (1986).

6. The historical process of impoverishment is discussed briefly by Pachón (1996), and also in the congressional debate on the creation of CNK (Wilches 1998, n.22).

7. There are other smaller settlements of Nasa, as well as settlements of mestizos and Guambiano, that will not be discussed here.

8. A review of CNK's Web site in June 2006 (www.nasakiwe.gov.co) indicates that the agency is still alive but to a certain extent living on "past glory."

9. Author's interview with Jorge Inseca, June 1995.

10. The following documents were consulted to better understand the conflict between Tóez and CNK: memorandum from Gustavo Wilches Chaux (director of CNK) to Gladys Jimeno Santoyo (director of Indigenous Affairs), Luis Fernando Munera, and Carlos Vicente De Roux, Popayán, December 7, 1994; letter to Victoriano Cruz, Rodrigo Atillo, Jorge Eliécer [*sic*], and Floresmiro Lectamo (all leaders in Tóez) from Gustavo Wilches Chaux, Popayán, December 15, 1994; letter to Horacio Serpa Uribe (minister of the Interior) from Gustavo Wilches Chaux, Popayán, December 23, 1994; letter to Gustavo Wilches Chaux from the Indigenous Cabildo of Tóez, Popayán, January 18, 1995; letter to Jorge Inseca (governor of Tóez) from Gustavo Wilches Chaux, Popayán, February 2, 1995; and letter to Gustavo Wilches Chaux from Jorge Inseca, La Selva, February 11, 1995. Don Jorge Inseca made these documents available to me; copies are now in my personal collection.

11. The following communications from the Division of Indigenous Affairs contradict CNK's plans in more detail: letter from Carlos Cesár Perafán (adviser to Indigenous Affairs) to Gladys Jimeno Santoyo and the CNK board, Bogotá, December 21, 1994; and letter from Carlos Cesár Perafán to Gladys Jimeno Santoyo, Bogotá, January 4, 1995. Copies of these documents are in my personal collection.

12. Author's interview with Inseca, June 1995.

13. Another version, unsubstantiated, has it that CCF refused to help the community build a new school unless the Catholic church withdrew its teachers.

14. In the community's development plan, produced five years later, these events are politely glossed over: "After a while, as a result of some internal problems which presented themselves within the resettlement, the sections

of La Troja [and] Quebraditos decided to look for another place. . . . In spite of all this dispersion, there remains a population of 583 people in the Nasa community of Juan Tama, *continuing staunch in their organization, authority and own autonomy*" (emphasis added) (Comunidad de Juan Tama 2002, 9–10).

15. Ironically, these teachers from the Prefectura who were obliged to leave Juan Tama are now very active in Itaibe, working with CRIH, the Regional Indigenous Council of Huila.

16. Don Rubén and his wife also survived the earthquake disaster, and they moved with their entire family to the new community. This is the same Don Rubén briefly described in the introduction.

17. The initial list presented contained the names of sixty-five families that did not jibe with the figures collected in a census conducted three months before the disaster. Closer inspection by CNK revealed that some thirty people listed had no legitimate roots in San José and their claims were disallowed, much to the anger of the local leadership. This charge, of course, can be leveled at all the resettlements: the availability of new resources had a magnetic effect on many people who might not normally have qualified, given that records were poor and eligibility criteria broad.

18. In contrast, at the same time the families in Tóez Caloto were living in a proper tent city, with large, relatively comfortable tents for the leaders, and smaller tents for the others, but all laid out as if in a military encampment.

19. In 1996, a mestizo schoolteacher commented that the proponents of alternative development are often more "indigenous" than the people themselves.

20. Wilches (1998, 216) himself took exception to this statement in an earlier publication (Rappaport and Gow 1997), arguing that the social background of CNK staff was irrelevant to an understanding of what they have achieved. I respectfully disagree: their involvement provided CNK with the necessary political credibility to get the job done in a relatively transparent manner.

3. Development Planning

1. My wife and I helped pay for the costs of preparing the plan.

2. In contrast to the other two plans, I neither witnessed nor participated in the process in Juan Tama, due partly to bad timing (I was not in the country when the process was under way) and later due to lack of security (I was unable to travel there and talk directly with the participants).

3. Although the Christian Children's Fund provided assistance with agriculture, nutritional support for small children, financial support for construction of the school, and management training for members of the cabildo and the Parent Teacher Association, it was not directly involved in preparing the plan.

4. At that time there were no shamans living in either San José or Cxayu'ce.

4. Local Knowledge, Different Dreams

1. There is already a rich and critical body of literature on the concept of "alternative development," questioning just how alternative it is, given the propensity of mainline development institutions, and this includes many NGOs, to absorb, dilute, and repackage some of its more political tenets (Nederveen Pieterse 1998).

2. As Sillitoe (2002, 8) points out, local knowledge is known by a variety of terms, including indigenous knowledge, rural people's knowledge, insider knowledge, indigenous technical knowledge, traditional environmental knowledge, people's science, and folk knowledge.

3. Be that as it may, Purcell and Onjoro (2002, 172–73) provide an impressive, but partial list of the "particular cultural domains" in which indigenous knowledge successfully complements Western "scientific" knowledge, including health, ecology, and the environment; food and agriculture; ethnopharmacology; agronomy; astronomy; and disaster management.

4. A somewhat more restricted definition is provided by Ellen (1998, 238) who writes that knowledge is "local, orally transmitted, a consequence of practical engagement, reinforced by experience, empirical rather than theoretical, repetitive, fluid and negotiable, shared but asymmetrically distributed, largely functional, and embedded in a more encompassing cultural matrix" (cited in Schonhuth 2002, n. 2).

5. This was not the case with the Quintín Lame Armed Movement (MAQL), which carefully consulted the local shamans before undertaking any military action.

6. While this concept of counterdevelopment has yet to be fully exploited, Hodgson and Schroeder (2002) have examined the problems associated with countermapping in East Africa, mapping against dominant power structures. In their analysis of four Tanzanian case studies, they conclude that countermapping is no panacea or quick fix for resource management problems in a context where there is a long history of deep-seated ani-

mosities between the state and the local population. To achieve their objectives, such efforts must be accompanied by parallel efforts in the legal and political domains.

7. Author's interview with Felipe Morales, July 1996.

8. Author's interview with Jorge Inseca, July 1999.

9. Ibid.

10. Author's interview with Miguel Ángel Achipiz, April 2000.

11. The first document was produced by Nydia Yasnó, Gerardo Gutierrez, and Miguel Ángel Achipiz; the second by Adela Mulcué, Nydia Yasnó, and Miguel Ángel Achipiz; and the third by a team of teachers.

12. The bibliography lists several references, including a PEB publication titled *Lo que cuentan nuestros abuelos* (What our grandparents say; CRIC n.d. 1), and one wonders if this may have been the principal "special source" of the appendix.

13. These responses were elicited during a couple of English classes that I taught in the school in March 2000.

14. This was Pacho Rojas, the same person who collaborated with the preparation of Juan Tama's development plan, discussed in the previous chapter.

15. Author's conversation with Inocencio Ramos, March 2000.

16. This leader, who now lives in Cxayu'ce, has four children, all of whom are teachers. The daughter in question has two sons, the second of whom teaches in Cxayu'ce and is paid through CRIC. In addition, she holds the position of nurse in the community, and as such receives a regular salary. Another leader, a well-respected and feared shaman who also lives in Cxayu'ce, also has four children, two of whom are schoolteachers. Both leaders were briefly mentioned in the introduction.

17. He had taken a leave of absence for one year from his teaching position in the community to fulfill the onerous responsibilities, time-wise and financial, of being governor. The following year, the treasurer of the cabildo, also a schoolteacher, did the same. They felt that this was the only way they could properly and effectively serve the community.

18. See also La Revista de El Espectador (2002, 6–9). The people in question, the Yanaconas, a peasant group in the process of recovering their indigenous past, are famous for their excellent music. For more on this issue, see Zambrano (1998).

19. Author's conversation with Vicente Pinzón, March 2000.

5. Nasa of the North, Tensions of Modernity

A somewhat different version of this chapter appeared in my article "Desde afuera y desde adentro: La planificación indígena como contra-desarrollo," in Joanne Rappaport, ed., *Retornando la mirada: Una investigación colaborativa interétnica sobre el Cauca a la entrada del milenio*, 65–96 (Popayán: Editorial Universidad del Cauca, 2005).

1. The types of information to be presented here are a reflection of the political realities of contemporary Cauca. In the case of the north, I suspect that it has been physically dangerous to do research there since the time of La Violencia. With the exception of Findji and Rojas's ethnography of Jambaló (Findji and Rojas 1985), there has been little or no research conducted there. An exception is the recent study by Hernández Delgado (2004, chap. 3). Each time I have gone to Toribío, I have always been accompanied by people from the municipality who guaranteed my personal security. On one visit, I "discovered" Padre Ulcué's report in the *casa parroquial* and the Consolata Fathers allowed me to make a copy. The municipality kindly lent me Toribío's 1998 development plan to copy.

2. I first heard this vanguard argument advanced in the 1999 workshop in Toribío, discussed in more detail later in this chapter.

3. This section draws heavily on the second part of the book by Beltrán and Mejía (1989). Somewhat less hagiographic than Roattino's book, it does contain some interesting information about Padre Ulcué and what he did in Toribío, supported by some valuable documentation. As far as I know, Mejía Salazar was a Laurita who worked with Padre Ulcué and was one of the authors of the plan discussed later in this chapter (Ulcué, Mejía, and Florez 1980).

4. During the Assembly, there had been strong comments voiced against missionary work, in this case presumably the Catholic Church, for its criticism of coca chewing and *chicha,* as well as against other entities, such as the Summer School of Linguistics and other religious sects, that were viewed as more insidious and more dangerous because they wished to destroy indigenous culture (Beltrán and Mejía 1989, 110).

5. Padre Ulcué's life and death also appear to have galvanized the activities of the Consolata Fathers in the region. Though they are regarded with some suspicion for their missionary efforts, they are also viewed as politically astute, committed to the indigenous cause, and physically fearless.

6. This figure is based on the number of names listed in the report and differs

radically from the figure of eight hundred given by Beltrán and Mejía. The smaller figure may include only the "official" participants.

7. Information on the Nasa Project is drawn from information I gathered over the years, as well as from a recent publication (Hernández Delgado 2004, 109–32). While the project has recently received international recognition from the United Nations and other entities, the indigenous leaders and the Consolata Fathers have carefully cultivated its public image. Given the security risks mentioned earlier, and the fact that outside visitors, national or international, need the blessing (literally) of the local authorities, the available literature tends to be very favorable, at times verging on the hagiographic on account of the association with the memory of Padre Ulcué. This is the case with a more recent publication (Wilches-Chaux 2005).

8. The full title is *Por la autonomía de los pueblos indígenas frente a los conflictos que atentan nuestro proyecto de vida* (In support of the autonomy of the indigenous communities in the face of the conflicts which commit crimes against our life plan).

9. This was not the first—or the last—statement of this kind. In 1985, the indigenous movement issued the Declaration of Vitoncó, which was highly critical of the various armed groups operating in the region, but particularly of the MAQL, discussed in more detail in the next chapter (Beltrán and Mejía 1989, 123). Similar denunciations, protests, and marches have followed the 1998 declaration, most often sparked by the assassination of indigenous leaders.

10. Gros (1991, 190–93), in an article originally published in 1981, also provides information about the creation of these communal enterprises, but from a much more favorable perspective.

11. CRIC (1999b) is an exception: in a publication on indigenous women the external problems are graphically depicted as illegal crops, armed groups, and the state.

6. Beyond Development

1. Fraser (1997, 97, n.33) carefully explains why she prefers the concept of public to that of community. The former implies a plurality of perspectives, an arena that is unbounded and open-ended, whereas the latter connotes consensus, implying a bounded and fairly homogenous group. But one could also argue that a "public" is composed of several "communities."

2. For information on Quintín Lame, I have relied primarily on Castillo (1971, 1987) and Rappaport (1998), and to a lesser extent on Castrillón Arboleda (1973), a novelist, curator of the Archivo Central del Cauca, and a member of one of Popayán's aristocratic families. From the perspective of Castillo (1987, 165), Castrillón Arboleda's work is more "a historical novel than a biography, in the sense that he uses some accurate historical information and combines it with anecdotes and literary narratives, often reflecting the traditional attitudes of the Colombian upper classes towards the Indians."

3. Also summarized in Rappaport (1998, 114).

4. Castrillón Arboleda (1973, chaps. 17 and 20) believes they were in favor of armed revolution but provides no concrete evidence to substantiate the claim. Rappaport (1998, 116), based on research in the Archivo Fundación Colombia Nuestra in Cali, indicates that interviews conducted with some of Lame's associates in Tierradentro describe in detail some of his military tactics, thereby lending credence to his support of violence.

5. Since Castillo (1987) also includes an English translation of Lame's book, I have chosen to cite this rather than translate from the original Spanish in the original edition (Lame 1971 [1939]).

6. Castrillón Arboleda is here directly quoting from the annual report that the secretary of government presented to the governor in 1916, which covers the events of the previous year. Hence, the events discussed must have taken place in 1915, and not 1916 as he claims in the text. There are various discrepancies of this sort regarding dates, with Castrillón Arboleda accusing Castillo, a much more careful researcher, of various inaccuracies.

7. Cited by Castillo (1987, 169) who judges this account to be "the most common version prevailing among the white population." A member of the Vicentian Fathers, Father González was also active in the privatization of resguardo lands (Rappaport 1998, 112). He and his work are still roundly detested by indigenous people in Cauca.

8. Cited in Castillo (1987, 168).

9. Lame was severely beaten up in the process, and there is a picture of him taken at this time with his face bloodied, and his feet in fetters (Castrillón Arboleda 1973, 195).

10. Cited in Rappaport (1998, 137).

11. There are many perspectives from which to analyze Lame and his work; for example Castillo (1987, 2004) focuses, among other things, on his religious

thought, Rappaport (1998, 2004) is more interested in his intellectual and historical role, whereas Romero (2004) emphasizes the philosophical and pedagogical aspects of his book.

12. Lame's book has recently been republished (2004), and includes chapters by Castillo, Rappaport, and Romero. Castillo's chapter was originally published in 1971.

13. More explicitly, according to Lame: "I had the lines of the telegraph cut, gathered 600 Indians, and resolved myself to defend the Indian race." This comes from an interview that Lame gave in his old age to representatives of the Ministry of Agriculture, quoted in Castillo (1987, 167).

14. Cited also in Rappaport (1998, 136–37).

15. Interview with Francisco Gembuel in 1996 (El Colectivo n.d., n.p.). In the mid-1990s, the Quintines worked on their own oral history and produced a document, never published, which contains interviews with many of the protagonists (El Colectivo n.d.). The Quintines themselves conducted the interviews.

16. Interview with Alfonso Peña in July 1999, conducted by Joanne Rappaport. He was later the Quintines' representative to the Constitutional Assembly in 1991 (El Colectivo n.d.).

17. Interview with Gildardo Peña in October 1992, conducted by Ricardo Peñaranda (Peñaranda 1998, 66–67).

18. Interview with Gildardo Peña, conducted by Myriam Amparo Espinosa (Espinosa 1996, 80).

19. I have intentionally avoided discussing the military aspects of the Quintines' activities because this is not central to my present argument. These actions and the political ramifications, particularly the relationships with the other armed groups in the region, are discussed in some detail in Peñaranda (1998) and Caballero (n.d.).

20. Interview with Celmo Secué in 1996 (El Colectivo). This type of relationship with the guerrillas continued until recently.

21. Interview with Gildardo Peña in May 1995, conducted by Ricardo Peñaranda (Peñaranda 1998, 178).

22. The proposal, titled *Proyecto de reforma constitutional presentado por el delgado del Movimiento Indígena Quintín Lame,* is cited in Peñaranda (1998, 220).

23. Barrington Moore (1978, xii–xiv) has provocatively pointed out that the term *moral outrage,* with its overtones of condescension, often suggests "the agonies of intellectuals trying to interpret, judge, and change the world. It

smacks too much of the preacher." As such, it fails to capture the tone and concreteness of much popular anger, better articulated by the term *injustice*. I prefer to use both terms, since I have seen this moral outrage expressed in public by people from all walks of life in Cauca.

24. Information on the march is drawn from my own interviews with participants; various newspaper reports in *Unidad,* a CRIC publication (2004); and a CRIC pamphlet (2005).

Conclusion: Countering Development

1. This point is also made by Clammer (2002, 59).
2. Here Nordstrom draws on the work of Corbin (1972) and Mimica (1991).
3. Here Nordstrom draws on the work of Pettman (1996) and Rawls (1971).
4. Uvin is quoting from a document prepared by the Human Rights Council of Australia (2001, section 3).
5. Information on what happened at La María in May was gathered during a trip to Popayán in July 2006 when I talked with participants, including the leadership of CRIC; read the reports in *El Liberal,* the local daily newspaper; viewed a recent CRIC documentary (CRIC/USAID 2006), which includes a section on the violence perpetrated at La María; and reviewed a recent CRIC publication that succinctly summarizes the movement's demands and proposals (2006).

Bibliography

Agrawal, Arun. 1996. "Poststructuralist Approaches to Development: Some Critical Reflections." *Peace and Change* 21(4): 464–77.

———. 1999. "On Power and Indigenous Knowledge." In Darrell F. Posey, ed., *Cultural and Spiritual Values of Biodiversity,* 177–80. Nairobi and London: UN Environmental Programme and Intermediate Technology Publications.

Alvarez, Sonia E., Evelina Dagnino, and Arturo Escobar. 1998. "Introduction: The Cultural and the Political in Latin American Social Movements." In Sonia E. Alvarez, Evelina Dagnino, and Arturo Escobar, eds., *Cultures of Politics Politics of Cultures: Re-visioning Latin American Social Movements,* 1–29. Boulder: Westview Press.

Anderson, Benedict. 1991. *Imagined Communities: Reflections on the Origin and Spread of Nationalism,* rev. ed. New York: Verso.

Appadurai, Arjun. 1996. *Modernity at Large: Cultural Dimensions of Globalization.* Minneapolis: University of Minnesota Press.

———. 2000. "Grassroots Globalization and the Research Imagination." *Public Culture* 12(1): 1–19.

———. 2004. "The Capacity to Aspire: Culture and the Terms of Recognition." In Vijayendra Rao and Michael Walton, eds., *Culture and Public Action,* 59–84. Stanford, Calif.: Stanford University Press.

Arce, Alberto, and Norman Long. 2000. "Reconfiguring Modernity and Development from an Anthropological Perspective." In Alberto Arce and Norman Long, eds., *Anthropology, Development and Modernities: Exploring Discourses, Counter-Tendencies and Violence,* 1–31. New York: Routledge.

Arcila Vélez, Graciliano. 1989. *Los indígenas páez de Tierradentro, Cauca, Colombia.* Medellín: Editorial Universidad de Antioquia.

Asociación de Damnificados del Resguardo Indígena de Tóez (ADRIT). 1995. *Estudio de factibilidad: Construcción de un colegio de enseñanza diversificada.* Tóez Caloto.

Baba, Marietta. 1999. "Theories of Practice in Anthropology: A Critical Appraisal." In Carole E. Hill and Marietta L. Baba, eds., *The Unity of Theory and Practice in Anthropology: Rebuilding a Fractured Synthesis,* 17–44. Washington: National Association of Practicing Anthropologists / American Anthropological Association.

Barona Becerra, Guido, and Cristóbal Gnecco Valencia. 2001, "Introducción: Territorios posibles." In Guido Barona Becerra and Cristóbal Gnecco Valencia, eds., *Historia, geografía y cultura del Cauca: Territorios possibles,* 1:9–19. Popayán: Editorial Universidad del Cauca.

Becerra, Yolanda. 2000. "Etnoeducación y Perspectivas." Presented at workshop in Nuevo Tóez, Caloto.

Beltrán Peña, Francisco, and Lucila Mejía Salazar. 1989. *La utopia mueve montañas: Álvaro Ulcué Chocué.* Bogotá: Editorial Nueva América.

Bennett, John W. 1988. "Anthropology and Development: The Ambiguous Engagement." In John W. Bennett and John R. Bowen, eds., *Production and Autonomy: Anthropological Studies and Critiques of Development,* 81–105. Lanham, Md.: University Press of America.

———. 1996. "Applied and Action Anthropology: Ideological and Conceptual Aspects." *Current Anthropology* Supplement (February): S23–S53.

Bentz, Marilyn. 1997. "Beyond Ethics: Science, Friendship, and Privacy." In Thomas Biolsi and Larry J. Zimmerman, eds., *Indians and Anthropologists: Vine Deloria, Jr., and the Critique of Anthropology,* 120–32. Tucson: University of Arizona Press.

Berman, Marshall. 1983. *All That is Solid Melts into Air: The Experience of Modernity.* New York: Verso.

Bernal Villa, Segundo E. 1953. "Aspectos de la cultura páez: Mitología y cuentos de la parcialidad de Calderas, Tierradentro." *Revista Colombiana de Anthropología* 1(1): 279–309.

———. 1954a. "Economía de los páez." *Revista Colombiana de Antropología* 3: 291–309.

———. 1954b. "Medicina y magia entre los paeces." *Revista Colombiana de Anthropología* 2: 219–64.

———. 1955. "Bases para el studio de la organización social de los páez." *Revista Colombiana de Antropología* 4: 165–88.

Berry, Wendell. 2002. "The Idea of a Local Economy." In Stephen R. Kellert and Timothy J. Farnham, eds., *The Good in Nature and Humanity: Connecting Science, Religion, and Spirituality with the Natural World,* 199–211. Washington: Island Press.

Billson, Janet M. 1993. *Complexities of Involuntary Resettlement in World Bank Projects: Task Manager Focus Group Report*. Washington: World Bank.

Biolsi, Thomas, and Larry J. Zimmerman. 1997. "Introduction: What's Changed, What Hasn't?" In Thomas Biolsi and Larry J. Zimmerman, eds., *Indians and Anthropologists: Vine Deloria, Jr., and the Critique of Anthropology*, 3–24. Tucson: University of Arizona Press.

Bolaños, Graciela, Abelardo Ramos, Joanne Rappaport, and Carlos Miñana. 2004. *¿Que pasaría si la esculea . . . ? 30 Años de construcción de una educación propia*. Popayán: Programa de Educación Bilingüe e Intercultural (PEBI/CRIC).

Caballero, Henry. n.d. Coordinadora Guerrillera Simon Bolívar. In Surgimiento de Quintín Lame. Popayán: Colectivo de Historia de Quintín Lame.

Cabildo, Taitas, and Comisión de Trabajo del Pueblo Guambiano. 1994. *Plan de vida del pueblo guambiano*. Territorio Guambiano-Silvia: Cabildo del Pueblo Guambiano.

Cabildos Indígenas del Norte, Nororiente y Oriente del Departamento del Cauca. 1998. *Por la autonomía de los pueblos indígenas frente a los conflictos que atentan nuestro proyecto de vida*. Jambaló: Mimeo.

El Cabuyo/CRIC. 1996. *Proyecto educativo comunitario: Construcción de una escuela intercultural*. Popayán: PEB-CRIC.

Cámara del Comercio del Cauca. 2000. *Tendencias ocupacionales a mediano plazo en las empresas beneficiarias de la Ley Páez en el departamento del Cauca*. Popayán: Cámara del Comercio del Cauca.

Camayo, Mélida, and Luz Mery Niquinás. 1997. "'Kwe's' Tul como estrategia pedagógica y cultural." *Çxayu'çe (Revista de Etnoeducación)* 2: 4–8.

Cannon, Terry. 1994. "Vulnerability Analysis and the Explanation of 'Natural' Disasters." In Ann Varley, ed., *Disasters, Development and Environment*, 13–30. Chichester: Wileys.

Cardona, Omar Darío. 1995. "Otro relato acerca del desastre de Páez." *Desastres & Sociedad* 4(3): 141–58.

Carvajal, Edmundo. 1995. *Censo de población el en area del desastre de Tierradento, Cauca, CRIC-Nasa Kiwe: Análisis descriptivo de la producción y usos del suelo e impacto del desastre del 6 de junio de 1994 en la región de Tierradentro*. Popayán: CRIC/CNK.

Castillo, Elizabeth. 1998. "Socialización política en comunidades indígenas de los Andes colombianos." In María Lucía Sotomayor, ed., *Modernidad, identidad y desarrollo: Construcción de sociedad y re-creación cultural en contextos de modernización*, 131–40. Bogotá: Instituto Colombiano de Antropología.

275

Castillo Cárdenas, Gonzalo. 1971. "Manuel Quintín Lame: Luchador e intelectual indígena del siglo xx." In Manuel Quinín Lame, *En defensa de mi raza*, xi-xlv. Bogotá: Comité de Defensa del Indio.

———. 1987. *Liberation Theology from Below: The Life and Thought of Manuel Quintín Lame*. Maryknoll, N.Y.: Orbis Books.

———. 2004. "Manuel Quintín Lame: Luchador e intelectual indígena del siglo xx." In Manuel Quintín Lame, *Los pensamientos del indio que se educó dentro de las selvas colombianas*, 13–49. Popayán: Biblioteca del Gran Cauca.

Castrillón Arboleda, Diego. 1973. Indio Quintín Lame. Bogotá: Tercer Mundo.

Centro de Educación, Capacitación e Investigación para el Desarrollo Integral de las Comunidades (CECIDIC). 1999a. *Licenciatura en economía y desarrollo*. Introductory course. First workshop: February 22–26, 1999. Toribío.

———. 1999b. *Licenciatura en economía y desarrollo*. Introductory course: April 26–30, 1999. Toribío.

Centro Etnoeducativo Tóez (CET). 1996. *Caminos de indentidad páez: Participación de la familia y la comunidad en la propuesta curricular del preescolar bilingüe*. Toéz Caloto.

———. 1997. *Proyecto etnoeducativo institucional "Caminos de identidad nasa."* Nuevo Toéz.

Cernea, Michael M. 1991. "Knowledge from Social Science for Development Policies and Projects." In Michael M. Cernea, ed., *Putting People First: Sociological Variables in Rural Development*, 1–41. 2d ed. New York: Oxford University Press.

———. 1993. "Anthropological and Sociological Research for Policy Development on Population Resettlement." In Michael M. Cernea and Scott E. Guggenheim, eds., *Anthropological Approaches to Resettlement: Policy, Practice, and Theory*, 13–58. Boulder, Colo.: Westview Press.

———. 1997. "The Risks and Reconstruction Model for Resettling Displaced Populations." *World Development* 25(10): 569–87.

Chambers, Robert. 1997. *Whose Reality Counts? Putting the First Last*. London: Intermediate Technology Publications.

Chatterjee, Partha. 2004. *The Politics of the Governed: Reflections on Popular Politics in Most of the World*. New York: Columbia University Press.

Clammer, John. 2002. "Beyond the Cognitive Paradigm: Majority Knowledges and Local Discourses in a non-Western Donor Society." In Paul Sillitoe, Alan Bicker, and Johan Pottier, eds., *Participating in Development: Approaches to Indigenous Knowledge*, 43–63. New York: Routledge.

Clifford, James. 1983. "Power and Dialogue in Ethnography: Marcel Griaule's Initiation." In George W. Stocking Jr., ed., *Observers Observed: Essays on Ethnographic Fieldwork,* 121–56. Madison: University of Wisconsin Press.

———. 1986. "Introduction: Partial Truths." In James Clifford and George Marcus, eds., *Writing Culture: The Poetics and Politics of Ethnography,* 1–26. Berkeley: University of California Press.

———. 1988. "On Ethnographic Self-Fashioning: Conrad and Malinowski." In James Clifford, *The Predicament of Culture: Twentieth Century Ethnography, Literature, and Art,* 92–113. Cambridge, Mass.: Harvard University Press.

El Colectivo de Historia del Quintín Lame. n.d. *Surgimiento del Quintín Lame.* Popayán: Fundación Sol y Tierra.

Comunidad de Juan Tama. 2002. *Plan de vida: Comunidad nasa Juan-Tama Santa Leticia Moscopán.* Santa Leticia: Comunidad de Juan Tama.

Conroy, Michael E., Douglas L. Murray, and Peter M. Rosset. 1996. *A Cautionary Tale: Failed U.S. Development Policy in Central America.* Boulder, Colo.: Lynne Rienner.

Consejo Regional Indígena del Cauca (CRIC). 1990. *Elaboración de currículo en comunidades indígenas paeces.* Popayán: CRIC.

———. 1994. *Amapola: Solución o destrucción?* Documentary. Directed by María Stella Hernández and Nelson Freddy Osorio. Popayán.

———. 1996a. *PICKWE THA', SA'T JUAN TAMA YATA: El Cerro Juan Tama es la Casa del Cacique Juan Tama.* Edited by Manuel Sisco and Gina Danira Díaz Mendoza. Popayán: CRIC.

———. 1996b. *Nasa Tul: La Huerta Nasa.* Documentary. Directed by Jesús Bosque. Popayán.

———. 1997. *Conclusiones: Décimo congreso regional indígena del Cauca.* Popayán: CRIC.

———. 1999a. "Programas económicos CRIC." Paper presented at the Taller de Economía y Desarrollo, CECIDIC, Toribío, April 26–30.

———. 1999b. *Hilando Vida: Programa Mujer Indígena CRIC.* Pamphlet. Popayán: CRIC.

———. 1999c. *Congreso Extraordinario Indígena Regional del Cauca.* Pamphlet. Territorio Indígena Guambiano La María-Piendamo: CRIC.

———. 2001. *Acta XI Congreso Regional Indígena del Cauca.* Popayán: CRIC.

———. 2004. *Unidad.* September.

———. 2005. *Caminar la palabra.* Popayán: CRIC.

———. 2006. *Cumbre Itinerante y Permanente de Organizaciones Sociales "Pedro Maricio Pascue" La María-Piendamo.* Pamphlet. Popayán: CRIC.

———. n.d.1. *Lo que cuentan nuestros abuelos*. Pamphlet. Popayán: CRIC.

———. n.d.2. *La María, Piendamó territorio de convivencia, diálogo y negociación: Territorio y autonomía*. Pamphlet. Popayán: CRIC.

CRIC/FST. 1999. *Territorio de Convivencia, Diálogo y Negociación*. La María, Piendamo: CRIC/FST.

CRIC/USAID. 2006. *Territorio, Vida y Derechos Humanos*. Documentary. Created by Indepaz/Punto de Encuentro. Popayán.

Cooke, Bill, and Uma Kothari, eds. 2001. *Participation: The New Tyranny?* New York: Zed Books.

Corbin, Henry. 1972. Mundus Imaginalis, or the Imaginary and the Imaginal. *Spring: An Annual of Archtypal Psychology and Jungian Thought*: 1–19.

Corporación Nasa Kiwe (CNK). 1995. *Primer semestre: Informe resúmen de actividades realizadas entre julio y diciembre de 1994*. Popayán: CNK.

———. 2005. www.nasakiwe.org (official Web site).

Corrales, Martha Elena. 1998. "Abriendo caminos, fortaleciendo espacios: Licenciatura en etnoeducación de la Universidad del Cauca." In Jorge Luis González Bermúdez, ed., *Memorias del primer congreso universitario de etnoeducación*, 61–69. Riohacha: Universidad de la Guajira.

Corrales, Martha Elena, and Cristina Simmonds. 2001. "Educación alternativa." In Guido Barona Becerra and Cristóbal Gnecco Valencia, eds., *Historia, geografía y cultura del Cauca: Territorios possibles*, 1:423–36. Popayán: Editorial Universidad del Cauca.

Cowen, Michael P., and Robert W. Shenton. 1995. "The Invention of Development." In Jonathan Crush, ed., *Power of Development*, 27–43. New York: Routledge.

Crush, Jonathan. 1995. "Introduction: Imagining Development." In Jonathan Crush, ed., *Power of Development*, 1–23. New York: Routledge.

D'Andrade, Roy. 1995. "Moral Models in Anthropology." *Current Anthropology* 36(3): 399–408.

Departamento del Cauca. 2001. *"En minga por el Cauca." Plan de desarrollo departamental 2001–2003*. Popayán: Consejo de Gobierno Departamental.

Dover, Robert V. H., and Joanne Rappaport. 1996. "Introduction. Ethnicity Reconfigured: Indigenous Legislators and the Colombian Constitution of 1991." Special issue of the *Journal of Latin American Anthropology* 1(2): 2–17.

Downing, Theodore E. 1996. "Mitigating Social Impoverishment When People Are Involuntarily Displaced." In Christopher McDowell, ed., *Understanding Impoverishment: The Consequences of Development-Induced Displacement*, 33–48. Providence, R.I.: Berghahn Books.

Edelman, Marc. 2001. "Social Movements: Changing Paradigms and Forms of Politics." *Annual Review of Anthropology* 30: 285–317.

Ellen, R. F. 1998. "Comment." *Current Anthropology* 39(2): 238–39.

Escobar, Arturo. 1991. "Anthropology and the Development Encounter: The Making and Marketing of Development Anthropology." *American Ethnologist* 18: 658–82.

———. 1992. "Planning." In Wolfgang Sachs, ed., *The Development Dictionary: A Guide to Knowledge as Power,* 132–45. Atlantic Highlands, N.J.: Zed Books.

———. 1995a. *Encountering Development: The Making and Unmaking of the Third World.* Princeton, N.J.: Princeton University Press.

———. 1995b. "Imagining a Post-Development Era." In Jonathan Crush, ed., *Power of Development,* 211–27. New York: Routledge.

———. 1997. "Cultural Politics and Biological Diversity: State, Capital, and Social Movements in the Pacific Coast of Colombia." In Richard G. Fox and Orin Starn, eds., *Between Resistance and Revolution: Cultural Politics and Social Protest,* 40–64. New Brunswick. N.J.: Rutgers University Press.

———. 2001. "Culture Sits in Places: Reflections on Globalism and Subaltern Strategies of Localization." *Political Geography* 20: 139–74.

Escuela de Pensamiento Nasa. n.d. *Autoridad y pensamiento nasa: Guías para la discusión participativa.* Popayán: Fundación para la Comunicación Popular.

Espinosa, Myriam Amparo. 1996. *Surgimiento y andar territorial del Quintín Lame.* Quito: Abya-Yala.

———. 1998. "Práctica social y emergencia armada en el Cauca." In María Lucía Sotomayor, ed., *Modernidad, identidad y desarrollo: Construcción de sociedad y re-creación cultural en contextos de modernización,* 111–30. Bogotá: Instituto Colombiano de Anthropología.

———. 2005. "Movimientos sociales en La María-Piendamó, territorio de convivencia, diálogo y negociación." In Joanne Rappaport, ed., *Retornando la mirada: Una investigación colaborativa interétnica sobre el Cauca a la entrada al milenio,* 129–51. Popayán: Editorial Universidad del Cauca.

Espinosa, Myriam Amparo, and Luis Alberto Escobar. 2000. "El tejido espacial en la elaboración de planes de vida en Tierradentro." *Utopia* 11: 23–32.

Fairhead, James. 1993. "Representing Knowledge: The 'New Farmer' in Research Fashions." In Johan Pottier, ed., *Practising Development: Social Science Perspectives,* 187–204. New York: Routledge.

Fajardo Sánchez, Luis Alfonso, Juan Carlos Gamboa, and Orlando Villanueva Martínez. 1999. *Manuel Quintín Lame y los Guerrilleros de Juan Tama (Multiculturalismo, Magia y Resistencia).* Madrid: Nossa y Jara Editores.

Fals Borda, Orlando. 1981. *La ciencia y el pueblo: Nuevas reflexiones sobre la investigación-acción*. Bogotá: Asociación Colombiana de Sociología.

Ferguson, James. 1994. *The Anti-Politics Machine: "Development," Depoliticization, and Bureaucratic Power in Lesotho*. Minneapolis: University of Minnesota Press.

Fernandez, James W., and Mary Taylor Huber. 2001. "Coda: Irony, Practice, and the Moral Imagination." In James W. Fernandez and Mary Taylor Huber, eds., *Irony in Action: Anthropology, Practice, and the Moral Imagination*, 261–64. Chicago: University of Chicago Press.

Field, Les W. 1996. "State, Anti-State, and Indigenous Entities: Reflections upon a Páez *Resguardo* and the New Colombian Constitution." *Journal of Latin American Anthropology* 1(2): 98–119.

———. 1999. "Complicities and Collaborations: Anthropologists and the 'Unacknowledged Tribes' of California." *Current Anthropology* 40(2): 193–209.

Findji, María Teresa, and Víctor Daniel Bonilla. 1995. "Tragedia, cultura y luchas de los paeces." *Desastres & Sociedad* 4 (3): 105–18.

Findji, María Teresa, and José María Rojas. 1985. *Territorio, economía y sociedad páez*. Cali: Universidad del Valle/CIDSE.

Fishman, Joshua A. 1991. *Reversing Language Shift: Theoretical and Empirical Foundations of Assistance to Threatened Languages*. Clevedon, U.K.: Multilingual Matters.

———. 1999. "Comments and Reflections." *Anthropology & Education Quarterly* 30(1): 116–24.

Flacks, Richard. 2004. "Knowledge for What? Thoughts on the State of Social Movement Studies." In Jeff Goodwin and James M. Jasper, eds., *Rethinking Social Movements: Structure, Meaning, and Emotion*, 135–53. Oxford: Rowman and Littlefield.

Foley, Douglas. 1999. "The Fox Project: A Reappraisal." *Current Anthropology* 40(2): 171–91.

Foucault, Michel. 1991. "Governmentality." In Graham Burchell, Colin Gordon, and Peter Miller, eds., *The Foucault Effect: Studies in Governmentality*, 87–104. Chicago: University of Chicago Press.

Fox, Jonathan. 1997. "The Political Construction of Social Capital in Rural Mexico." In Peter Evans, ed., *State-Society Synergy: Government and Social Capital in Development*, 119–49. International and Area Studies, Research Series 94. Berkeley: University of California Press.

———. 1998. "When Does Reform Policy Influence Practice?" In Jonathan A.

Fox and L. David Brown, eds., *The Struggle for Accountability: The World Bank, NGOs, and Grassroots Movements,* 303–44. Cambridge, Mass.: MIT Press.

Franck, Thomas M. 2001. "Are Human Rights Universal?" *Foreign Affairs* 80(1): 191–204.

Fraser, Nancy. 1997. "Rethinking the Public Sphere: A Contribution to the Critique of Actually Existing Democracy." In *Justice Interruptus: Critical Reflections on the "Postsocialist" Condition,* 69–98. New York: Routledge.

Friedmann, John. 1987. *Planning in the Public Domain: From Knowledge to Action.* Princeton: Princeton University Press.

——. 1992. *Empowerment: The Politics of Alternative Development.* Cambridge, Mass.: Blackwell.

Fundación Sol y Tierra (FST). 1994. *Yu 'Up'hku* (*The Waters Have Given Birth*). Documentary. Directed by Nelson Freddy Osorio. Popayán.

——. 1995a. *Formación integral e investigación, Pueblo Nuevo, Centro de Capacitación "Luis Angel Monroy."* Popayán: FST.

——. 1995b. *Plan de desarrollo resguardo indígena de Vitoncó municipio de Páez-Cauca, años 1996–1997–1998. Elaborado por la comunidad indígena y el cabildo de Vitoncó.* Popayán: FST.

——. 1998. *Plan de vida plan de desarrollo en comunidades indígenas del Cauca.* Documentary. Directed by Henry Caballero. Popayán.

Galjart, B. 1981. "Counterdevelopment: A Position Paper." *Community Development Journal* 16(2): 88–96.

Gaonkar, Dilip Parameshwar. 1999. "On Alternative Modernities." *Public Culture* 11(1): 1–18.

Gardner, Katy, and David Lewis. 1996. *Anthropology, Development and the Post-Modern Challenge.* Chicago: Pluto Press.

Gatter, Philip. 1993. "Anthropology in Farming Systems Research: A Participant Observer in Zambia." In Johan Pottier, ed., *Practising Development: Social Science Perspectives,* 153–86. New York: Routledge.

Geertz, Clifford. 1988. *Works and Lives: The Anthropologist as Author.* Stanford, Calif.: Stanford University Press.

Giddens. Anthony. 1984. *The Constitution of Society: An Outline of the Theory of Structuration.* Cambridge: Polity Press.

Giroux, Henry A. 1988. *Teachers as Intellectuals: Toward a Critical Pedagogy of Learning.* Granby, Mass.: Bergin and Garvey.

Gómez, Herinaldy. 2001. "Culturas jurídicas indígenas." In Guido Barona Becerra and Cristóbal Gnecco Valencia, eds., *Historia, geografía y cultura del*

Cauca: Territorios possibles, 1:337–60. Popayán: Editorial Universidad del Cauca.

Gómez, Herinaldy, and Carlos Ariel Ruíz. 1997. *Los paeces: Gente territorio: Metáfora que perdura.* Popayán: Fundación para la Comunicación Popular and Universidad del Cauca.

González, Fr. David. n.d. *Los paeces o genocidio y luchas indígenas en Colombia.* Bogotá: La Rueda Suelta.

González Arias, José Jairo. 1992. *Espacios de exclusión: El estigma de las repúblicas independients 1955–1965.* Bogotá: CINEP.

Gow, David D. 1994. *Planning as a Rational Act: Constructing Environmental Policy in Uganda.* Working Paper no. 181. Boston: Boston University, African Studies Center.

———. 1997. "Can the Subaltern Plan? Ethnicity and Development in Cauca, Colombia." *Urban Anthropology* 26(3–4): 243–92.

———. 1998. "¿Pueden los subalternos planificar? Etnicidad y desarrollo en Cauca, Colombia." In María Lucía Sotomayor, ed., *Modernidad, identidad y desarrollo: Construcción de sociedad y recreación cultural en contextos de modernización,* 185–224. Bogotá: Instituto Colombiano de Antropología.

———. 2002. "Anthropology and Development: Evil Twin or Moral Narrative?" *Human Organization* 61(4): 299–313.

Gow, David D., and Joanne Rappaport. 2002. "The Indigenous Public Voice: The Multiple Idioms of Modernity in Native Cauca." In Jean Jackson and Kay B. Warren, eds., *Indigenous Movements, Self-Representation in Latin America,* 47–80. Austin: University of Texas Press.

Green, Maia. 2000. "Participatory Development and the Appropriation of Agency in Southern Tanzania." *Critique of Anthropology* 20(91): 67–89.

Greene, Linda. 1995. "Living in a State of Fear." In Carolyn Nordstrom and Antonius C. G. M. Robben, eds., *Fieldwork under Fire: Contemporary Studies of Violence and Survival,* 105–27. Berkeley: University of California Press.

Griaule, Marcel. 1965 [1948]. *Conversations with Ogotommeli.* Translated by R. Butler and A. Richards. London: Oxford University Press.

Grillo, Ralph D. 1997. "Discourses of Development: The View from Anthropology." In Ralph. D. Grillo and R. L. Stirrat, eds., *Discourses of Development: Anthropological Perspectives,* 1–33. New York: Berg.

El Grillote, Taller de Títeres. 2000. *Capacitación en teatro de títeres como estrategia para proceso de recuperation cultural.* Documentary (unedited version). Cali.

Gros, Christian. 1991. *Colombia indígena: Identitad cultural y cambio social.* Bogotá: CEREC.

Guegía Hurtado, Carlos Alberto, María Marleny Caicedo de Cachimba, and Hugo Dorado Zuñiga. 1997. *Kwe's kiwe's hiyuka: Conozcamos nuestro territorio.* Popayán: Fond Mixto de Cultura del Cauca.

Gupta, Akhil. 1998. *Postcolonial Developments: Agriculture in the Making of Modern India.* Durham, N.C.: Duke University Press.

Gupta, Akhil, and James Ferguson. 1997. "Culture, Power, Place: Ethnography at the End of an Era." In Akhil Gupta and James Ferguson, eds., *Culture, Power, Place: Explorations in Critical Anthropology,* 1–30. Durham, N.C.: Duke University Press.

Harrell-Bond, Barbara. 1986. *Imposing Aid: Emergency Assistance to Refugees.* Oxford: Oxford University Press.

Harrison, Lawrence E., and Samuel P. Huntington, eds. 2000. *Culture Matters: How Values Shape Human Progress.* New York: Basic Books.

Harvey, Neil. 1998. *The Chiapas Rebellion: The Struggle for Land and Democracy.* Durham, N.C.: Duke University Press.

Henze, Rosemary, and Kathryn A. Davis. 1999. "Authenticity and Identity: Lessons from Indigenous Language Education." *Anthropology & Education Quarterly* 30(1): 3–21.

Hernández Delgado, Esperanza. 2004. *Resistencia civil artesana de paz: Experiencias indígenas, afrodescendientes y campesinas.* Bogotá: Editorial Pontificia Universidad Javeriana.

Herrera Rivera, Luz Angela. 2003. *Región, desarrollo y acción colectiva: Movimiento de integración del Macizo Colombiano.* Bogotá: CINEP.

Herzfeld, Michael. 1999. "Hybridity in an Arid Field." *Anthropological Quarterly* 72(30): 131–35.

Hetherington, Kevin. 1998. *Expressions of Identity: Space, Performance, Politics.* Thousand Oaks, Calif.: Sage.

Hewitt, Kenneth. 1983. "The Idea of Calamity in a Technocratic Age." In Kenneth Hewitt, ed., *Interpretations of Calamity: From the Viewpoint of Human Ecology,* 3–32. London: Allen and Unwin.

———. 1997. *Regions of Risk: A Geographical Introduction to Disasters.* Harlow, U.K.: Addison Wesley Longman.

Heyman, Josiah M. 2003. "The Inverse of Power." *Anthropological Theory* 3(2): 139–56.

Hickey, Sam, and Giles Mohan. 2005. "Relocating Participation within a Radical Politics of Development." *Development and Change* 36(2): 237–62.

Hirschman, Albert O. 1984. *Getting Ahead Collectively: Grassroots Experiences in Late America.* New York: Pergamon Press.

Hobart, Mark. 1993. "Introduction: The Growth of Ignorance?" In Mark Hobart, ed., *An Anthropological Critique of Development: The Growth of Ignorance,* 1–30. New York: Routledge.

Hodgson, Dorothy. 2002. "Comparative Perspectives on the Indigenous Rights Movement." *American Anthropologist* 104(4): 1037–49.

Hodgson, Dorothy L., and Richard A. Schroeder. 2002. "Dilemmas of Counter-Mapping Community Resources in Tanzania." *Development and Change* 33(1): 79–100.

Hornberger, Nancy. 2000. "Bilingual Education Policy and Practice in the Andes: Ideological Paradox and Intercultural Possibility." *Anthropology & Education Quarterly* 31(2): 173–201.

Horowitz, Michael M., Dolores Koenig, Curt Grimm, and Yacouba Konate. 1993. "Resettlement at Manantali, Mali: Short-Term Success, Long-Term Problems." In Michael M. Cernea and Scott E. Guggenheim, eds., *Anthropological Approaches to Resettlement: Policy, Practice, and Theory,* 229–50. Boulder, Colo.: Westview Press.

Howell, Jude, and Jenny Pearce. 2001. *Civil Society and Development: A Critical Exploration.* Boulder, Colo.: Lynne Rienner.

Human Rights Council of Australia. 2001. *Submission to the Joint Standing Committees on Foreign Affairs, Defense and Trade Inquiry into the Link Between Aid and Human Rights.* Canberra: Human Rights Council of Australia, February.

Hurtado, Abelino Dagua, Misael Aranda, and Luis Guillermo Vasco. 1998. *Guambianos: Hijos del arcoiris y del agua.* Bogotá: Fondo de Promoción de la Cultura, Fundación Alejandro Angel Escobar, Los Cuatro Elementos, and CEREC.

Ibeas, Juan. 1999. "Guerrilla indígena en Colombia. El Movimiento Armado Quintín Lame: De la lucha armada a la vida política legal." In Luis Alfonso Fajardo Sánchez, Juan Carlos Gamboa, and Orlando Villanueva Martínez, eds., *Manuel Quintín Lame y los guerrilleros de Juan Tama (multiculturalismo, magia y resistencia),* 197–226. Madrid: Nossa y Jara Editores.

Ignatieff, Michael. 2001a. *Human Rights as Politics and Idolatry.* Princeton, N.J.: Princeton University Press.

———. 2001b. "Are Human Rights Universal?" *Foreign Affairs* 80(1): 191–204.

Ingeominas. 1995. *Zonificación para usos del suelo el la cuenca del Río Páez.* Bogotá: Ingeominas.

Jackson, Jean E. 1990. "'I Am a Fieldnote': Fieldnotes as a Symbol of Professional Identity." In Roger Sanjek, ed., *Fieldnotes: The Making of Anthropology,* 3–33. Ithaca, N.Y.: Cornell University Press.

——. 2002. "Contested Discourses of Authority in Colombian National Indigenous Politics: The 1996 Summer Takeovers." In Jean Jackson and Kay B. Warren, eds., *Indigenous Movements, Self-Representation in Latin America*, 81–122. Austin: University of Texas Press.

Jaramillo Salgado, Diego. 2001. "Un gobierno alternativo en una región olvidada de Colombia: Entrevista al taita Floro Alberto Tunubalá Paja, gobernador del departamento del Cauca." *Journal of Iberian and Latin American Studies* 7(2): 151–66.

——. 2005. "Procesos de resistencia de los movimientos sociales en el Cauca y la experiencia de un gobierno alternativo." *Utopía* 21: 19–40.

Jasper, James M. 1997. *The Art of Moral Protest: Culture, Biography, and Creativity in Social Movements*. Chicago: University of Chicago Press.

Jimeno, Myriam. 2001. "Violence and Social Life in Colombia." *Critique of Anthropology* 21(3): 221–46.

Kabeer, Naila. 2005. "Introduction: The Search for Inclusive Citizenship: Meanings and Expressions in an Interconnected World." In Naila Kabeer, ed., *Inclusive Citizenship: Meanings and Expressions*, 1–27. New York: Zed Books.

Kearney, Michael. 1996. *Reconceptualizing the Peasantry: Anthropology in Global Perspective*. Boulder, Colo.: Westview Press.

Kendrick, Thomas D. 1957. *The Lisbon Earthquake*. Philadelphia: Lippincott.

Kirk, Robin. 2003. *More Terrible than Death: Massacres, Drugs, and America's War in Colombia*. New York: Public Affairs.

Kirsch, Stuart. 2002. "Anthropology and Advocacy: A Case Study of the Campaign against the Ok Tedi Mine." *Critique of Anthropology* 22(2): 175–200.

Lame, Manuel Quintín. 1922. "Por mi desventurada raza." *El Espectador,* January 22.

——. 1971 [1939]. *En defensa de mi Raza*. Edited and with an introduction by Gonzalo Castillo. Bogota: Comité de Defensa del Indio.

——. 2004. *Los pensamientos del indio que se educó dentro de las selvas colombianas.* Popayán: Biblioteca del Gran Cauca.

La María. 2000a. *Del silencio a la palabra. Seminario taller gestores de convivencia, diálogo y negociación.* Popayán: Resguardo Guambiano La María Piendamó.

——. 2000b. *Memorias: Encuentro de organizaciones sociales — construcción de alternativas al Plan Colombia.* Popayán: Resguardo Guambiano La María Piendamó.

León, Juanita. 2004. *No somos machos, pero somos muchos: Cinco crónicas de resistencia civil en Colombia.* Bogotá: Grupo Editorial Norma.

Long, Norman. 1992. "From Paradigm Lost to Paradigm Regained? The Case
for an Actor-Oriented Sociology of Development." In Norman Long and
Ann Long, eds., *Battlefields of Knowledge: The Interlocking of Theory and Practice in Social Research and Development*, 16–43. New York: Routledge.

López Garcés, Carlos Alfredo. 1995. *Censo de población CRIC-Nasa Kiwe en
la zona de desastre del 6 de junio de 1994: Análisis descriptivo del medio ambiente
en Tierradentro*. Popayán: Consejo Indígena del Cauca / Corporación Nasa
Kiwe.

Lubkemann, Stephen C. 2002. "Refugees." In *World at Risk: A Global Issues
Sourcebook*, 522–44. Washington: Congressional Quarterly Press.

Luykx, Aurolyn. 1996. "From *Indios* to *Profesionales:* Stereotypes and Student
Resistance in Bolivian Teacher Training." In Bradley A. Levinson, Douglas
Foley, and Dorothy C. Holland, eds., *The Cultural Production of the Educated
Person: Critical Ethnographies of Schooling and Local Practice*, 239–72. Albany:
State University of New York Press.

MacClancy, Jeremy, ed. 2002. *Exotic No More: Anthropology on the Front Line*.
Chicago: University of Chicago Press.

Malinowski, Bronislaw. 1989 [1967]. *A Diary in the Strict Sense of the Term*.
Stanford, Calif.: Stanford University Press.

Malkki, Lisa H. 1995. "Refugees and Exile: From 'Refugee Studies' to the
National Order of Things." *Annual Review of Anthropology* 24: 495–523.

Margold, Jane A. 1999. "From 'Cultures of Fear and Terror' to the Normaliza-
tion of Violence." *Critique of Anthropology* 19(1): 63–88.

Maskrey, Andrew. 1994. "Comunidad y desastres en América Latina:
Estrategias de intervención." In A. Lavall, ed., *Viviendo en riesgo: Com-
unidades vulnerables y prevención de desastres en América Latina*, 25–57.
Bogotá: Tercer Mundo Editores.

Meneses Lucumi, Lucía Eugenía. 2000. "De la montaña al Valle: Tradición y
cambio el el resguardo de Tóez, Caloto." Undergraduate thesis presented to
the Department of Anthropology. University of Cauca, Popayán.

Mimica, Jadran. 1991. "The Incest Passions: An Outline of the Logic of Iqwaye
Social Organization." *Oceania* 62(1): 34–58.

Moore, Barrington. 1978. *Injustice: The Social Bases of Obedience and Revolt*.
New York: M. E. Sharpe.

Mosse, David. 2001. " 'People's Knowledge,' Participation and Patronage:
Operations and Representations in Rural Development." In Bill Cooke and
Uma Kothari, eds., *Participation: The New Tyranny*, 16–35. New York: Zed
Books.

Mulcué Mulcué, Adela, and Nydia María Yasnó González. n.d. *Participación de la familia y la comunidad en la propuesta pedagógica del grado cero del* CET. Manuscript, copy in D. Gow's personal collection.

Municipio de Toribío. 1998. *Plan de Desarrollo 1998–2000*. Toribío: Municipio de Toribío.

Nash, June. 1976. "Ethnology in a Revolutionary Setting." In Michael Rynkiewich and James Spradley, eds., *Ethics and Anthropology: Dilemmas in Fieldwork,* 148–66. New York: Wiley.

Nederveen Pieterse, Jan. 1998. "My Paradigm or Yours? Alternative Development, Post-Development, Reflexive Development." *Development and Change* 29: 343–73.

Neiman, Susan. 2002. *Evil in Modern Thought: An Alternative History of Philosophy*. Princeton, N.J.: Princeton University Press.

Nolan, Riall. 2002. *Development Anthropology: Encounters in the Real World*. Boulder, Colo.: Westview Press.

Nordstrom, Carolyn. 1997. *A Different Kind of War Story*. Philadelphia: University of Pennsylvania Press.

Nustad, Knut G. 2001. "Development: The Devil We Know?" *Third World Quarterly* 22(4): 79–89.

Nyambu-Musembi, Celestine. 2005. "Towards an Actor-Oriented Perspective on Human Rights." In Naila Kabeer, ed., *Inclusive Citizenship: Meanings and Expressions,* 31–49. New York: Zed Books.

Nygren, Anja. 1999. "Local Knowledge in the Environment-Development Discourse: From Dichotomies to Situated Knowledges." *Critique of Anthropology* 19(3): 267–88.

Oliver-Smith, Anthony. 1996. "Anthropological Research on Hazards and Disasters." *Annual Review of Anthropology* 25: 303–28.

Ortiz, Sutti. 1979. "The Estimation of Work: Labour and Value among Paez Farmers." In Sandra Wallman, ed., *Social Anthropology of Work,* 207–28. New York: Academic Press.

Ortner, Sherry B. 1995. "Resistance and the Problem of Ethnographic Refusal." *Comparative Studies in Society and History* 37(1): 173–93.

——. 1999. "Thick Resistance: Death and the Cultural Construction of Agency in Himalayan Mountaineering." In Sherry B. Ortner, ed., *The Fate of "Culture": Geertz and Beyond,* 136–63. Berkeley: University of California Press.

Pachón, Jimena. 1996. "Los nasa o la gente páez." In Jimena Pachón, Diana Olivaris, and Luis Eduardo Wiener, eds., *Geografía humana de Colombia:*

Región andina central, 89–150. Bogotá: Instituto Colombiano de Cultura Hispánica.

Partridge, William L. 1987. "Toward a Theory of Practice." In Elizabeth M. Eddy and William L. Partridge, eds., *Applied Anthropology in America,* 211–36. New York: Columbia University Press.

Paz, José Manuel. 2001. "Estructura de la tenencia de la tierra: 1973–1997." In Guido Barona Becerra and Cristóbal Gnecco Valencia, eds., *Historia, geografía y cultura del Cauca: Territorios possibles,* 1:199–215. Popayán: Editorial Universidad del Cauca.

Peet, Richard, with Elaine Hartwick. 1999. *Theories of Development.* New York: Guildford Press.

Peñaranda, Ricardo. 1998. *Historia del Movimientos Armado Quintín Lame.* Masters's thesis in history, Universidad Nacional, Bogotá.

Perdomo, Adonías. 2005. "Actores de autoridad: Una mirada desde el pueblo nasa de Pitayó." In Joanne Rappaport, ed., *Retornando la mirada: Una investigación colaborativa interétnica sobre el Cauca a la entrada del milenio.* 97–117. Popayán: Editorial Universidad del Cauca.

Peters, Pauline. 2000. "Encountering Participation and Knowledge in Development Sites." In Pauline Peters, ed., *Development Encounters: Sites of Participation and Knowledge,* 3–14. Cambridge, Mass.: Harvard Institute for International Development.

Pettman, Jan Jindy. 1996. *Worlding Women: A Feminist International Politics.* London: Routledge.

Pigg, Stacey Leigh. 1997. " 'Found in Most Traditional Societies': Traditional Medical Practitioners between Culture and Development." In Frederick Cooper and Randall Packard, eds., *International Development and the Social Sciences: Essays on the History and Politics of Knowledge,* 259–90. Berkeley: University of California Press.

Piñacué, Susana. 2005. "Liderazgo y poder: Una cultura de la mujer nasa." In Joanne Rappaport, ed., *Retornando la mirada: Una investigación colaborativa interétnica sobre el Cauca a la entrada del milenio,* 55–64. Popayán: Editorial Universidad del Cauca.

Pizarro, Eduardo. 1996. *Insurgencia sin revolución.* Bogotá: Tercer Mundo.

Platteau, Jean-Philippe. 1994. "Behind the Market Stage Where Real Societies Exist." *Journal of Development Studies* 30: 533–77.

Posey, Darrell. 2002. "Upsetting the Sacred Balance: Can the Study of Indigenous Knowledge Reflect Cosmic Connectedness?" In Paul Sillitoe, Alan

Bicker, and Johan Pottier, eds., *Participating in Development: Approaches to Indigenous Knowledge,* 24–42. New York: Routledge.

Programa de Educacion Bilingüe (PEB/CRIC). 2000a. *Centros educativos comunitarios intercultural bilingüe. CECIBs. Juan Tama — Santa Leticia; López Adentro — Cornito; Delicias — Buenos Aires.* Popayán: CRIC.

———. 2000b. *CXA' KUTY'A — Volver a nacer.* Documentary. Directed by Emiluth Collo. Popayán.

Puerto Chávez, Fernando. 1995. *Censo de población el en area del desastre de Tierradento, Cauca, CRIC-Nasa Kiwe: Análisis descriptivo de los principales indicadores de morbilidad y mortalidad en los municipios de Páez e Inzá por el desastre del 6 de junio.* Popayán: CRIC/CNK.

Purcell, Trevor, and Elizabeth Akinyi Onjoro. 2002. "Indigenous Knowledge, Power and Parity: Models of Knowledge Integration." In Paul Sillitoe, Alan Bicker, and Johan Pottier, eds., *Participating in Development: Approaches to Indigenous Knowledge,* 162–88. New York: Routledge.

Quarles van Ufford, Philip, Ananta Kumar Giri, and David Mosse. 2003. "Interventions in Development: Towards a New Moral Understanding of Our Experiences and an Agenda for the Future." In Philip Quarles van Ufford and Ananta Kumar Giri, eds., *A Moral Critique of Development: In Search of Global Responsibilities,* 4–40. New York: Routledge.

Rahnema, Majid. 1992. "Participation." In Wolfgang Sachs, ed., *The Development Dictionary: A Guide to Knowledge as Power,* 116–31. Atlantic Highlands, N.J.: Zed Books.

Ramírez, María Clemencia. 2001a. *Entre el estado y la guerrilla:identidad y ciudadanía en el movimiento de los campesinos cocaleros del Putumayo.* Bogotá: Instituto Colombiano de Antropología e Historia.

———. 2001b. "Los movimientos cívicos como movimientos sociales en el Putumayo: El poder visible de la sociedad civil y la construcción de una nueva ciudadanía." In Mauricio Archila and Mauricio Pardo, eds., *Movimientos sociales, estado y democracia en Colombia,* 127–49. Bogotá: CES/Universidad Nacional de Colombia/ICANH.

Rao, Vijayendra, and Michael Walton. 2004. "Culture and Public Action: Relationality, Equality of Agency, and Development." In Vijayendra Rao and Michael Walton, eds., *Culture and Public Action,* 3–36. Stanford, Calif.: Stanford University Press.

Rapley, John. 2002. *Understanding Development: Theory and Practice in the Third World,* 2d ed. Boulder, Colo.: Lynne Rienner.

Rappaport, Joanne, ed., 1996. "Ethnicity Reconfigured: Indigenous Legislators and the Colombian Constitution." Special issue of the *Journal of Latin American Anthropology* 1(2).

———. 1998 [1990]. *The Politics of Memory: Native Historical Interpretation in the Colombian Andes.* Durham, N.C.: Duke University Press.

———. 2004. "Manuel Quintín Lame Hoy." In Manuel Quintín Lame, *Los pensamientos del indio que se educó dentro de las selvas colombianas,* 51–101. Popayán: Biblioteca del Gran Cauca.

———. 2005a. *Intercultural Utopias: Public Intellectuals, Cultural Experimentation, and Ethnic Pluralism in Colombia.* Durham, N.C.: Duke University Press.

———, ed. 2005b. *Retornando la mirada: Una investigación colaborativa interétnica sobre el Cauca a la entrada del milenio.* Popayán: Editorial Universidad del Cauca.

Rappaport, Joanne, and David D. Gow. 1997. "Cambio dirigido, movimiento indígena y estereotipos del indio: El estado colombiano y la reubicación de los nasa." In María Victoria Uribe and Eduardo Restrepo, eds., *Antropología de la modernidad,* 361–99. Bogotá: Instituto Colombiano de Antropología.

Rawls, John. 1971. *A Theory of Justice.* Cambridge, Mass.: Harvard University Press.

República de Colombia. 1991. *Nueva Constitución Política de Colombia.* Pasto: Minilibrería Jurídica Moral.

Resguardo de San José. 1999. *Plan de vida 2000–2004.* Popayán: Comunidad del Resguardo de San José / Empresa Asociativa de Trabajo "El Telar."

La Revista de El Espectador. 2002. "La conversación: No sólo a las Farc, resistimos a todos los actores de la guerra." August 4, 6–9.

Richards, Paul. 1993. "Cultivation: Knowledge or Performance?" In Mark Hobart, ed., *An Anthropological Critique of Development: The Growth of Ignorance.* 61–78. New York: Routledge.

Roattino, Ezio. 1986. *Álvaro Ulcué nasa pal: Sangre india para una tierra nueva.* Bogotá: CINEP.

Robins, Steven. 2003. "Whose Modernity? Indigenous Modernities and Land Claims after Apartheid." *Development and Change* 34(2): 265–85.

Roe, Emory. 1994. *Narrative Policy Analysis: Theory and Practice.* Durham, N.C.: Duke University Press.

Rojas M., Alejandro Axel. 1994. *Censo de población en el area del desastre de Tierradentro, Cauca, CRIC-Nasa Kiwe: Herramientas de planeación para los planes de reconstrucción: La región de Tierradentro, análisis general e impacto del desastre del 6 de junio de 1994: Características generales de la población.* Popayán: CRIC/CNK.

Romero, Fernando. 2004. "Aspectos pedagógicos y filosóficos en *Los pensamientos del indio que se educó dentro de las selvas colombianas* de Manuel Quintín Lame." In Manuel Quintín Lame, *Los pensamientos del indio que se educó dentro de las selvas colombianas,* 111–38. Popayán: Biblioteca del Gran Cauca.

Rondinelli, Dennis A. 1993. *Development Projects as Policy Experiments,* 2d ed. New York: Routledge.

Ruano, S. William, and Carolina Forgioni A. 2000. *"Yu'c ech wala" (El dueño de la montaña grande): Escrita con paeces para paeces del reasentamiento de Tóez, Municipio de Caloto.* Cali: Taller de Títeres El Grillote/Fondo Mixto de Cultura del Cauca.

Rubinstein, Robert A. 1986. "Reflections on Action Anthropology: Some Developmental Dynamics of an Anthropological Tradition." *Human Organization* 45(3): 270–79.

Ruiz Sánchez, Carlos Ariel. 2000. *Multiculturalismo, etnicidad y cultivos ilícitos.* Popayan: FUNCOP.

Sahlins, Marshall. 1999. "What is Anthropological Enlightenment? Some Lessons of the Twentieth Century." *Annual Review of Anthropology* 28: i–xxiii.

Samper, Mady. 2000. *Senderos de la amapola: Testimonios de indígenas y campesinos sobre cultivos ilícitos.* Bogotá: Planeta.

Scheper-Hughes, Nancy. 1995. "The Primacy of the Ethical." *Current Anthropology* 36(3): 409–20.

Schonhuth, Michael. 2002. "Negotiating with Knowledge at Development Interfaces: Anthropology and the Quest for Participation." In Paul Sillitoe, Alan Bicker, and Johan Pottier, eds., *Participating in Development: Approaches to Indigenous Knowledge,* 139–61. New York: Routledge.

Scott, James C. 1985. *Weapons of the Weak: Everyday Forms of Peasant Resistance.* New Haven, Conn.: Yale University Press.

Sevilla Casas, Elías. 1986. *La pobreza de los excluidos: Economía y sobrevivencia en un resguardo indígena del Cauca, Colombia.* Quito: Editorial Abya-Yala/Ethnos.

Sillitoe, Paul. 2002. "Participant Observation to Participatory Development: Making Anthropology Work." In Paul Sillitoe, Alan Bicker, and Johan Pottier, eds., *Participating in Development: Approaches to Indigenous Knowledge,* 1–23. New York: Routledge.

Sluka, Jeffrey A. 1995. "Reflections on Managing Danger in Fieldwork: Dangerous Anthropology in Belfast." In Carolyn Nordstrom and Antonius C. G. M. Robben, eds., *Fieldwork under Fire: Contemporary Studies of Violence and Survival,* 276–94. Berkeley: University of California Press.

Spivak, Gayatri Chakravorty. 1988. "Can the Subaltern Speak?" In Cary Nelson and Larry Grossberg, eds., *Marxism and the Interpretation of Culture,* 271–313. Urbana: University of Illinois Press.

———. 1996. "Subaltern Talk: Interview with the Editors." In Donna Landry and Gerald MacLean, eds., *The Spivak Reader,* 287–308. New York: Routledge.

Steinberg, Ted. 2000. *Acts of God: The Unnatural History of Natural Disaster in America.* New York: Oxford University Press.

Stull, Donald D., Jerry A. Schultz, and Ken Cadue. 1987. "In the People's Service: The Kansas Kickapoo Technical Assistance Project." In Donald D. Stull and Jean J. Schensul, eds., *Collaborative Research and Social Change: Applied Anthropology in Action,* 33–54. Boulder, Colo.: Westview Press.

Taussig, Michael. 2004. *Law in a Lawless Land: Diary of a* Limpieza *in Colombia.* New York: New Press.

Tax, Sol. 1958. "The Fox Project." *Human Organization* 17: 17–19.

———. 1975. "Action Anthropology." *Current Anthropology* 16: 171–77.

Trinh, T. Minh-ha. 1991. *When the Moon Waxes Red: Representation, Gender and Cultural Politics.* London: Routledge.

Turner, Victor. 1969. *The Ritual Process: Structure and Anti-Structure.* Chicago: Aldine.

———. 1974. *Drama, Fields, and Metaphors: Symbolic Action in Human Society.* Ithaca, N.Y.: Cornell University Press.

Turner, Victor, and Edith Turner. 1978. *Image and Pilgrimage in Christian Culture.* New York: Columbia University Press.

Ulcué Chocué, Álvaro, Lucila Mejía, and Ana Bertile Florez. 1980. *Seminarios realizado* [sic] *con los cabildos de Toribío, San Francisco, Tacueyó.* Part 1, Del 8 al 12 de septiembre de 1980. Part 2, Del 27 al 29 de abril de 1981. Bogotá: CENPRODES.

Uvin, Peter. 1998. *Aiding Violence: The Development Enterprise in Rwanda.* West Hartford, Conn.: Kumarian Press.

———. 2004. *Human Rights and Development.* Bloomfield, Conn.: Kumarian Press.

Van Cott, Donna Lee. 2000. *The Friendly Liquidation of the Past: The Politics of Diversity in Latin America.* Pittsburgh: University of Pittsburgh Press.

Van de Wetering, Maxine. 1982. "Moralizing in Puritan Natural Science: Mysteriousness in Earthquake Sermons." *Journal of the History of Ideas* 43(3): 417–38.

Vasco Uribe, Luis Guillermo. 2002a. *Entre selva y páramo: Viviendo y pensando la lucha indígena*. Bogotá: Instituto Colombiano de Antropología e Historia.

———. 2002b. "Replanteamiento del trabajo de campo y la escritura etnográficos." In Luis Guillermo Vasco, ed., *Entre selva y páramo: Viviendo y pensando la lucha indígena*, 452–86. Bogotá: Instituto Colombiano de Antropología e Historia.

Warner, Lloyd. 1947. *The Social System of the Modern Factory*. Oxford: Oxford University Press.

Warren, Kay B. 1998. *Indigenous Movements and Their Critics: Pan-Maya Activism in Guatemala*. Princeton, N.J.: Princeton University Press.

Whiteley, Peter. 1997. "The End of Anthropology (at Hopi?)." In Thomas Biolsi and Larry J. Zimmerman, eds., *Indians and Anthropologists: Vine Deloria, Jr., and the Critique of Anthropology*, 177–207. Tucson: University of Arizona Press.

———. 1998. "Introduction: The Predicament of Hopi Ethnography." In *Rethinking Hopi Ethnography*, 1–45. Washington: Smithsonian Institution Press.

Wilches Chaux, Gustavo. 1995a. "Tierra de la gente: Principios orientadores de la Corporacion Nasa Kiwe: Tierra de la gente." *Desastres & Sociedad* 4(3): 91–104.

———. 1995b. "Particularidades de un desastre." *Desastres & Sociedad* 4(3): 119–39.

———. 1998. *En el borde del caos*. Popayán: FONAM/FUNCOP.

———. 2005. *Proyecto Nasa: La construcción del Plan de Vida de un pueblo que sueña*. Bogotá: PNUD.

Wilson, Richard Ashby. 2006. "Afterword to 'Anthropology and Human Rights in a New Key': The Social Life of Human Rights." *American Anthropologist* 108(1): 22–83.

Woost, Michael. 1997. "Alternative Vocabularies of Development? 'Community' and 'Participation' in Development Discourse in Sri Lanka." In R. D. Grillo and R. L. Stirrat, eds., *Discourses of Development: Anthropological Perspectives*, 229–53. New York: Berg.

Wood, Elizabeth Jean. 2001. "The Emotional Benefits of Insurgency in El Salvador." In Jeff Goodwin, James M. Jasper, and Francesca Polletta, eds., *Passionate Politics: Emotions and Social Movements*, 267–81. Chicago: University of Chicago Press.

Zambrano, Carlos Vladimir. 1998. "Conflictos y cambio en el proceso de modernización del Macizo Colombiano. Un caso de alteridad étnica." In María Lucía Sotomayor, ed., *Modernidad, identidad y desarrollo: Construcción de sociedad y re-creación cultural en contextos de modernización.* 379–97. Bogotá: Instituto Colombiano de Antropología.

———. 2001. "Conflictos por la hegemonía regional. Un análisis del movimiento social y étnico del Macizo Colombiano." In Mauricio Archila and Mauricio Pardo, eds., *Movimientos sociales, estado y democracia en Colombia,* 260–85. Bogotá: CES/Universidad Nacional de Colombia/ICANH.

Index

David D. Gow is Edgar P. Baker Professor of Anthropology and International Affairs at The George Washington University's Elliott School of International Affairs. Prior to becoming an academic, he worked for many years in the field of international development for USAID, FAO, the World Resources Institute, and the World Bank. He is the coeditor (with Elliott R. Morss) of *Implementing Rural Development Projects: Lessons from Aid and the World Bank Experiences* (1985).

Library of Congress Cataloging-in-Publication Data

Gow, David D.
Countering development : indigenous modernity and the
moral imagination / David D. Gow.
p. cm. — Includes bibliographical references and index.
ISBN-13: 978-0-8223-4148-2 (cloth : alk. paper)
ISBN-13: 978-0-8223-4171-0 (pbk. : alk. paper)
1. Indians of South America — Colombia — Cauca (Dept.) — Economic conditions. 2. Indians of South America — Colombia — Cauca (Dept.) — Government relations. 3. Indians of South America — Commerce — Colombia — Cauca (Dept.) 4. Economic development — Colombia — Cauca (Dept.) 5. Sustainable development — Colombia — Cauca (Dept.) 6. Cauca (Colombia : Dept.) — Economic conditions. I. Title.
F2269.1.C375G69 2008   307.1'41208998086153 — dc22
2007043970